ALLAN BEALT B.A.

Head of Geography Department
Moseley School, Birmingham

Chief Examiner, GCE Ordinary Level Geography
Associated Examining Board

Western Europe
A Systematic Geography

D1797570

Pitman Publishing

First Published 1977

Pitman Publishing Ltd
Pitman House, Parker Street, Kingsway, London WC2B 5PB
PO Box 46038, Banda Street, Nairobi, Kenya

Pitman Publishing Pty Ltd
Pitman House, 158 Bouverie Street, Carlton, Victoria 3053, Australia

Pitman Publishing Corporation
6 East 43 Street, New York, NY 10017, USA

Sir Isaac Pitman (Canada) Ltd
495 Wellington Street West, Toronto M5V IGI, Canada

The Copp Clark Publishing Company
517 Wellington Street West, Toronto M5V IGI, Canada

ISBN: 0 273 25267 4

Filmset at The Universities Press, Belfast Ltd and
printed by photolithography at The Pitman Press, Bath
893:56

Preface

Since the Second World War, Western Europe has developed a political and economic identity that is separate from the eastern part of the continent. The traditional country-by-country approach to the geography of Europe no longer seems suitable for an area where, in economic terms, national boundaries have become blurred, and powerful multi-national organizations have emerged. The book is designed to meet this changed environment, and the West European economy is analysed within eight major themes, following a section devoted to a description of the physical environment. This rationalized treatment of the geography of Western Europe has not been undertaken lightly, and it is hoped that a feeling for the essential diversity of the region has been retained.

The book has been prepared primarily for the use of students working towards GCE O-level (16+) examinations, and care has been taken to ensure the inclusion of material to cater for some of the latest syllabus changes of the examining boards. It is also anticipated that the text will offer a useful source of reference for all secondary school students. The various studies have been prepared in detail and offer the teacher the opportunity to select material for a range of abilities and interests. It is in the experience of many external examiners that the factual knowledge and reasoning capacity of a large number of candidates is either inadequate or superficial.

Most syllabuses examine the British Isles separately from Western Europe, and it is for this reason that no detailed British studies are included; although in some instances references are made for the purpose of comparison. The fundamental aim has been to offer an informative account of the geography of Western Europe, illustrated with maps, diagrams and photographs. It is expected that the information contained in the book will be amplified by the use of atlases and further visual material. In order to facilitate the student's understanding, a metric conversion table and a list of standard metric abbreviations used in the text appear on page 195.

I should like to express my appreciation for the assistance I have received from various public and private organizations; each of which is acknowledged in a later section. My thanks are also due to the many individuals who have provided information and advice.

v

Acknowledgments

The author and publishers wish to thank the following for the information and illustrations they have provided.

The Austrian Embassy, the Belgian Embassy, the Danish Embassy, the Dutch Embassy, the French Embassy, the Embassy of the Federal Republic of Germany, the Italian Embassy, the Norwegian Embassy, the Spanish Embassy, the Swedish Embassy, the Swiss Embassy.

The Belgian Tourist Office, the French Tourist Office, the German Tourist Office, the Italian Tourist Office, the Swiss Tourist Office.

The Aluminium Federation, the European Communities Press and Information Office, the Institute of Petroleum, the Petroleum Times, the Meteorological Office, the port authorities of Dunkirk and Antwerp.

Aerospatiale, Aktiengesellschaft, ASV Aluminium, Bayer, BP, Esso Europe Inc., Fred Olsen Ltd, Fullwood & Bland Ltd, Gesamtverband des Deutschen Steinkohlenbergbaus, Gulf Oil, IDG (Itrecht), KLM, 'La Bergerie', Baron Ph. de Rothschild SA, Lufthansa, Pechiney Ugine Kuhlmann, Philips Petroleum, Compagnie Nationale du Rhône, Renault, Skogsindustrins Informationschef Stockholm, Swissair, Texaco, A Thyssen-Hutte, USINOR, Volkswagen.

Economic statistics have been taken from various UN and EEC publications.

Specific acknowledgement for permission to reproduce the following illustrations is made to:

The Controller of Her Majesty's Stationery Office (Crown Copyright) (Fig. 2.7)

The Dutch Ministry of Foreign Affairs and Bart Hofmeester, Rotterdam (Figs 5.17, 16.8, 8.10)

The Embassy of the Federal Republic of Germany (Figs 13.3, 14.11)

EME Corporation, Pelham, New York (Fig, 1.2)

The French Government Tourist Office (Figs 14.16, 16.6)

LKAB (Figs 10.3, 10.4, 10.5, 10.6)

The Royal Danish Ministry for Foreign Affairs (Fig. 14.14(b)) and Aerodan (Fig. 14.14(c)); E. Fischer (Fig. 5.11); Nordisk Pressefoto A/S (Fig. 14.3)

The Royal Norwegian Ministry of Foreign Affairs (Fig. 16.14)

TB Tomlinson (Figs 1.9, 1.10, 1.12, 4.2)

Artist's reference: the prime source for map work in this book was the *Oxford Regional Economic Atlas: Western Europe.*

Contents

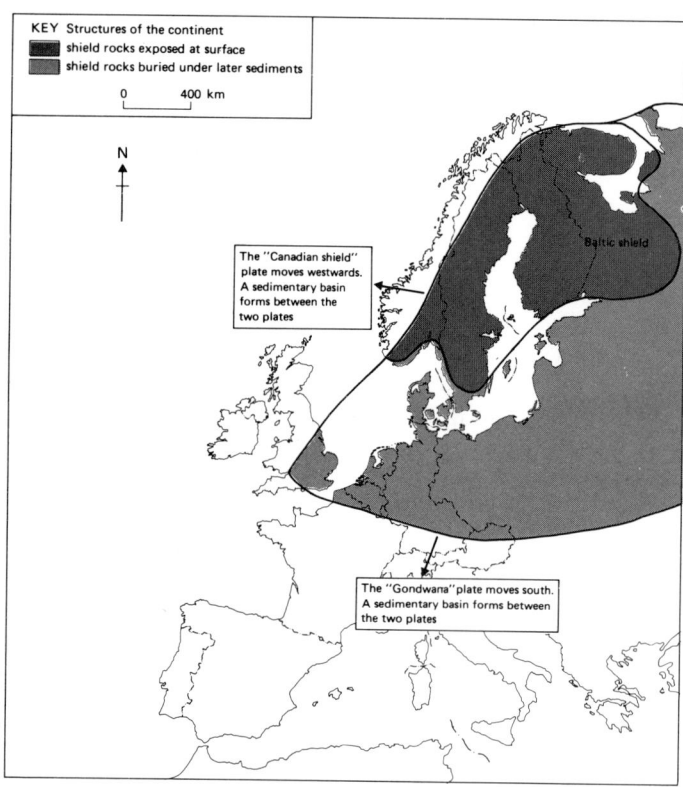

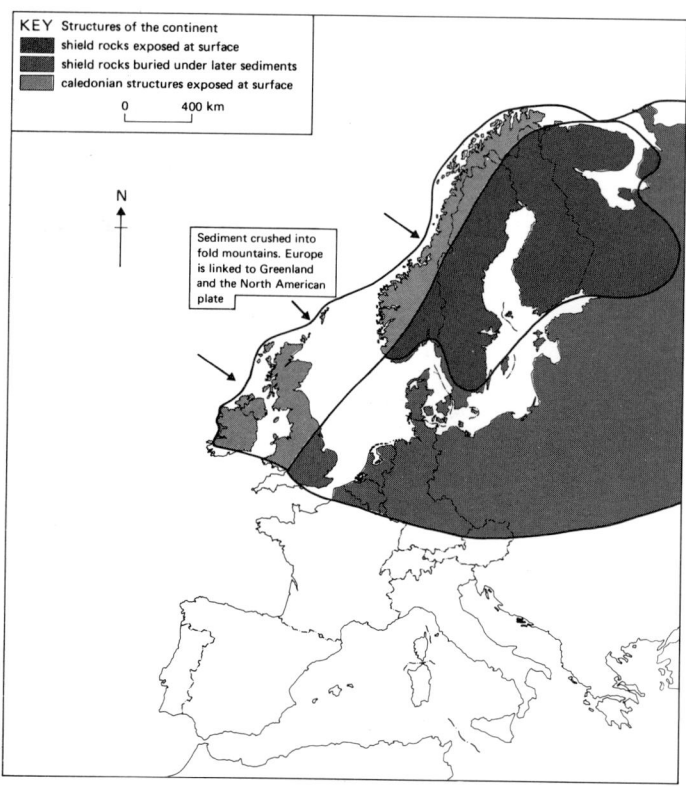

Figure 1.1(a–d) The evolution of the continent.

(**a**) (*left, above*) 1700 million years ago the super-continent Pangaea broke up and the fragments (plates) moved apart to form the nucleus of the continents. The Baltic Shield plate formed the nucleus of the continent of Europe

(**b**) (*left, below*) 420 million years ago the North American (Canadian Shield) plate moved eastwards to collide with Europe. The sediments which has formed in the basin between the two continents were compressed and folded into the north-east/south-west mountain ranges that exist in Scandinavia, the British Isles and eastern North America today (Caledonian structures). 3500 million years ago the Scandinavian and British sections parted

Figure 1.1(c) (*opposite, above*) 250 million years ago the African plate (a fragment of Gondwana) moved from the South West to crush sedimentary strata into west/east mountain ridges across the southern part of the North America/Europe plate (Hercynian mountains)

(**d**) (*opposite, below*) 60 million years ago the North American plate detached itself from Europe, and the Iberian area moved south to open up the Bay of Biscay. A second movement of the African plate northwards crushed sediments to form the Alpine mountains. A depression within this mountain system produced the Mediterranean Sea

1 Geology and structure

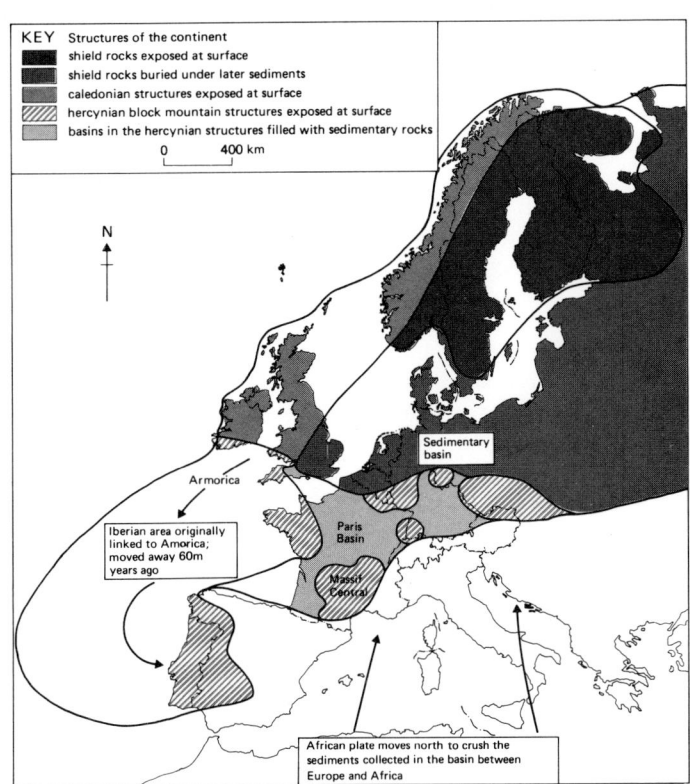

Since the theory of plate tectonics received general acceptance, the formation of the continents has been more clearly understood. The ancient basal rocks of the continents, partly covered by more recent sediments, are primarily of a low specific density and 'float' upon rocks of higher density, with a plasticity which allows for slow movements of between two and eighteen centimetres per year.

It is believed that approximately 300 million years ago the present continents were united in one super-continent which geologists have named 'Pangaea'. Since then, the original continent has fractured and sections have moved apart and periodically come together again, 'floating' upon the plastic mantle. Seas formed between the new continents, and sediments eroded from the land surface were deposited in them (see Fig. 1.1). These sediments were gradually compressed and cemented into distinctive strata until they were crushed into folds and cracked into faults by the movements of the continental plates. In this way the high fold mountain chains were added to the fragments of the ancient continent. In Europe only the Baltic Shield remains as a surface example of the original continent, although it is believed to underlie much of central Europe too.

A characteristic of the landscape of Europe is its variety. This stems from the presence of five major structural types: the Baltic Shield, the Caledonian Fold mountains, the Hercynian Block mountains, the Alps and the North European Plain.

The Baltic Shield

Underlying much of northern and central Europe is a mass of ancient metamorphic and igneous rock forming a gently-dipping plateau. It outcrops in Sweden and Finland, in

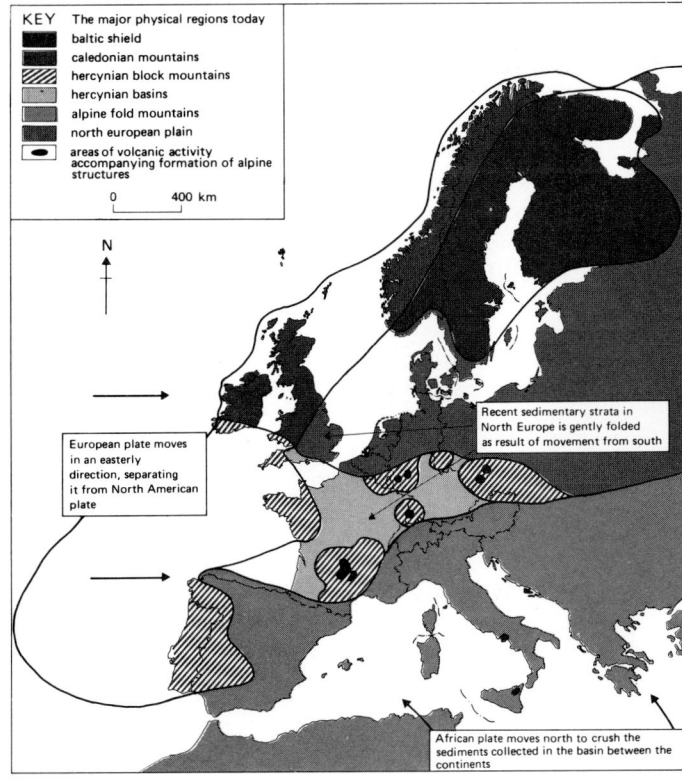

the form of an up-turned shield, the central depression being occupied by the Gulf of Bothnia.

The Shield has remained as a land area for the past 500 million years, and has undergone little of the submergence and sedimentation that has affected other parts of Europe. The original high landscape has been lowered by the agents of erosion and weathering to form a low plain reduced almost to sea level. Subsequent earth movements have raised this gentle surface to a plateau, into which many deep steep-sided valleys have been cut by the combined work of ice and water.

In the Norrland region of Sweden the Shield rises to over 600 m, but in Finland heights range from only 100 m in the south to 300 m in the north. The greater height and steeper gradient in northern Sweden has produced a number of straight well-developed river systems, which rise on the Scandinavian mountains and flow powerfully across the Shield surface. Rejuvenated rivers, like the Lule, Angerman, Indals and Dal, all have steep-sided valleys, and contain breaks in their long profiles caused by changes in rock hardness, producing numerous waterfalls and lakes.

Along the coast of the Gulf of Bothnia uplift of the land has revealed a narrow plain of marine sediments, which provides useful farmland in contrast to the more difficult environment of the plateau. Its seaward margin is made up of low swamp and mud flats which reflect the slight tidal scour experienced in the almost enclosed Baltic Sea.

Until about 20,000 years ago and for much of the preceding 1 million years the Shield had been buried under a slow-moving ice sheet, hundreds of metres thick. The effects of this recent glaciation have contributed a great deal to the landscape of the Shield. The North European ice sheet covered all but the highest and steepest areas of Scandinavia, much of the ice flowing off the Scandinavian mountains south-eastwards across the Shield. The existing valleys attracted the greatest thickness of ice and were deepened and steepened accordingly, while the plateau surface was scraped and smoothed into its present undulating appearance. Today the plateau contains many lakes which are the product of either over-deepening by the ice or morainic damming. Most of the lakes are long and narrow, following the line of the main north-west/south-east valleys.

The landscape of the lake plateau of Finland is similar in many respects: an undulating surface with an irregular cover of glacial moraine trapping innumerable lakes. The lower altitude of Finland means that the rejuvenation of river courses has been less spectacular; only the rivers of northern Finland, such as the Oulu and the Kemi, show incision on a scale comparable with the Swedish rivers. Glacial deposition has produced a prominent relief feature in southern Finland: the Salpausselka morainic ridge. It stretches over 250 km and rises to 100 m in places, forming a barrier which all rivers flowing southwards off the plateau have to cross.

The Caledonian Mountains

Once connected with the Appalachian mountains of North America, the Caledonian mountains now form the western section of the Scandinavian peninsula and the northern and western parts of the British Isles. The characteristic north-east/south-west trend of these mountains was caused by compression from the north-west which crushed the sedimentary rocks into a series of fold ridges. A long period of erosion followed which reduced the surface to a virtual plain, whereupon uplift of the land rejuvenated the river systems, which cut deeply into the level surface. The uplift tilted the region to make the western edge highest; consequently the drainage system is of long, easterly-flowing rivers and short, westerly-flowing ones. Only locally have the rivers developed the north-east/south-west lines of structure; this is best shown by the rivers flowing into the Trondheim and Oslo fjords.

Throughout the Scandinavian mountains the plateau origins of the region are shown by the major peaks which generally conform to heights of around 2000 m. The height is exceeded in the broader southern part of the mountains; in the Jotunheim massif several peaks are above this height, notably Galdhoppigen (2469 m) and Snohetta (2286 m). In the narrower central section the land lowers to form the Trondheim saddle, but rises again in the north with peaks above 2000 m.

The quartzites, slates and shales which comprise the Scandinavian mountains have been

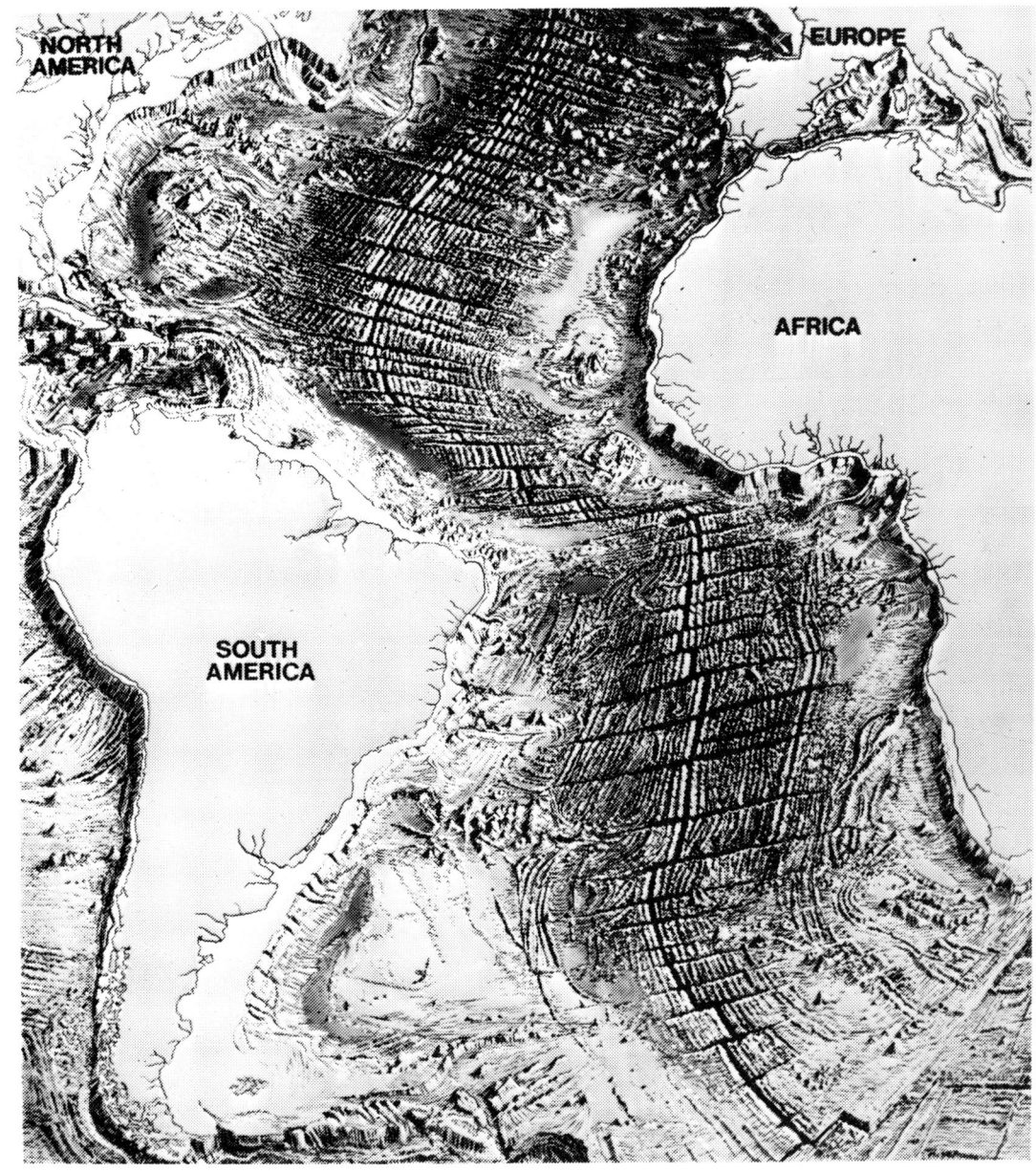

heavily metamorphosed and faulted. Consequently, in spite of the general north-east/south-west structure, there are often important local factors which determine the way a particular landscape has developed. This is clearly illustrated in Norway where east/west fault weaknesses have guided valley development. The valleys have been greatly deepened

Figure 1.2 The mid-Atlantic ridge. The separation of the Americas from Europe and Africa has allowed the periodic escape of new volcanic rock along the plate boundary. The rock lies in symmetrical bands which roughly follow the line of the boundary, the oldest being furthest away. (Copyright: E.M.E. Corporation; Pelham, New York)

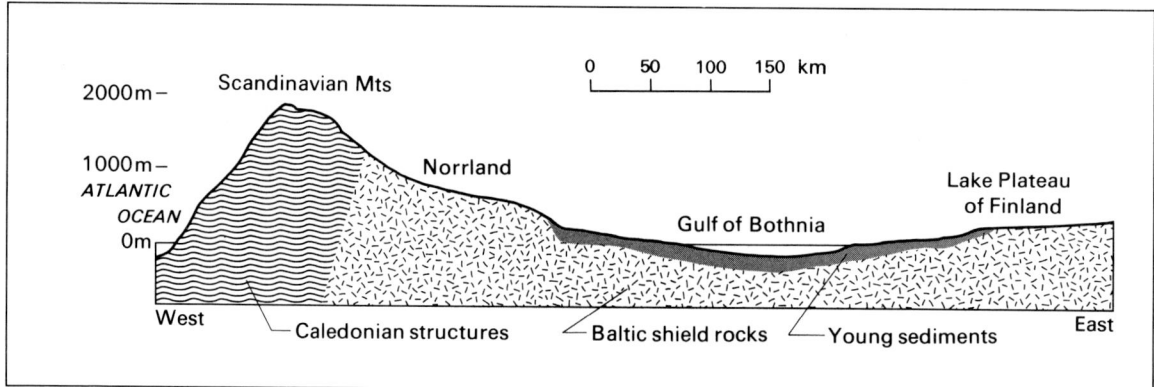

Figure 1.3 Section across the Baltic Shield

by westward-flowing glaciers; and the rise in sea level, following the melting of the ice, flooded them to produce such spectacular inlets as the Sogne, Hardanger and Nord fjords. The Sogne fjord, averaging 5 km in width, is 183 km long and is often as deep as its sides are high, namely 1000 m!

Along the western coasts of Norway and Scotland, chains of islands occur; these are remnants of former coastal ridges separated from the mainland by the rise in sea level that followed the recent Ice Age. The largest group is the Lofoten Islands, stretching between latitude 68° and 69°N. They have similar characteristics to the other islands of the Norwegian skerryguard, being deeply indented, bleak and barren; but unlike the smaller islands the land rises steeply to form rugged mountains over 1000 m in height.

Hercynian Block Mountains

A feature of the central zone of continental Europe is the rounded plateau blocks which rise abruptly from the gentle scarp and vale country. They are remnants of the Hercynian range of mountains which was formed 280 million years before the European and North American plates separated; these structures are repeated in the Appalachian mountains.

In Europe their preservation as upland blocks is the result of the down faulting which accompanied the severance of the North American plate 60 million years ago. It produced broad lowland troughs in the Hercynian structures, but left a number of steep-edged sections as plateaux. The structural upheaval caused widespread volcanic activity, a characteristic of these areas.

All of the uplands are roughly similar in that they have steep edges and rounded plateau surfaces. They differ individually according to the dominance of the following effects.

1 A consistent west/east trend to the ridges. This is most noticeable in the western section of the Hercynian mountains, known as Armorica, which includes the uplands in the south-west of the British Isles, Brittany and the Meseta. Here a characteristic west/east structure exists and the ridges, valleys and coastal indentations generally conform to this control.

2 The amount of fragmentation and dissection resulting from faulting. In the Central Uplands of Germany, the landscape is complicated by the quantity of faulting; deep fault-guided valleys (for example, the River Moselle), rift valleys (for example, the Rhine from Basle to Mainz) and horsts (for example, Harz mountains) are characteristic, and there are few large, uninterrupted plateau sections.

3 The effects of volcanic activity. Here the contrast between the Armorican landscape in the west and central European landscapes is apparent. In the west the volcanic activity was chiefly of the intrusive type, and the granite batholiths depended upon later denudation before they were revealed in the plateau of Dartmoor and ridges of Brittany. In the Eifel and Auvergne regions violent extrusive activity has occurred since the Alpine mountain-building period, and volcanic cones and craters disturb the smooth surfaces. Such action is not associated with instability along plate boundaries, and geologists believe that it is the result of the Eurasian plate moving over a

4

Figure 1.4 (*above*) Tongue of glacier ice extending from the Jostedals plateau icecap, Norway (also see Fig. 2.5)

Figure 1.5 (*below*) An explanation of the line of volcanic features which extend across Central Europe

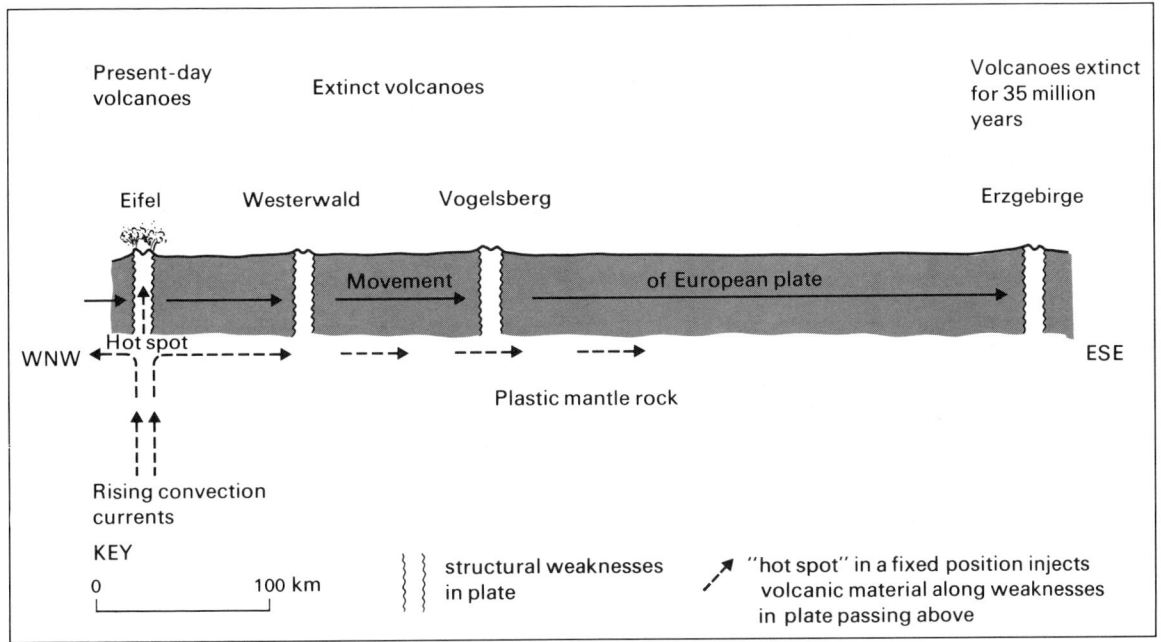

'hot spot' of rising convection currents in the molten zone below the crust. The Eifel are the youngest in a chain of volcanoes stretching from Poland westwards. It also suggests that the Eurasian plate is moving slowly eastwards, a theory supported by a similar movement

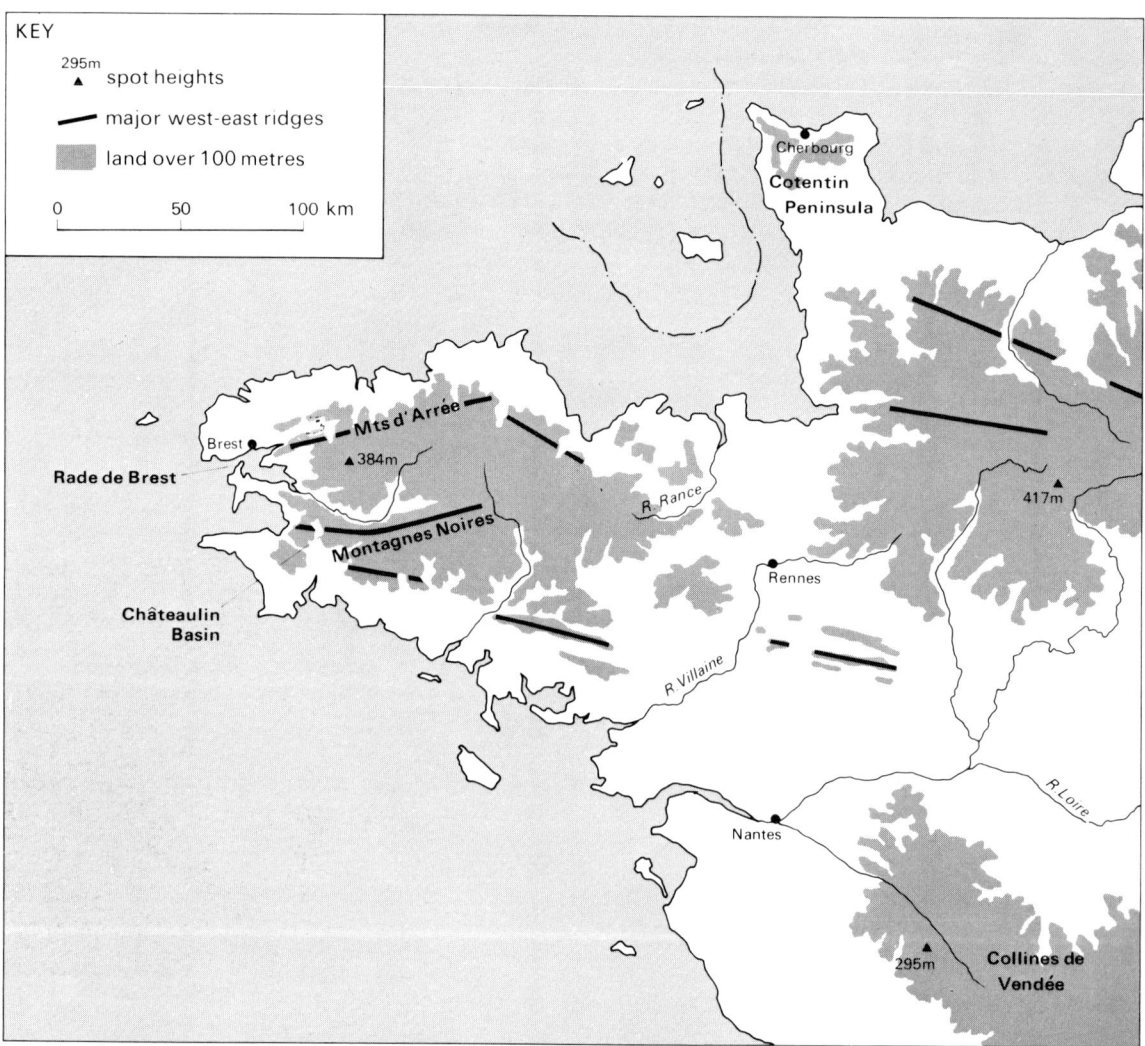

Cherbourg

**Cotentin
Peninsula**

Mts d'Arrée

Brest

▲384m

Rade de Brest

R. Rance

▲417m

Montagnes Noires

Rennes

**Châteaulin
Basin**

R. Villaine

R. Loire

Nantes

▲295m

**Collines de
Vendée**

Figure 1.6 Main relief and drainage features of Brittany

from the mid-Atlantic ridge area.

Between the plateau blocks are lowland troughs, in which later sediments accumulated to be gently folded into a series of anticlines and synclines. The processes of erosion have since breached the anticlines to form scarp and vale features with well-developed surface drainage systems.

Many of the relief features of France originated in the Hercynian period, and the following studies illustrate the principal landscape characteristics of that period.

Brittany
In Brittany the Hercynian uplands comprise ridges running approximately west to east, rising to between 200 and 400 m in height, and enclosing small steep-sided river basins. In the west of the region the Montagnes d'Arrée (384 m) and the Montagnes Noires (326 m) form smooth-topped ridges enclosing the Chateaulin Basin. This basin is drained by the River Aulne, its lower valley submerged by the post-glacial rise in sea level to form a ria, the Rade de Brest. The parallel ridges continue to the coast, where they protrude as twin rocky headlands. The higher ridges are formed of granite intrusions, and produce a landscape very similar to that of the moorlands of south-west England.

6

Paris Basin

The region is a broad saucer-shaped depression within the Hercynian structures, measuring 500 km from west to east and 300 km from north to south. Within the depression a succession of sedimentary strata, accumulated from Jurassic times, was later folded into a gentle syncline tilted slightly to the east. Erosion acting upon the fold structures has exposed the various sedimentary rocks and their varying degrees of resistance have produced a landscape of alternate scarps (côtes) and vales.

The region is drained primarily by the river Seine, which enters the basin from the Massif Central and then gathers tributaries flowing towards the centre of the saucer before breaching the low chalk escarpment in the west. It reaches the sea in a broad estuary. This drainage system cuts through the varied geological surface of outward-facing escarpments and broad vales. Each unit or 'pays' often differs slightly in relief and agricultural

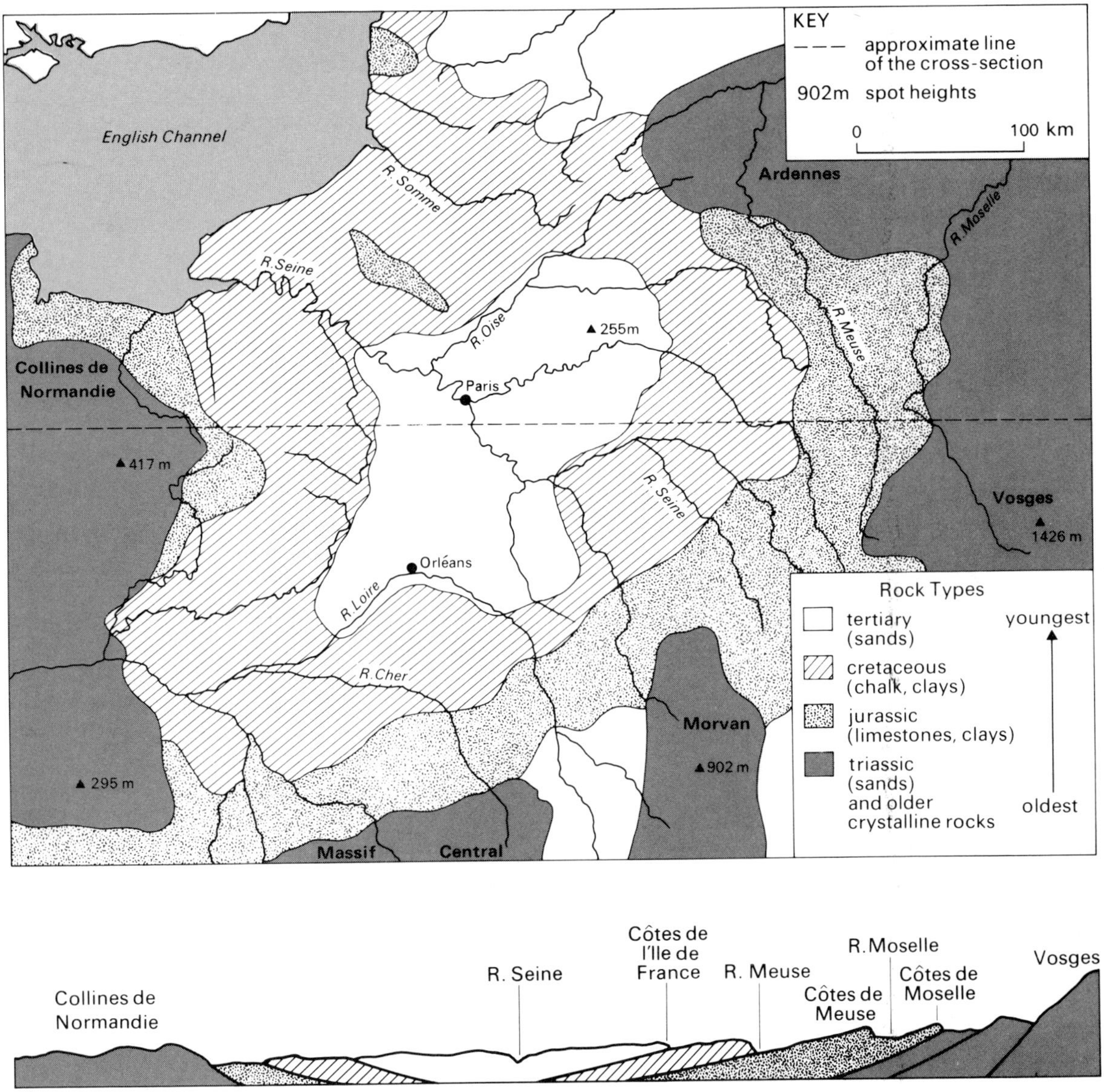

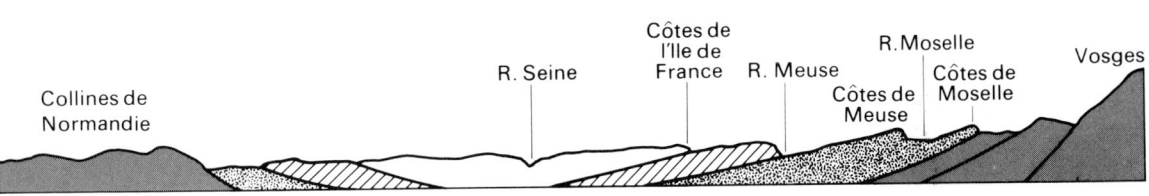

KEY

- – – approximate line of the cross-section

902m spot heights

0   100 km

English Channel

R. Somme

R. Seine

R. Oise

▲ 255m

Paris

Ardennes

R. Moselle

R. Meuse

Collines de Normandie

▲ 417 m

Vosges ▲ 1426 m

R. Seine

Orléans

R. Loire

R. Cher

▲ 295 m

Morvan

▲ 902 m

Massif   Central

Rock Types

tertiary (sands)	youngest
cretaceous (chalk, clays)	
jurassic (limestones, clays)	
triassic (sands) and older crystalline rocks	oldest

Collines de Normandie

R. Seine

Côtes de l'Ile de France

R. Meuse

Côtes de Meuse

R. Moselle

Côtes de Moselle

Vosges

Figure 1.7 A simplified map and cross-section illustrating the geology of the Paris Basin

7

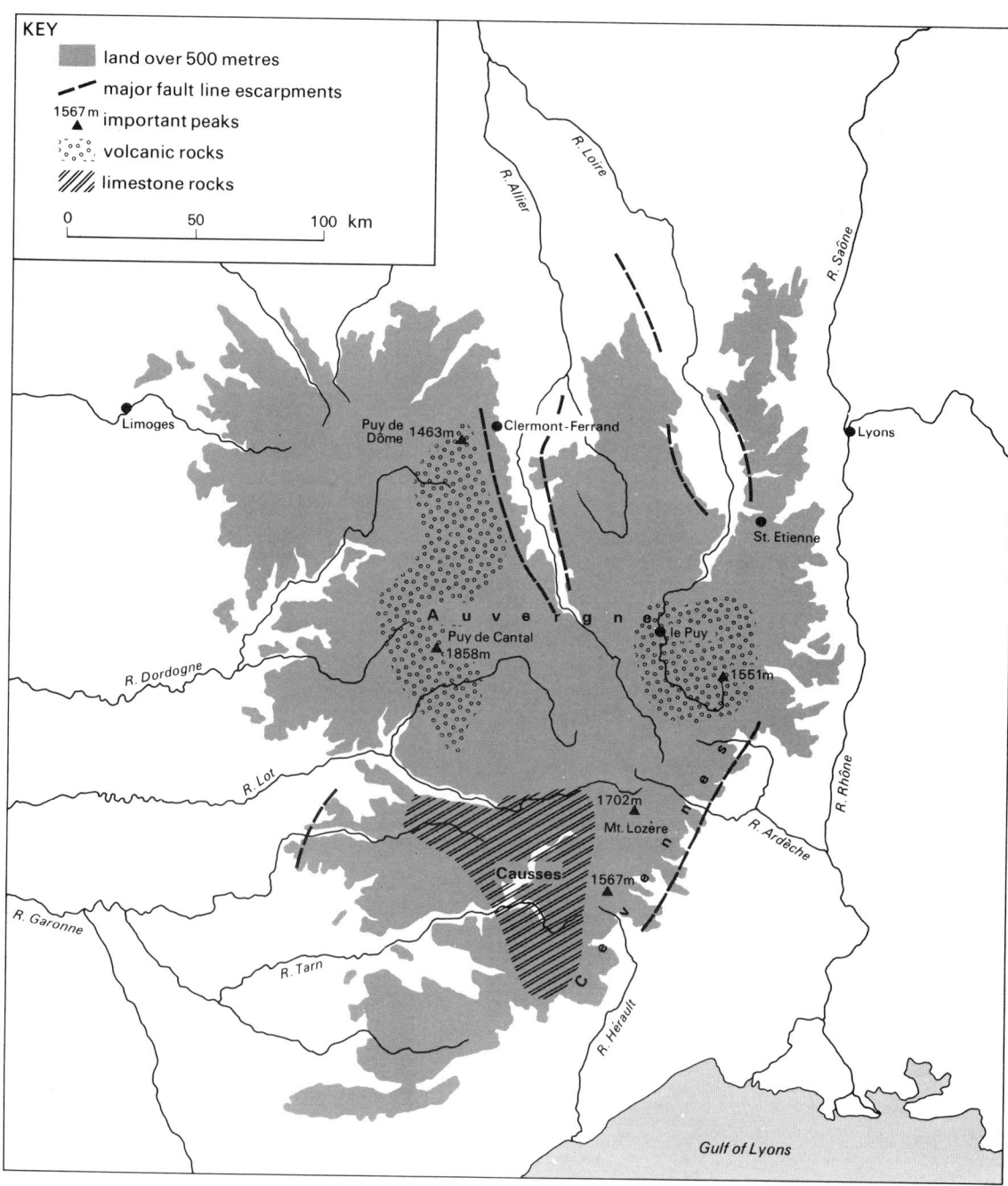

KEY

▓	land over 500 metres
– – –	major fault line escarpments
1567m ▲	important peaks
∴∴∴	volcanic rocks
///	limestone rocks

0   50   100 km

Limoges

Puy de Dôme 1463m▲ ● Clermont-Ferrand

● Lyons

St. Etienne

R. Loire

R. Allier

R. Saône

A u v e r g n e

Puy de Cantal ▲ 1858m

le Puy ● ▲ 1551m

R. Dordogne

R. Lot

R. Rhône

1702m ▲
Mt. Lozère

R. Ardèche

Causses 1567m ●

R. Garonne

R. Tarn

R. Hérault

Gulf of Lyons

Figure 1.8 The main relief and drainage features of the Massif Central

development from its neighbour. The dissection by the Seine and its tributaries also provides natural valley corridors for routes to follow towards the centre of the basin, and helps to explain the position of Paris near the centre of the 'saucer'.

Massif Central

The Massif Central is a faulted plateau block which averages 1000 m in height, but is highest in the scarp of the Cevennes which marks the south-east edge of the region (Mt Lozère 1702 m). The land dips gently away from the

Figure 1.9 Gorge on the river Tarn.
With reference to the photograph:
(**a**) describe the principal features of relief and drainage in the area;
(**b**) describe and explain the distribution of (i) settlements, and (ii) communications

scarp as rolling countryside, dissected by deep steep-sided valleys, until the Hercynian structures end in the west at a plateau edge 300 m high. The rocks of the Massif are granites and ancient sedimentaries, but in the larger valleys recent sediments offer a more suitable surface for farming.

In contrast to the Cevennes scarp, which is cut into by short swift-flowing streams (such as the Ardèche) flowing in steep, narrow valleys, the plateau is crossed by the headwater systems of two of France's major rivers: the Loire and Garonne. These systems dominate the drainage and cut deep valleys into the plateau. The most spectacular valleys are those of the Dordogne, Lot and Tarn as they follow weaknesses in the limestone rocks which yield a landscape of rugged gorges, cliffs and caves.

The volcanic activity which accompanied the building of the Alps was mostly of the extrusive type and finds its fullest development in the Auvergne. In the north of the region the volcanoes are of the acid lava type, rich in silica, of high viscosity and forming steep convex-sided domes or 'puys'. The highest of these is the Puy de Dome (1463 m). Elsewhere, ash and cinder cones predominate. Further south the volcanic masses of Mt Dore and Cantal are of a less viscous, basaltic lava and have more familiar volcanic forms. In the south-east of the Auvergne occur several pinnacles of volcanic rock, remnants of lava plugs which have resisted erosion longer than the ash and lava flanks of the cones.

As can be seen from the foregoing account, it is the Hercynian structures which probably offer the most varied of the landscapes in Western Europe, and through this variety help to explain the provincial style of much of France.

The Alpine Fold Mountains

The mountain ranges which dominate the landscape of Southern Europe are among the most recent structural additions to the continent. Between 70 and 20 million years ago, the African plate moved to crush the sedimentary rocks that lay to the north against the Hercynian surfaces of central Europe. The sedimentary strata were severely folded and

9

Figure 1.10 Acid lava cones on the Auvergne plateau, Central France

Figure 1.11 The Rhône Glacier (top left) now occupies a large corrie basin, having progressively retreated from the main valley

faulted into a series of curving west/east ridges containing numerous igneous intrusions. In the Hercynian structures north of the Alps this upheaval was marked by gentle folding in the sedimentary basins, and volcanic activity and faulting in the hill blocks. Many geologists believe that a revived movement of the African plate is underway, suggested by the seismic (earthquake) activity in southern Italy, North Africa, the Balkan peninsula, Turkey and the Middle East.

During and since the fold movement, the surface of the Alps has been continuously affected by the agents of erosion, particularly running water and ice, so that the mountains have been dissected into a steep, rugged landscape. However, a consistent pattern is clearly visible, with several major mountain chains curving across southern Europe. The only significant breaks in the system are those between the Apennines and Atlas mountains and between the Sierra Nevada and Pyrenees.

The highest ranges are found in the Maritime Alps, where Mont Blanc (4810 m), the Jungfrau (4158 m) and the Matterhorn (4478 m) present rugged surfaces that are almost entirely the work of weathering. The major valleys in the Alps, such as the Rhône, Rhine, Inn and Drava, follow the general west/east structure, and while the sides present difficult surfaces for settlement, the larger valley floors are filled with glacial and river sediments which offer good farmland and important routeways. Although high and imposing, the Alps do not constitute a great physical barrier like the Himalayas, and in addition to the major west/east valley routeways, there are numerous passes like the Brenner, St Gotthard and Mont Cenis to carry communication across the ridges.

Although the results of the recent glaciation are chiefly erosional, on the Swiss Plateau and along the edge of the North Italian Plain deposition has had important effects too. Morainic debris was left by the melting glaciers in irregular, hummocky mounds across the principal lines of drainage. This caused lakes to form, of which Lucerne and Zurich are examples in Switzerland, and Como and Garda in Italy. The patchy deposition of sands and gravels, carried beyond the moraines by streams flowing from the melting ice, has also been an important influence on drainage and settlement in Bavaria and in

Figure 1.12 The Zugspitze (2951 m) in southern Bavaria

11

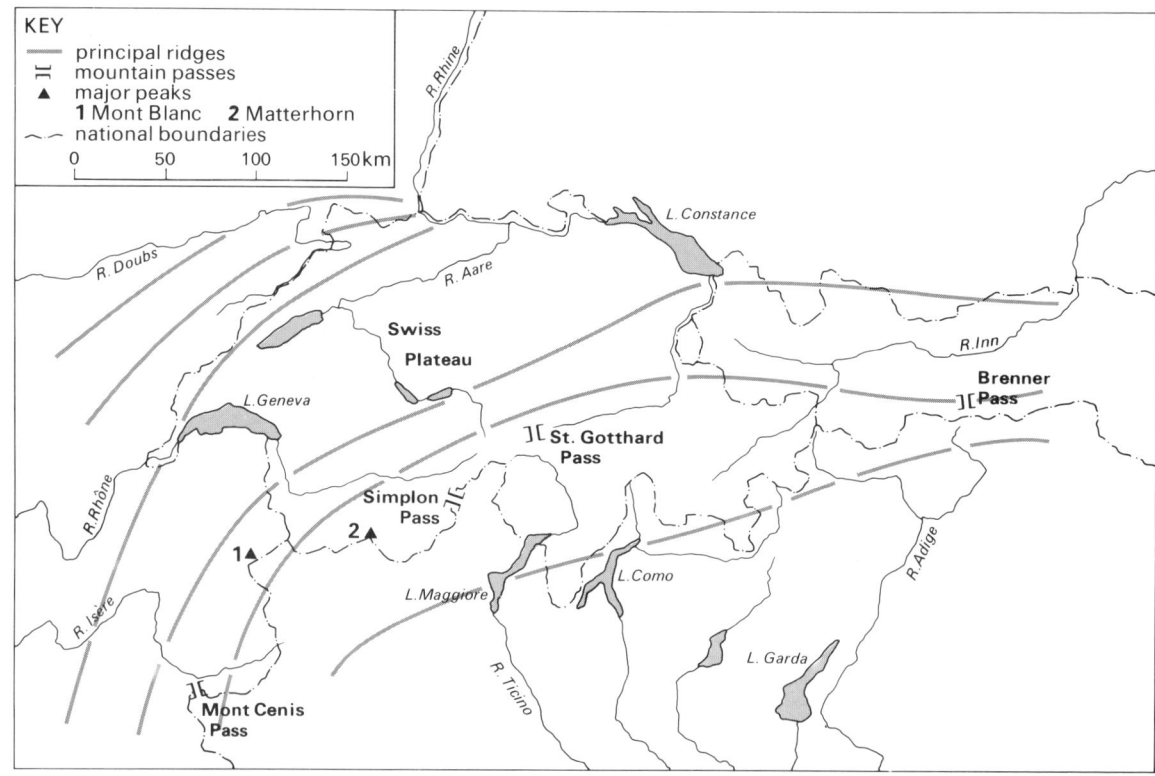

Figure 1.13 The structure and drainage of the Alps

...•... the Fontanali line and
important towns sited
nearby
—— rivers

0   200 km

Figure 1.14 The fontanali line

northern Italy. The close relationship between the 'fontanali line' and the sites of some of the important north Italian cities is shown in Figs 1.14 and 1.15.

Volcanic Activity in Southern Italy

As stated earlier, the Alpine ridges in Italy include a wide range of active volcanic features. The most famous is Mount Vesuvius (1277 m), which has had long periods of quiet, punctuated by violent eruptions of ash and lava—in AD 79 the towns of Pompeii and Herculaneum were destroyed. The top of the cone was removed during this eruption and a new cone, Monte Somma, has since developed within the crater. Around the foot of the mountain the black lava has weathered into a fertile soil, which supports a population density of over 800 per sq. km.

The other active volcanoes are Stromboli (962 m) and Etna (3263 m), although there is geological evidence of earlier activity along much of the west coast. Stromboli and Etna both erupt more frequently than Vesuvius; Stromboli being noted for the ejection of pyroclasts (solids) and Etna for the violence of its eruptions from numerous separate craters.

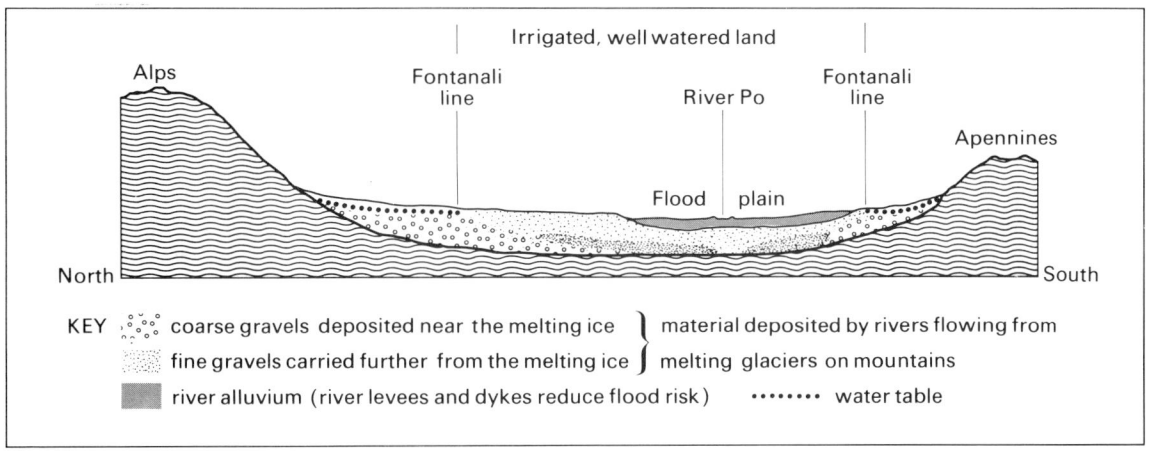

Figure 1.15 Sketch section across the North Italian Plain. The fontanali line marks the zone where the water table breaks surface to provide a reliable water supply for irrigation and domestic use. It is discontinuous and less important in the southern part of the plain than in the north

Figure 1.16 Mount Vesuvius (1277 m) and the settlements around its lower slopes

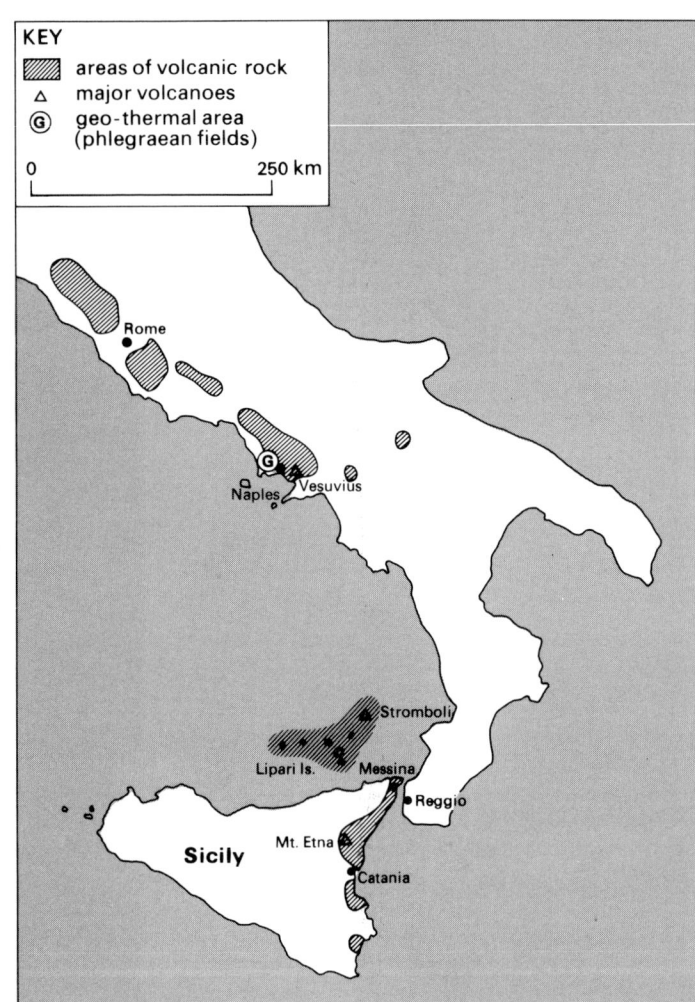

The lava outpourings which occurred between April and June 1971 came from three separate craters and descended over 1000 m, obliterating 200 hectares of orchards and vineyards before halting. The Etna area is a particularly unstable one; the Straits of Messina occupy a fault zone, and the towns of Messina and Reggio have both been severely damaged by earthquakes in the past.

Several minor volcanic features occur in areas where violent activity has virtually ceased. West of Naples, near Pozzuoli, are the Phlegraean Fields, an ancient, gentle-sided crater containing geo-thermal springs named Solfatara, which emit gas and steam. Similar springs near Lardarello in Tuscany have been harnessed to generate electricity. The emission of warm-water mineral springs has also been utilized at several spa and medicinal centres, such as Lucca.

North European Plain

The surface of the North European Plain is largely the product of the recent Ice Age which has affected Europe over the past one

Figure 1.17 (*left*) The volcanic area in southern Italy

Figure 1.18 (*below*) Glacial deposition in northern Europe. Note how the line marking the limit of the final glacial phase follows the route taken by the Lower Elbe. The river course is guided by the morainic ridge left by the melting ice. Other examples where a similar influence is exercised by morainic deposition can be seen where the rivers turn westwards or north-westwards

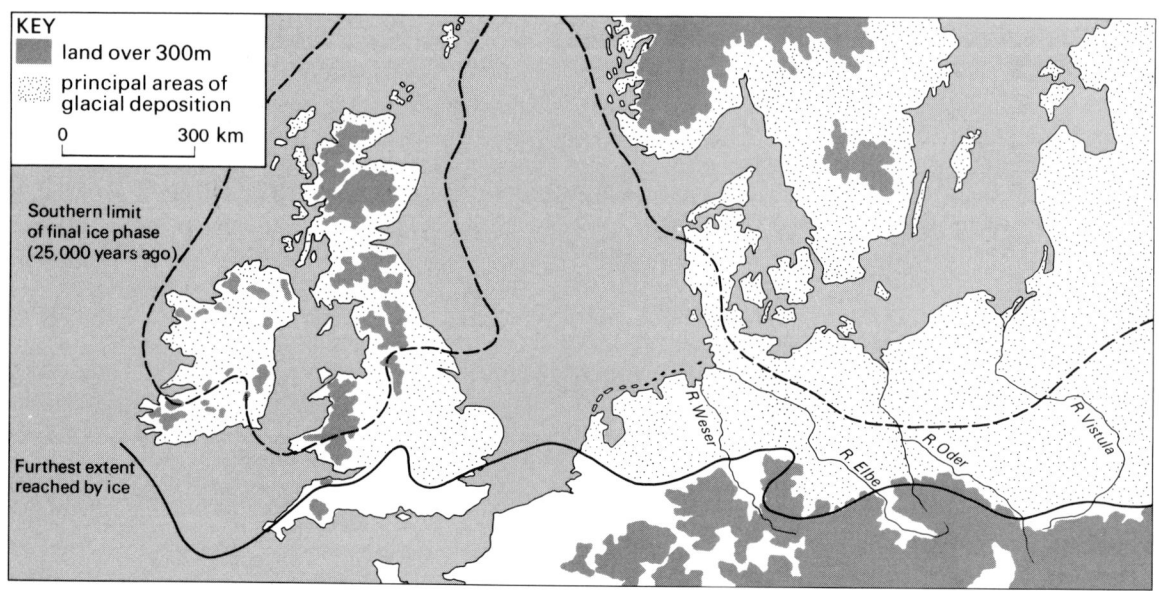

Southern limit of final ice phase (25,000 years ago)

Furthest extent reached by ice

million years. The ice moving from the north made four separate advances onto continental Europe, separated by periods of climatic improvement. During these periods the ice sheets melted and their fronts retreated to more northerly latitudes and to a few high mountain areas. Some geologists believe that the present mild period is another pause between ice advances. A fall of 3°C in the mean annual temperature of the British Isles could result in the formation of permanent icecaps on the plateaux of the Highlands of Scotland.

Figure 1.19 Gently-rolling boulder-clay landscape in Zealand, Denmark

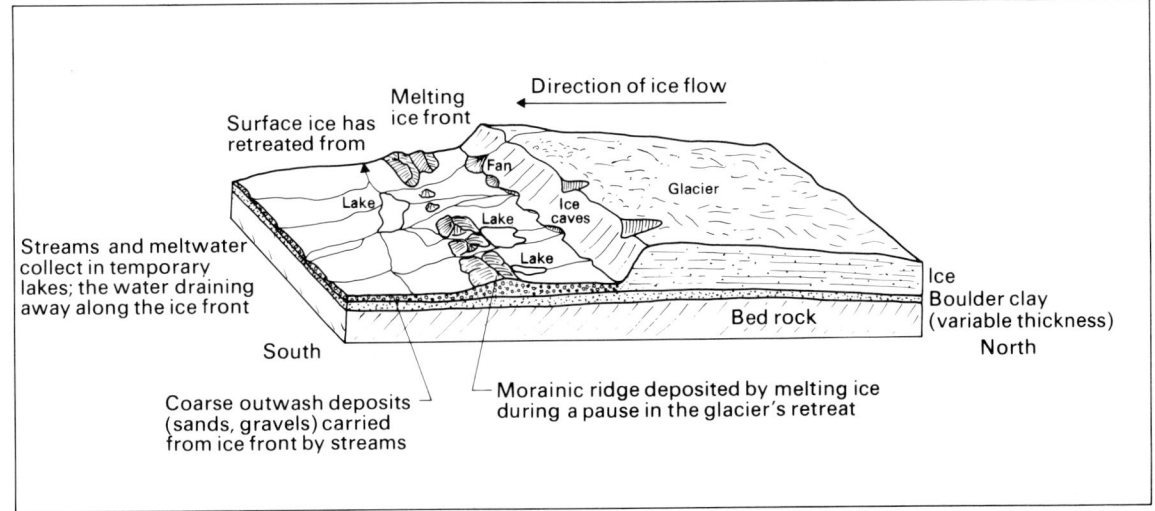

Figure 1.20(a) A reconstruction showing the formation of a glacial lowland plain

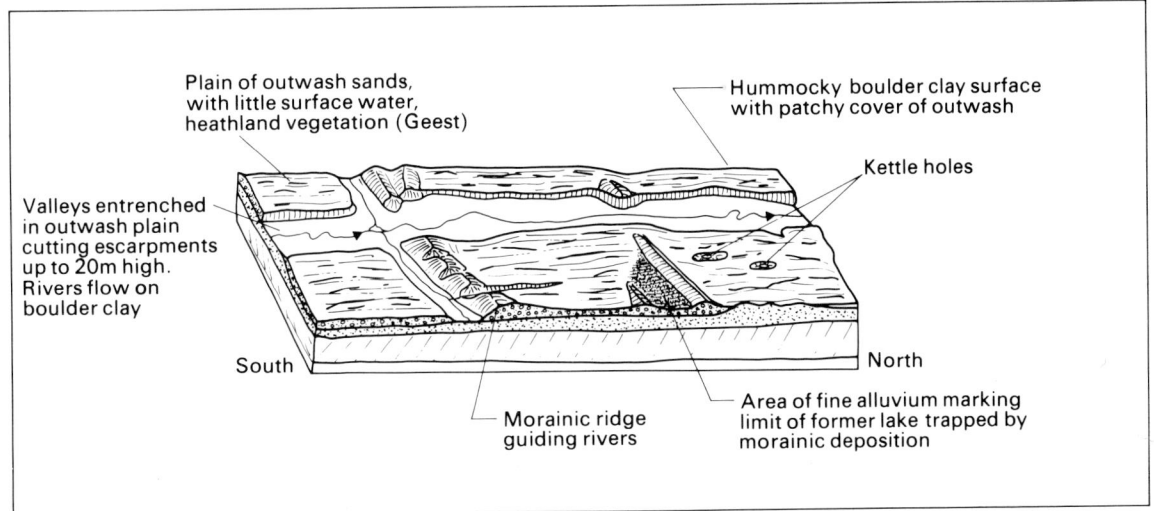

Figure 1.20(b) The same glacial lowland plain after ice has left the area

The erosional effects of the glaciation are best seen in Norway and Switzerland, while depositional features occur widely on the North European Plain. In places, the boulder clay, outwash and alluvial deposits of successive ice retreats were laid upon earlier deposition. Each type of deposition produces a characteristic surface so that the North European Plain, in spite of its generally low relief, offers a variety of landscapes. In north Germany, western Jutland and the eastern Netherlands, outwash sands predominate and have formed a heathland or 'geest' surface. Where the rivers Rhine, Ems, Weser and Elbe cross the geest, broad trenches have been cut and the rivers often flow on the boulder clay beneath. River alluvium has been deposited in these trenches and their damp surface is in marked contrast to the dry heathland. The morainic ridges are an important influence on the direction of the drainage. Most major rivers flowing northwards show several instances of having been diverted along the line of the ridges before breaking through to the sea. At the coast the river Rhine has formed a delta, while the north German rivers have long, deep estuaries.

An effect of the Ice Age which is apparent throughout Western Europe is the fluctuation in the levels of land and sea. During the periods of ice advance the weight of glacier ice depressed the floating European 'plate' into the underlying plastic mantle rocks. When the ice melted, an immediate submergence of coastal valleys occurred to form fjords, rias and isolated chains of islands. Gradually, the depressed European plate is recovering its former position, and in doing so has revealed islands and raised beaches while providing shallow-water conditions to encourage deposition in the narrow fjords and rias. The coast of Europe illustrates the features of both a submerged and rising shoreline.

Questions

1. For each of the following landscape types—block mountains, a shield area, a lowland plain:

(a) name an example;
(b) draw a sketch map to show its location;
(c) describe its characteristic surface features.

2. Name *three* different areas in Europe that have been affected by the recent Ice Age. Describe and explain the characteristic landscape features of each.

3. With reference to Fig. 1.8 and the text, answer the following questions on the Massif Central.
(a) Suggest reasons to explain the deep valleys of (i) the Upper Lot and Tarn, and (ii) the Upper Loire and Allier.
(b) Describe the pattern of drainage in the area.
(c) Account for the distribution of the peaks shown on the map.

4. With reference to Fig. 1.13 describe how the pattern of mountain ridges has influenced drainage.

5. Find out all you can about the subject 'plate tectonics'. The following references will prove helpful:
Nigel Calder: *The Restless Earth*, BBC Publications (1972);
John Dewey: 'Plate Tectonics', *Scientific American*, vol. 226, No 5, pp. 56–68 (May 1972);
HMSO (Geological Museum) *The Story of the Earth*.

6. Make a copy of the map in Fig. 1.14 and name *three* of the lakes shown.

7. With reference to Fig. 1.16
(a) describe the shape of Mount Vesuvius;
(b) explain with the aid of diagrams how the mountain has been formed;
(c) suggest reasons to explain the concentration of settlement on the lower slopes.

2 Climate

Europe has been described as a 'peninsula of peninsulas', and it is the dominant influence of the sea which gives the continent its main climatic characteristics. Clearly, other factors exert local influence, but above all else it is the penetration of the moderating effects of the Atlantic Ocean which determines the West European type of climate. Its significance becomes less towards the east; the difference between summer and winter temperatures widens, and rainfall declines. The indented character of the European coastline allows the moderating influence of the sea and the southwest prevailing winds to penetrate deeply into the continent. A comparison between selected European and North American towns illustrates the particular benevolence of the European climate (*see table below*).

Distance from the sea, latitude and altitude are the major considerations in determining the climate of an area.

Distance from the Sea

Land and water surfaces react differently to the solar heat they receive. On land, only a thin surface layer is heated or cooled, the ground below being relatively unaffected by seasonal changes in temperature. The sea, being liquid, can distribute the solar heat it receives both horizontally and, to some extent, vertically; so that in summer heat is dispersed through the water to make sea temperatures cooler than those on the land. In winter, heat is lost rapidly from the land surface by radiation, while the sea, having its heat less concentrated near the surface, loses less and has a higher temperature.

Europe, with its deeply indented shoreline, is influenced by the ability of the surrounding seas to act as 'heat reservoirs' in winter, so that temperatures are very mild for the latitude of the continent: the coastline of northern Norway is 15°C warmer than the average for the latitude, and ports are ice free throughout winter. The prevailing south-westerly winds and the ocean current, the North Atlantic Drift, carry tropical maritime air northwards to restrict the effects of cold, dry winds blowing outwards from the Polar 'high' pressure belt. Where the warm maritime air meets the cold Polar air, depressions frequently occur and continue eastwards across the European lowlands before dispersing over continental Europe. Places distant from the sea, or shut off from its influence by a relief barrier, have a noticeably wider temperature range; this increases from 11°C at Brest, to 19°C at Berlin and 28°C at Moscow.

The influence of the sea as a cooling agent in summer is less effective; only exposed coastal sites receive summer temperatures which are lower than average for their latitude. In summer, the ability of the land surface of Europe to absorb solar heat is a main influence upon the temperature, and a low pressure belt extends across the continent. As a result, summer rainfall in Western

	Station	Latitude	Longitude	Height above sea level	Average January	Average July	Range	Rainfall
West Coast	Brest	48°N	5°W	64·6 m	7°C	18°C	11	736 mm
	Seattle	47°N	122°W	37·3 m	5°C	15°C	10	1214 mm
Interior	Kiev	50°N	31°E	179·2 m	−4°C	19°C	23	533 mm
	Regina	50°N	105°W	571·5 m	−18°C	18°C	36	381 mm

Europe is less frequently associated with the passage of depressions from the west, but more often caused by rising currents of warm air bringing heavy but localized storms.

Latitude

The control of latitude upon temperature is less marked in Europe than in other continents, because of the strength of the maritime influence. The latitudinal spread is from 36°N to 71°N, a span which neatly confines Europe to the temperate zone. The angle of the sun's rays, which largely determines the amount of solar heat received, is nowhere sufficient to cause wide seasonal changes in temperature. The difference in the angle of the sun at mid-day between Hammerfest (71°N) and Gibraltar (36°N) is 35°. Likewise, latitudinal variations in the length of daylight are not as wide as in other continents. At the Equator almost exactly twelve hours daylight and twelve hours darkness are experienced throughout the year; towards the poles the length of daylight increases during summer and decreases during winter. The effect of the increased summer daylight as one travels northwards in part compensates for the reduction in intensity caused by the more acute angle of the sun's rays.

Height Above Sea Level

The principal effect of increased altitude is to reduce the mean temperature at an average rate of 3°C per 500 m. This fall in temperature is caused by the thinner air at high altitudes which, in particular, lacks water vapour and carbon dioxide. Because of high relative density these gases are at their greatest concentration in areas of low altitude, where they readily absorb solar heat. In high areas the air is less able to absorb heat, and radiation from the ground at night goes on unrestricted by the presence of a cover of dense air. Conversely, in low areas the denser air keeps temperatures higher and more constant.

High land usually experiences heavier precipitation than similarly placed lowlands. The combined rain and snowfall is particularly high where a relief barrier lies across the route of an on-shore prevailing wind, as in southwest Norway. The mechanics of relief rainfall are illustrated in Fig. 2.2.

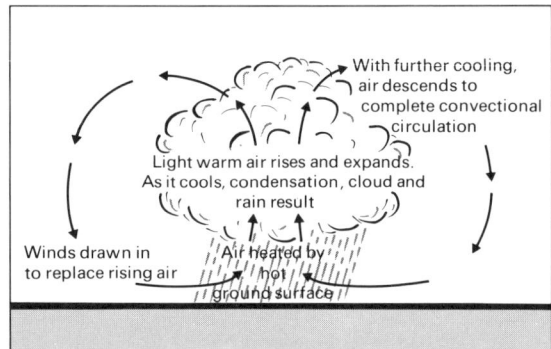

Figure 2.1 Convectional rainfall (chiefly in summer)

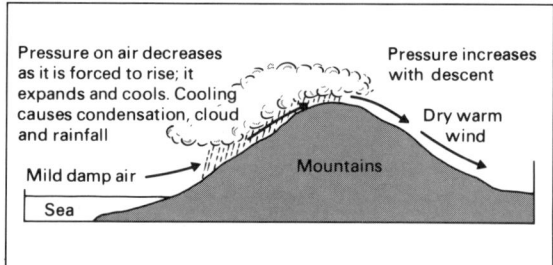

Figure 2.2 Relief rainfall

The Climatic Regions of Europe

Europe is in a zone where air from four diverse sources, maritime, polar, continental and tropical, mixes. The nature of the coastline and west/east direction of the mountains and valleys allows these influences to spread and interact. Occasionally the continent comes under the domination of one influence, but usually its severe effects are avoided. Hence, the overriding characteristic of the climate is its mildness and lack of extremes. By reference to Fig. 2.3, the influence of the continental land mass can be observed at Warsaw and Gällivare, while Palermo shows the familiar summer drought of Mediterranean areas. Overall, however, the variation in European climates is less than that shown within the temperate zone of any other continent.

1 Tundra* Region

The region is characterized by a short growing season, with winters lasting 8–9 months. In the short summers, only the ground surface thaws, causing floods in the low-lying areas,

---

* The word 'tundra' is used here to define a climatic region rather than a type of vegetation.

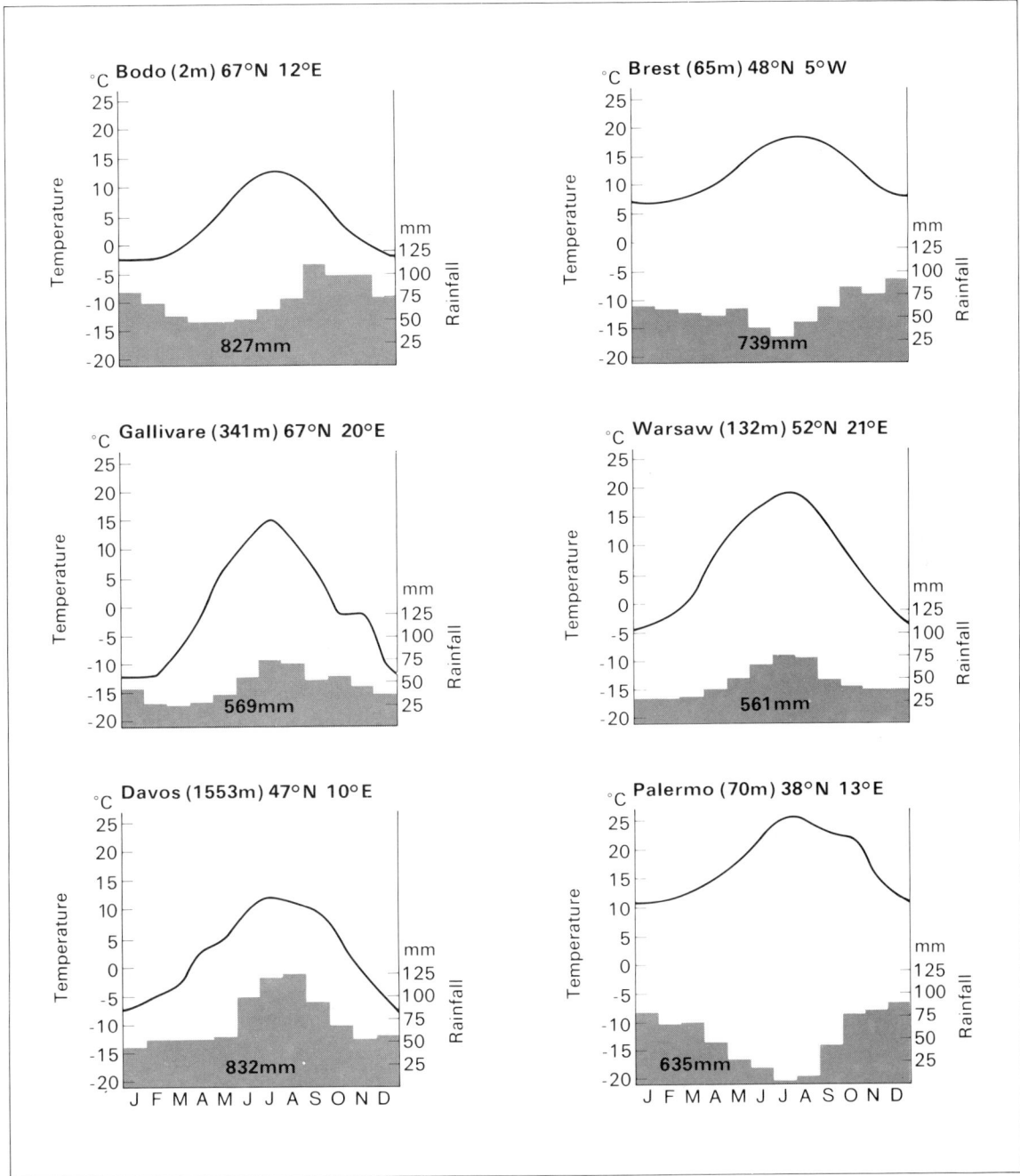

Figure 2.3 Climate graphs of selected European stations

and a vegetation cover of mosses, lichens, low-growing shrubs and short, flowering plants becomes established. The climatic conditions are the result of three main factors:

(a) the northern latitude, which produces long cold winters and short summers;

(b) the area is cut off by the mountain chain of Norway from the mild influence of the Atlantic;

(c) the dry, cold winds coming from the Polar and continental high-pressure systems in winter.

19

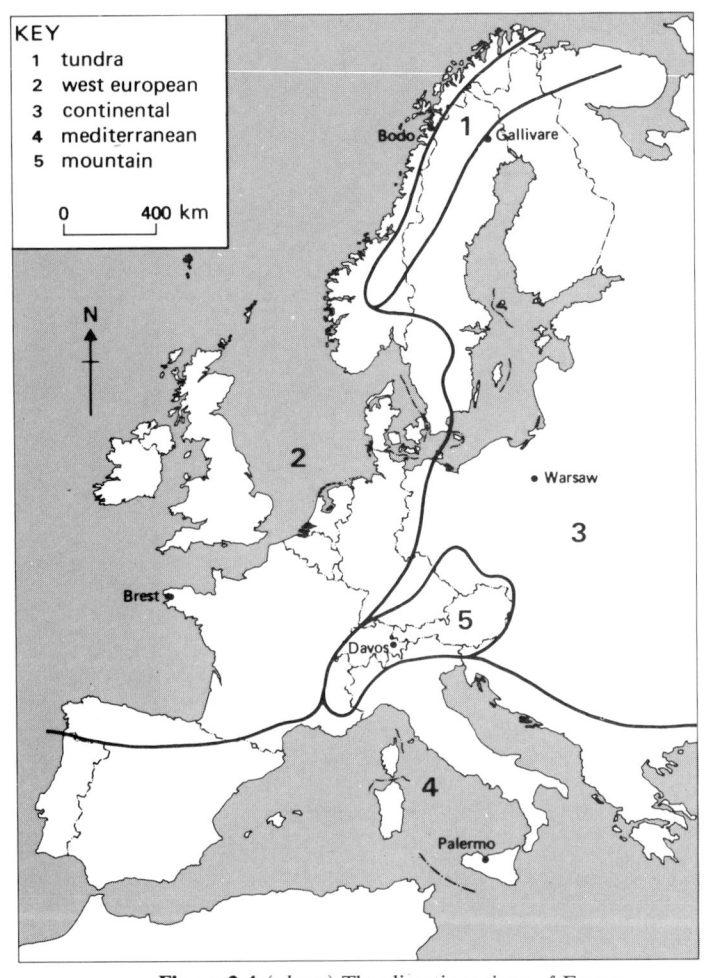

KEY
1 tundra
2 west european
3 continental
4 mediterranean
5 mountain

0   400 km

N

Bodo
Gallivare
1
2
Warsaw
3
Brest
5
Davos
4
Palermo

Figure 2.4 (*above*) The climatic regions of Europe

The area extends south of the Arctic Circle to include the high plateau regions of Norway where the increased altitude, averaging 1500 m, cancels out the influence of the more southerly latitude and causes tundra conditions to persist. In central and southern Norway the sunnier, warmer summers encourage the development of a wider range of mountain plants than in the north. A permanent snow cover exists above 1500 m in southern Norway, forming such plateau icecaps as the Jostedals and Fogelfonn; but permanent snow is present above 750 m in the colder north.

Precipitation, most of it in the form of snow, varies with an area's exposure to maritime air currents. It ranges from over 1250 mm in the southern plateau areas to under 500 mm in northern Scandinavia. Snow is frequently redistributed by blizzards, which add a further hazard to life in these areas.

2 The West European Region   *C.T.W.C.*

In this region the maritime influence has its greatest effect, and the climate is mild in winter and warm in summer with an annual temperature range of less than 16°C. Precipitation, largely in the form of rain, is more consistent and reliable than in any other part of the continent, and totals reach 1250 mm on exposed coastal sites, but fall to 500 mm in more sheltered inland areas. The cause of

Figure 2.5 (*below*) The Jostedals icecap

Figure 2.6 Depression tracks across Western Europe

Mechanism. In the temperate latitudes warm maritime air masses move north-east to meet cold polar air extending south. The warm air rises over the cold causing an area of low pressure to form. Both polar and maritime air are drawn in to take its place and an anti-clockwise circulation is set up, spiralling towards the centre of the depression. The warm front marks the slope where warm air rides above the cold; the water vapour in the air condensing on nucleii to form cloud and rain. The cold front marks the zone where cold polar air is drawn towards the centre of the depression, meeting and replacing the warm air by driving underneath it. Some of the warm air is cooled, and a narrow cloud and rain belt results. As the depression progresses eastwards the cold front travels faster and gains on the warm front until they meet and the warm sector is raised above surface level to form an occlusion. An occlusion is classified as 'warm' if the cold air at the rear of the depression is less cold than that at the front, and 'cold' if the reverse situation exists

Passage. In Europe the passage of depressions is most marked in winter along a front between latitude 40°N and 60°N. As the depressions, separated by ridges of high pressure, move eastwards onto the European coast, they deepen and produce stormy weather conditions. However, the weather accompanying the passage is usually predictable, its approach being heralded by a gradual thickening and lowering of the cloud layer until the warm front has passed. Temperatures rise with the arrival of the warm sector until the south-west wind is replaced by a north-east one to mark the arrival of the cold front. Following the passage of the cold front and its rain belt, skies clear and temperatures fall as cold air moves in again

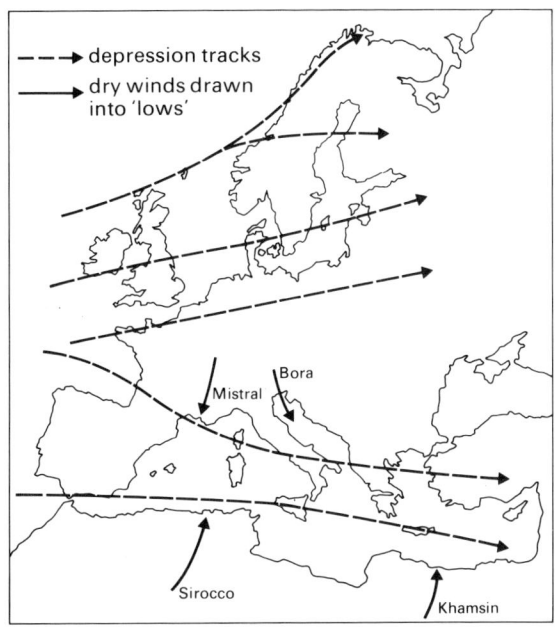

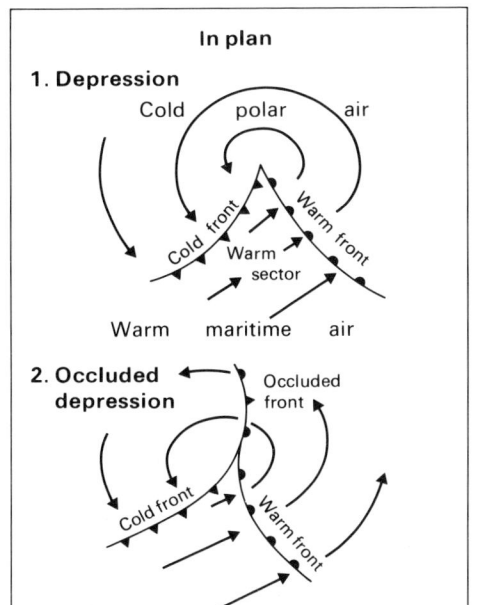

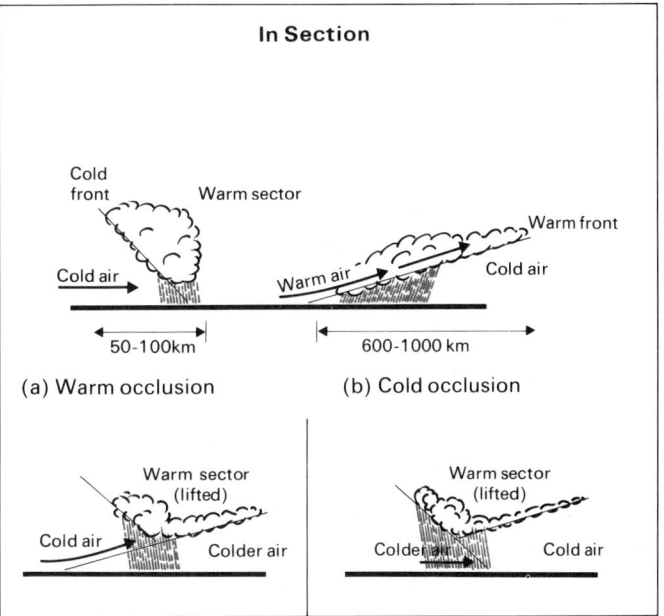

21

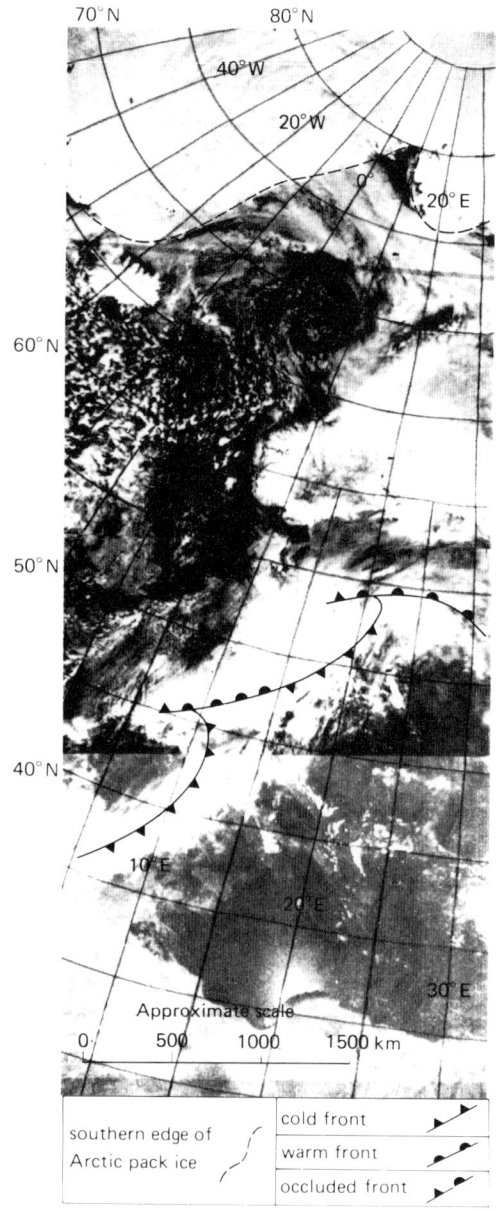

Figure 2.7 Satellite photograph of weather conditions over Europe at 09.45 on 20 April 1970. A system of two depressions is shown over central Europe with a ridge of High Pressure.

With reference to the photograph answer the following questions.

(a) On an outline map of Europe note the main weather features shown on the photograph. With the help of an atlas, mark and label: (i) an area of High Pressure, and (ii) the position of the warm and cold fronts over Central Europe. Summarize the weather conditions associated with each.

(b) Describe and account for the extent of the Arctic pack ice shown on the photograph

most of the precipitation is the meeting of warm maritime air and cold polar air, which sets up a series of depressions which travel eastwards into Europe.

Depressions vary in size from 400 to 1200 km in diameter and travel at speeds of up to 25 k/h. The frequency at which depressions cross into Western Europe, particularly in winter, helps to explain the marked day-to-day changes in weather conditions, which characterize their passage.

Separating the 'low' pressure depressions are ridges of 'high' pressure which give more stable anticyclonic conditions. These ridges extend from the Polar and continental 'high' pressure zones in winter, giving cold, dry conditions, and from the Azores 'high' in summer, producing warm, dry weather.

The high nature of the relief of much of Western Europe frequently causes extremely low temperature and high precipitation—conditions which are not found at sea level. The plateau icecaps of south-west Norway illustrate how Arctic conditions can exist within a few miles of the sea. Some climatic stations in the mountains of Norway, Scotland and Wales, regularly record rainfall figures of over 2500 mm.

3 The Continental Region

The transition from the mild conditions of the west coast to the more extreme conditions of interior Europe is very gradual. In the North European Plain it is especially apparent, the low relief allowing maritime air to penetrate eastwards.

Without ever showing extreme continental conditions, central Europe has marked seasonal differences in temperature. The rain falls mainly in the summer and is of the convectional type. Distance from the Atlantic Ocean reduces the cooling influence of the sea, and high ground temperatures cause the air currents to rise. As the air rises it cools, and any water vapour in the air condenses around nucleii to form water particles. As condensation increases, the density of these particles becomes greater and clouds form, which gradually thicken and so appear darker. The particles of water, buffetted by the air currents, join and become heavy enough to fall as droplets of rain. If the convection is strong, violent storms of short duration, often accompanied by thunder and lightning, result.

The small winter precipitation decreases eastwards and is often in the form of snow. It results from depressions forming where the prevailing westerlies have carried maritime air eastwards to meet and be cooled by cold air moving from the continental 'high' over Asia.

4 The Mediterranean Region W.T.W.C.

The type of climate known as 'Mediterranean', or West Coast Warm Temperate, occurs on the west coast of all the continents centred upon latitudes 35°N and 35°S. It is one of the most easily identifiable of climates, being outstanding in the temperate region for its marked winter rainfall maximum and virtual summer drought. The winter temperatures are mild and the summer hot. The maritime character of the area determines the mild winters, and results in some cooling effects in the western Mediterranean in summer, but the dominant summer influence is the high pressure zone from which the northeast trade winds blow across the region towards the low pressure system over Africa. These winds are warm and dry and contrast with the mild, wet westerlies which carry the rain into the region in winter. The marked seasonal change in climate is the result of the movement of the permanent pressure belts, which put the region under the influence of the westerlies in winter, but the north-east trade winds in summer. Distance from the Atlantic Ocean controls the strength of the maritime influence and its effects are illustrated by a comparison of Gibraltar, Smyrna (Turkey) and Alexandria (*see table*).

The region having a true Mediterranean climate is limited to the immediate coastal areas. To the north, the climate develops the continental characteristics of a wider temperature range and increased summer rainfall, while inland from the North African coast rainfall decreases and desert conditions occur. The climate also loses some of its identity in the interior of the Iberian peninsula and in northern Italy, where continental characteristics become marked (see Fig. 2.7).

An interesting local feature of the Mediterranean region is the occurrence of dry winds drawn into the depressions crossing the area in winter. Such winds are the Mistral and Bora, funnelling southwards along the Rhône valley and northern Adriatic to bring cold dry conditions; and the Sirrocco and Khamsin

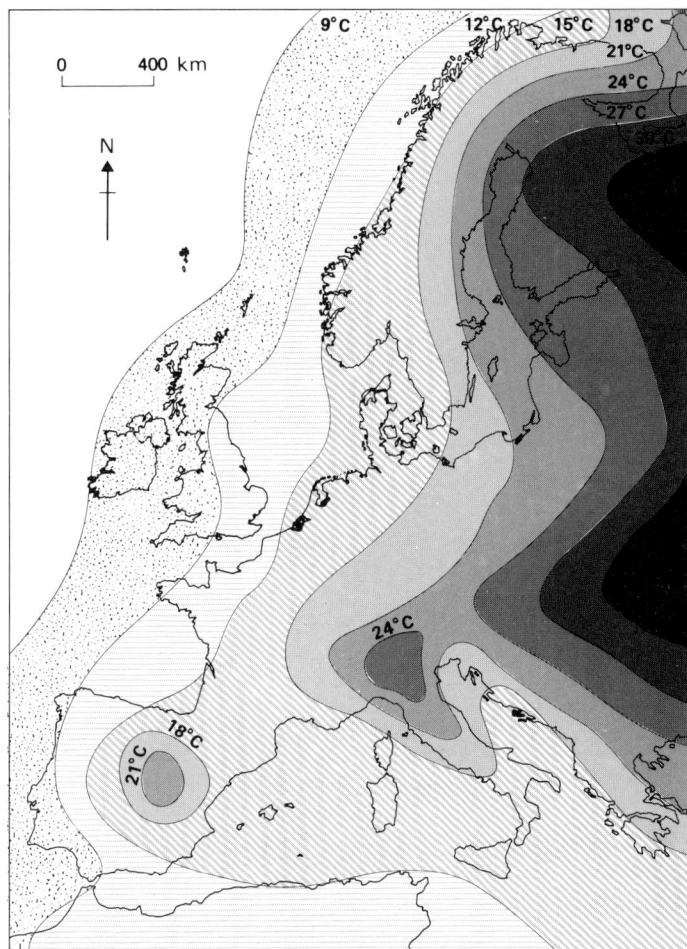

Figure 2.8 Isopleths showing the seasonal range of temperatures

Maritime influence upon selected Mediterranean stations			
	Gibraltar (36°N 5°W) Height 16·5 m	Smyrna (28°N 27°E) Height 20·1 m	Alexandria (31°N 30°E) Height 31·8 m
Rainfall total (%Nov-April)	907 mm(80%)	653 mm(83%)	206 mm(95%)
January temp.	13°C	8°C	14°C
July temp.	23°C	26°C	27°C

23

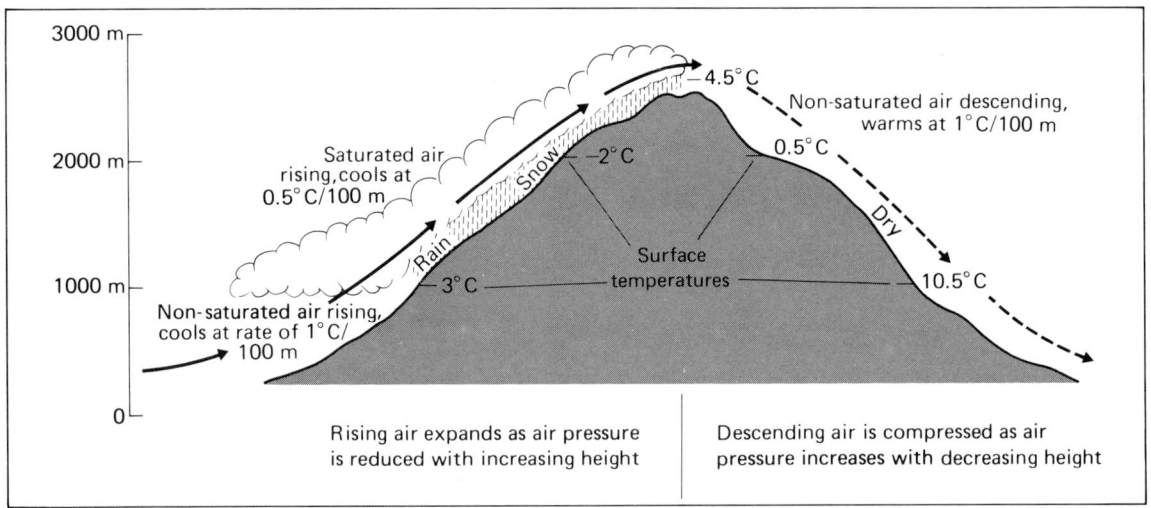

Figure 2.9 (*above*) The Föhn wind. Compare the temperatures at 1000 m on each side of the mountain

Figure 2.10 (*below*) Summer climatic conditions

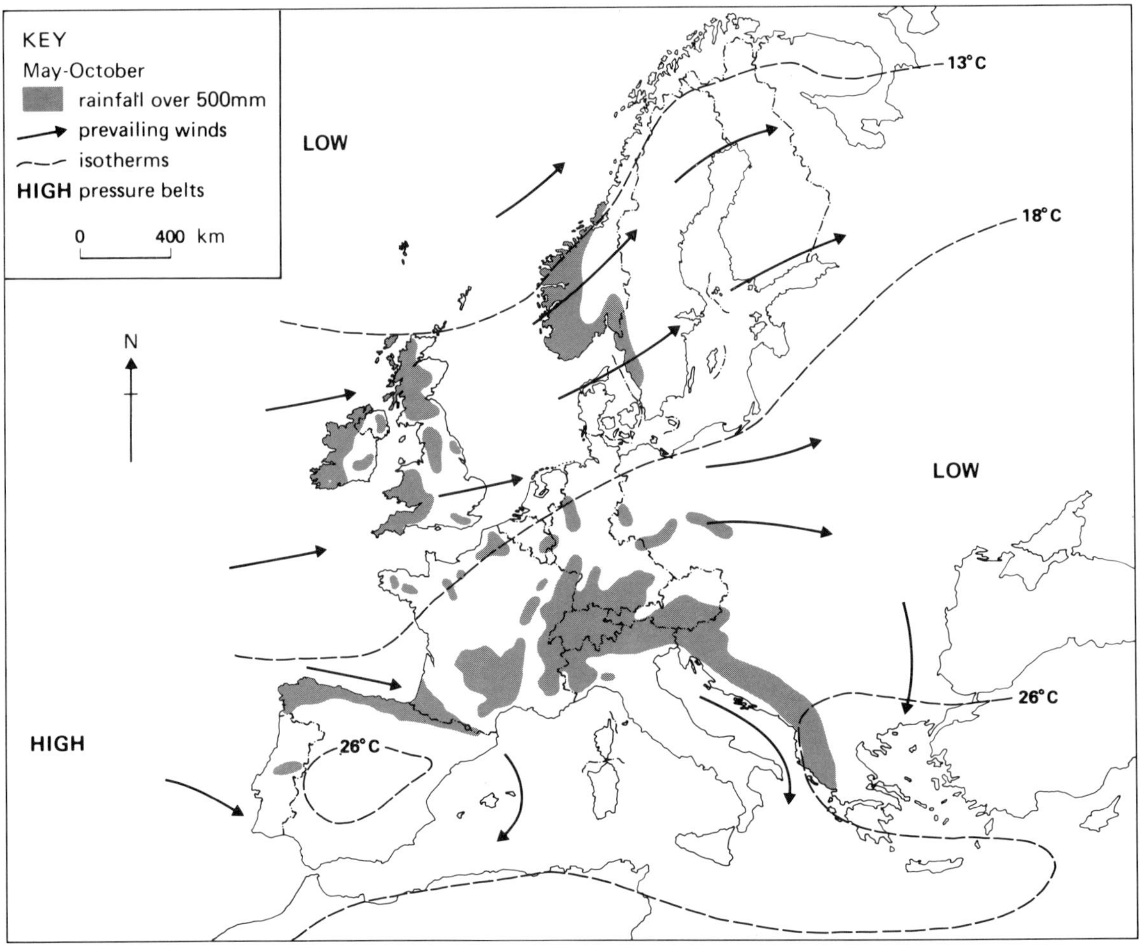

KEY
May-October
rainfall over 500mm
prevailing winds
isotherms
HIGH pressure belts

0   400 km

N

LOW

13°C

18°C

LOW

HIGH

26°C

26°C

winds blowing hot, dry air northwards off the Sahara Desert onto the North African coast.

Mountain Climates

The two principal mountain systems of Europe are the Caledonian ranges in the north-west and the Alpine ranges in the south, which rise to average heights of 1000 m and 2000 m respectively. In southern Norway the severity of the climate increases with height to produce tundra conditions on the plateau surfaces. In the Alps the range within the climate is more marked, due to the greater heights involved and the southerly latitude of the area. From the Mediterranean coast to the crests of the Maritime Alps in France, the mean temperatures gradually fall until a permanent snow line is reached at about 2000 m.

These climatic changes are reflected in the differences in vegetation.

The Alps lie across Europe where the West European and continental climatic regions to the north merge into the Mediterranean region in the south. Consequently, there is no general pattern to the precipitation; although the western Alps usually have a winter maximum, while the eastern Alps are further from the Atlantic Ocean and exhibit the continental characteristic of a summer maximum.

An important factor which influences the climate of particular mountain locations is aspect. A sunny southern or moist westerly aspect is more desirable for settlement and farming than the cooler and drier situations facing the north or east.

A feature of all mountain areas, but one which is particularly influential in the Alps, is

Figure 2.11 Winter climatic conditions

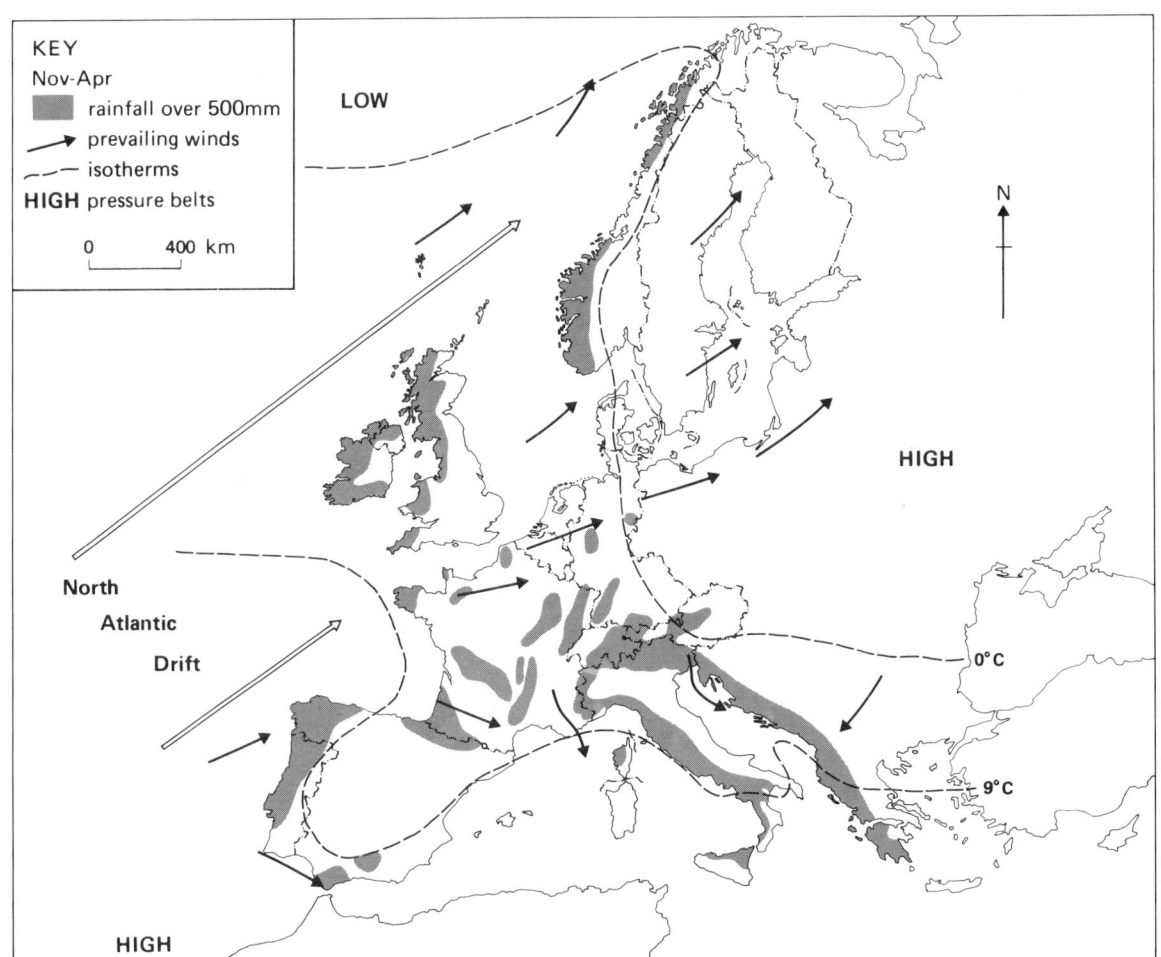

KEY
Nov–Apr
▨ rainfall over 500mm
→ prevailing winds
– – – isotherms
HIGH pressure belts

0   400 km

LOW

N

HIGH

North
Atlantic
Drift

0°C

9°C

HIGH

the föhn wind. It is a warm, dry wind which descends the mountain slopes in winter and early spring. Sometimes it helps to cause avalanches and forest fires, but it is also consistently beneficial in that it melts and clears the snow from the Alpine meadows and enables the early cultivation of crops in the valley bottoms. The föhn wind gives a simple illustration of the different rates at which air cools on rising and warms on descending. In Switzerland it is a north–south blowing wind and is most effective in a valley such as the Rhine above Lake Constance (Bodensee), which is aligned in that direction.

Clearly, mountain areas exhibit considerable variety in their climate, but in general one can expect temperatures to be cooler and precipitation higher than in equivalent sea-level locations.

Questions

1. List *four* important factors which help to determine the climate of Europe, and describe the influence of each.

2. Choose *three* contrasted climate graphs from Fig. 2.3, and suggest reasons for the differences they show.

3. With reference to Fig. 2.10, describe the summer climatic conditions of Europe. With reference to Fig. 2.11, describe the winter climatic conditions of Europe.

4. Imagine a period of 48 hours during which time a complete depression passes over your house. Describe and explain the weather that (*a*) heralded the approach of the depression, and (*b*) accompanied its passage.

5. For each of the following sets of statistics of European stations:
(*a*) suggest a location for the station;
(*b*) describe and explain its climate conditions;
(*c*) describe briefly the natural vegetation of the area.

| Station | Height above Sea level | Temperature | | | Rainfall | |
		January	July	Range	Total	Distribution Oct–Mar
A	12 m	−15°C	6°C	21°C	295 mm	187 mm
B	215 m	−2°C	20°C	22°C	635 mm	260 mm
C	65 m	7°C	25°C	18°C	817 mm	552 mm
D	9 m	7°C	15°C	8°C	1392 mm	817 mm

3 Soil and vegetation

The Composition of Soil

Soil is comprised of organic and inorganic materials; the former are primarily derived from decayed animals and plants and the latter from bedrock. It is the mixing, by moving water, of these two materials which gives each soil type its main characteristics. Of the two, the organic material is the more important, and it is chiefly the variations in rainfall effectiveness which determine the vegetation cover.

Organic Materials

The organic constituents in a soil are derived from the decay of plants and animals which have died and fallen to the ground. Decay is relatively rapid, and is carried out by bacteria and other soil organisms which are activated by oxygen obtained from percolating rainwater. The bacteria cause the organic material to decompose into soluble compounds which are distributed by water through the soil for plant systems to absorb.

A plant's nitrogen requirements are not met from this source, but direct from the air. Bacteria living within the nodules of leguminous plants (for example, pea and bean) absorb the nitrogen and convert it into a soluble form available to plants.

The decayed organic material is known as humus, and it is vital to the fertility of a soil. However, where the free movement of water in the soil is absent, waterlogging will occur to slow the breakdown of organic material. Where the pore-spaces are filled with water and there is little air in the soil, decay is slow, and damp, acid peat areas are formed.

Inorganic Materials

These materials in the soil primarily derive from the breakdown of the bedrock surface by weathering agents. They can, however, be redistributed far from where the original breakdown occurred. River water can carry silts and deposit them over flood plain areas in a sufficiently fine form to be readily absorbed and used in soils. Similarly, the deposition of fine wind-blown loess over large parts of central Europe occurred at the end of the recent Ice Age, and is available as soil without further reduction.

The principal weathering processes which act upon a rock surface are a result of temperature and chemical changes.

Temperature Changes

In temperate latitudes and high mountain areas day and night time temperatures rise above and fall below 0°C many times over a five- to eight-month period each year. Where water (or snow) has gathered in rock crevices and in the pore-spaces of rocks, freezing produces a 9 per cent expansion in volume which, when repeated many times, causes rocks to crack or disintegrate. On porous stony ground containing water this process will cause the surface to rise when frozen and fall when thawed. The heaving process helps reduce the debris in size and also concentrates the larger calibre stones on or near the surface. Surface heaving can be readily observed in winter, when potholes are formed on roads by stones being heaved upwards to break the tarmac surface; or when garden gates or garage doors jam on the raised ground. This freeze/thaw process will form soil particles as rock debris is continually broken down.

Where the daily range of temperatures experienced is very wide, although not necessarily falling below 0°C, similar destruction of the rock surface occurs. In the daytime during the summer in the Mediterranean areas, surface temperatures of 30–35°C are experienced; at night there is rapid heat loss through radiation and temperatures fall to as low as 10°C. Rock surfaces expand slightly in the day and contract slightly at night; when repeated many times this will cause boulders to crack open or layers to flake off.

Chemical Changes

Chemical change results in the alteration of the chemical composition of a rock so that part or all of the rock may be removed in the form of a soluble compound. Few rocks are soluble in pure water; but rainwater which has absorbed some carbon dioxide on passing through the atmosphere reaches the ground as a mild carbonic acid, in which many minerals will dissolve. Chemical weathering is seen at its most effective on limestone surfaces where the carbonic acid converts the insoluble calcium carbonate into a soluble form—calcium bicarbonate. This can then be removed in solution, leaving behind any impurities the limestone contained, to begin the soil forming process. This is well illustrated in the 'terra rosa' soils of the Mediterranean region.

The presence of water in soil has two purposes—to mix and distribute the organic and inorganic materials, and to provide for the needs of plant growth. Mixing is done by downward and upward movements through the soil. The former is the result of the normal gravitational flow of water and is known as *leaching*. The latter is found in areas which experience hot dry periods, when the evaporation of surface moisture causes the water in the soil to be drawn towards the surface. This is called *capillary action*. Both movements carry soluble compounds through the soil, darkening the areas where they gather, and profiles (soil cross-sections) develop—which are characteristic of the different climatic conditions. Damp conditions all the year round, as found in Western Europe, show a pronounced downward movement, and soils are darker in the lower part of their profile. In the drier Eastern European areas, soils have a profile which is darker in the upper layers. The amount of water available for plant growth depends upon (a) the rate of supply from the surface and (b) the rate at which the water passes through the soil.

The supply is largely dependent upon precipitation, and a variety of different situations exist.

Example 1: Northern Sweden. Here winter temperatures are low; the soil is often frozen and is unable to absorb moisture over a period of several months. When a thaw occurs, the quantity of run-off is too great for the soil to accept and the soil will be waterlogged for a time. Normal drainage through the soil only acts for a short period of the year.

Example 2: Belgian Plain. Mild temperatures and an evenly distributed precipitation allow water to be absorbed throughout the year, with only a small loss through evaporation in the summer.

Example 3: Ukraine. In a continental area temperatures are extreme; the ground is frozen in winter and little water is taken in, while in the higher rainfall season in summer there is considerable loss through evaporation.

Example 4: South-east Spain. In the Mediterranean area, the problem is not one of absorption but of an insufficient supply of water in the summer; and the weathering of the bed rock into soil is slow. The amount of winter rainfall stored in the soil is inadequate for all but the specially adapted xerophytic plants, and intensive cultivation is not possible without the aid of irrigation.

From the examples shown above, it is clear that rainfall totals alone are meaningless as indicators for plant growth, and that other climatic factors must be considered before the true rainfall effectiveness of an area can be discovered.

Equally important in supplying water to plants is the rate of movement of water through the soil. Water moves between the soil grains, and the size of grain determines how rapidly water will pass through. Relatively large grains such as sand (0·02–1 mm in size) offer wide pore spaces and water moves quickly through, while fine clays (up to 0·002 mm) offer smaller spaces and a slower movement. Pore space is further reduced by the thin film of water coating the surface of each soil grain, causing them to stick together. Fine grained clay soils hold a lot of water and are difficult to plough, hence they are termed 'heavy', 'wet' or 'cold' soils. The latter term is the result of their slowness to warm up in spring compared with drier sandy soils.

The ideal soil texture should be a compromise, with sufficient pore space to allow both the movement of water and of air, for without either, soil development will be immature and poor for plant growth.

The Soils of Europe

Although there is great variety of relief in Europe, the essentially temperate maritime nature of the climate has led to a forest vegetation cover which is missing only in high mountain areas and sandy heathlands, or where man's interference has disturbed the natural cover. Where there is a temperate climate and natural vegetation cover, the soils are likely to show common characteristics and a distribution related to that of climate and vegetation. Where mild, damp conditions prevail there is an overall downward movement in the soil which distributes the organic materials up to 1 m deep in the soil. Soils which are leached in this way are known as 'podzols'. In areas where the podzol is found, the forest cover is coniferous and has a thin humus layer formed from decayed needles and cones. Decomposition by bacteria is inactive in the cold winters but revives with the spring thaw, and water is released to leach the soluble materials from the upper layer (A horizon). The iron oxides accumulate in a narrow red-brown iron pan layer and the aluminium oxides in a wider light-brown layer below (B horizon). The deficient A horizon is left as a light ash-coloured sandy layer. The most common West European soils are variants of the podsol, and under a deciduous forest cover are known as 'Brown Forest' soils. They are similar in appearance to the podzol but lack the distinctive red-brown iron pan.

Eastwards into Central and Eastern Europe summer temperatures increase and the precipitation takes on a seasonal pattern. A summer maximum replaces the more even distribution of Western Europe. This limits leaching to the summer period, and then only the easily soluble material, such as calcium carbonate, is carried deep into the soil. The clayey particles which make up most of the humus are little affected, particularly as the hot sunny summers and dry winds aid evaporation and keep the top layers of the soil dry. The soils developing under such conditions are significantly different in appearance from the Brown Forest soils and are transitional between them and the 'chernozen' soils of the temperate grassland of Asia. The chernozen soil shows limited evidence of leaching, the A horizon being darker than the B horizon. The summer evaporation causes an upward or capillary movement of soluble materials, adding to the concentration of organic material in the upper layer (A horizon).

In the limestone areas of the Mediterranean most of the forest cover has been destroyed and 'terra rosa' soils have developed. As the soluble lime of the parent rock is slowly removed by percolating ground water only a few clay particles (impurities in the limestone) are left from which soil can be formed. It is estimated that 400 m of limestone must be dissolved for a terra rosa soil of 1 m thickness to remain. The scrub vegetation provides little organic matter for humus development. The soil therefore lacks the clearly zoned structure of the podzol, and has a characteristic red-brown appearance throughout. The clay particles have been stained this colour by iron oxides carried in water percolating from the surface.

The Natural Vegetation of Europe

The natural vegetation of an area is the product of climate, soil and structure, which combine to give a characteristic plant association such as coniferous forest or grassland. Vegetation is frequently but slowly modified by changes in climate and soil, but relatively rapidly by human interference. In Europe the areas of natural vegetation are limited to inaccessible and remote regions where human habitation is limited. Of the five associations shown in Fig. 3.3 only the Tundra/Alpine area

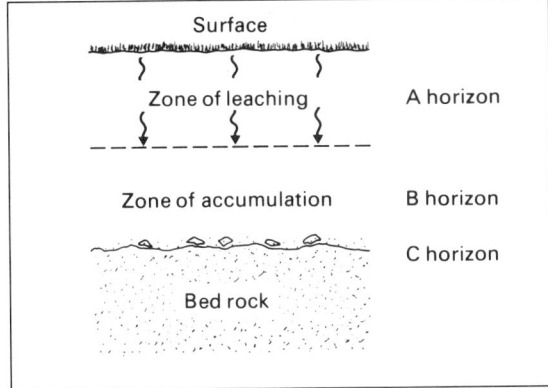

Figure 3.1 Soil horizons

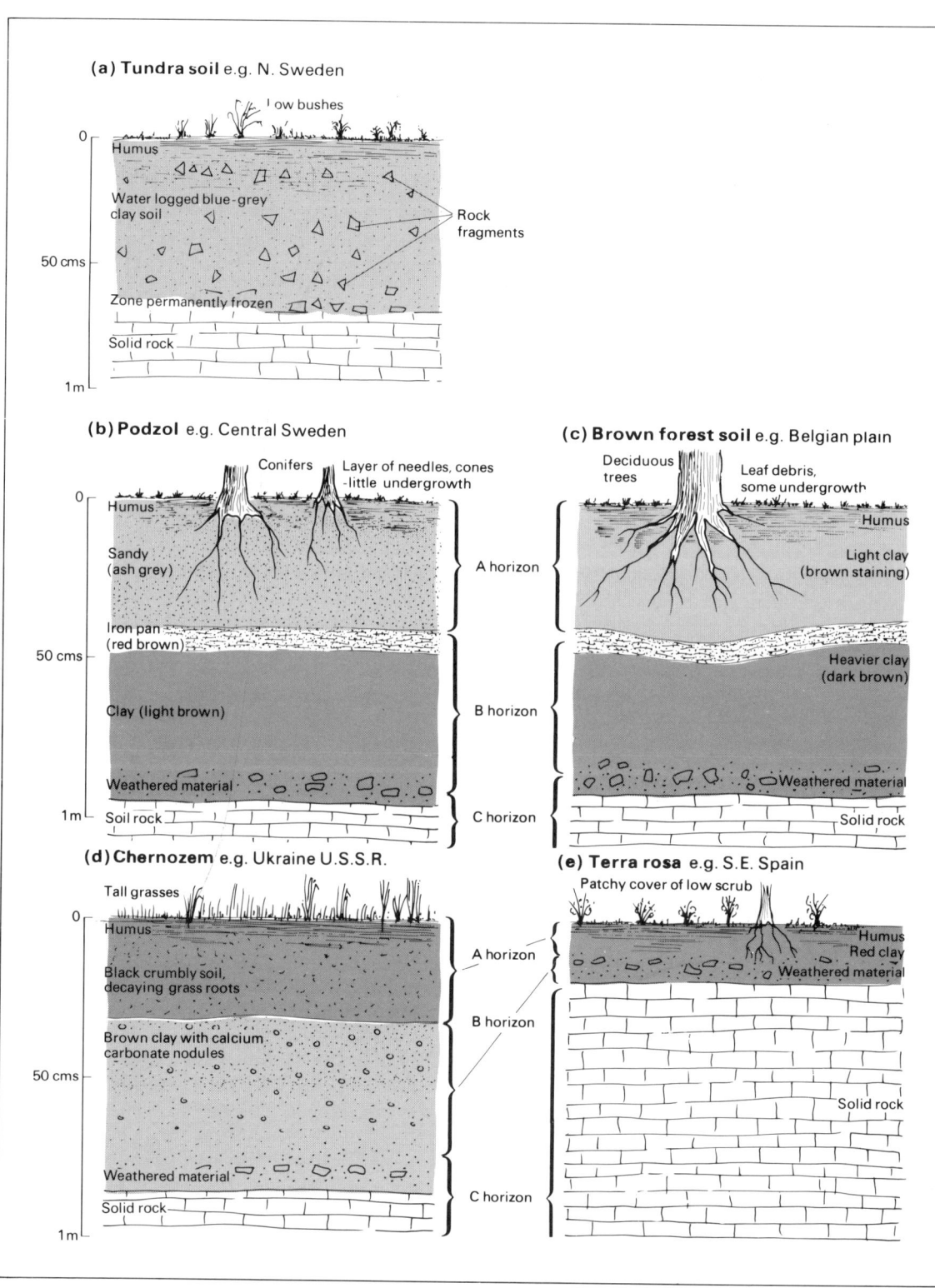

(a) Tundra soil e.g. N. Sweden

Low bushes

0

Humus

Water logged blue-grey clay soil

Rock fragments

50 cms

Zone permanently frozen

Solid rock

1m

(b) Podzol e.g. Central Sweden

Conifers   Layer of needles, cones -little undergrowth

0

Humus

Sandy (ash grey)

A horizon

Iron pan (red brown)

50 cms

Clay (light brown)

B horizon

Weathered material

1m Soil rock

C horizon

(c) Brown forest soil e.g. Belgian plain

Deciduous trees   Leaf debris, some undergrowth

Humus

Light clay (brown staining)

Heavier clay (dark brown)

Weathered material

Solid rock

(d) Chernozem e.g. Ukraine U.S.S.R.

Tall grasses

0

Humus

Black crumbly soil, decaying grass roots

A horizon

Brown clay with calcium carbonate nodules

B horizon

50 cms

Weathered material

C horizon

Solid rock

1m

(e) Terra rosa e.g. S.E. Spain

Patchy cover of low scrub

Humus
Red clay
Weathered material

Solid rock

Figure 3.2 (*above*) Specimen soil types in Europe

Figure 3.3 (*right*) The natural vegetation zones of Europe

30

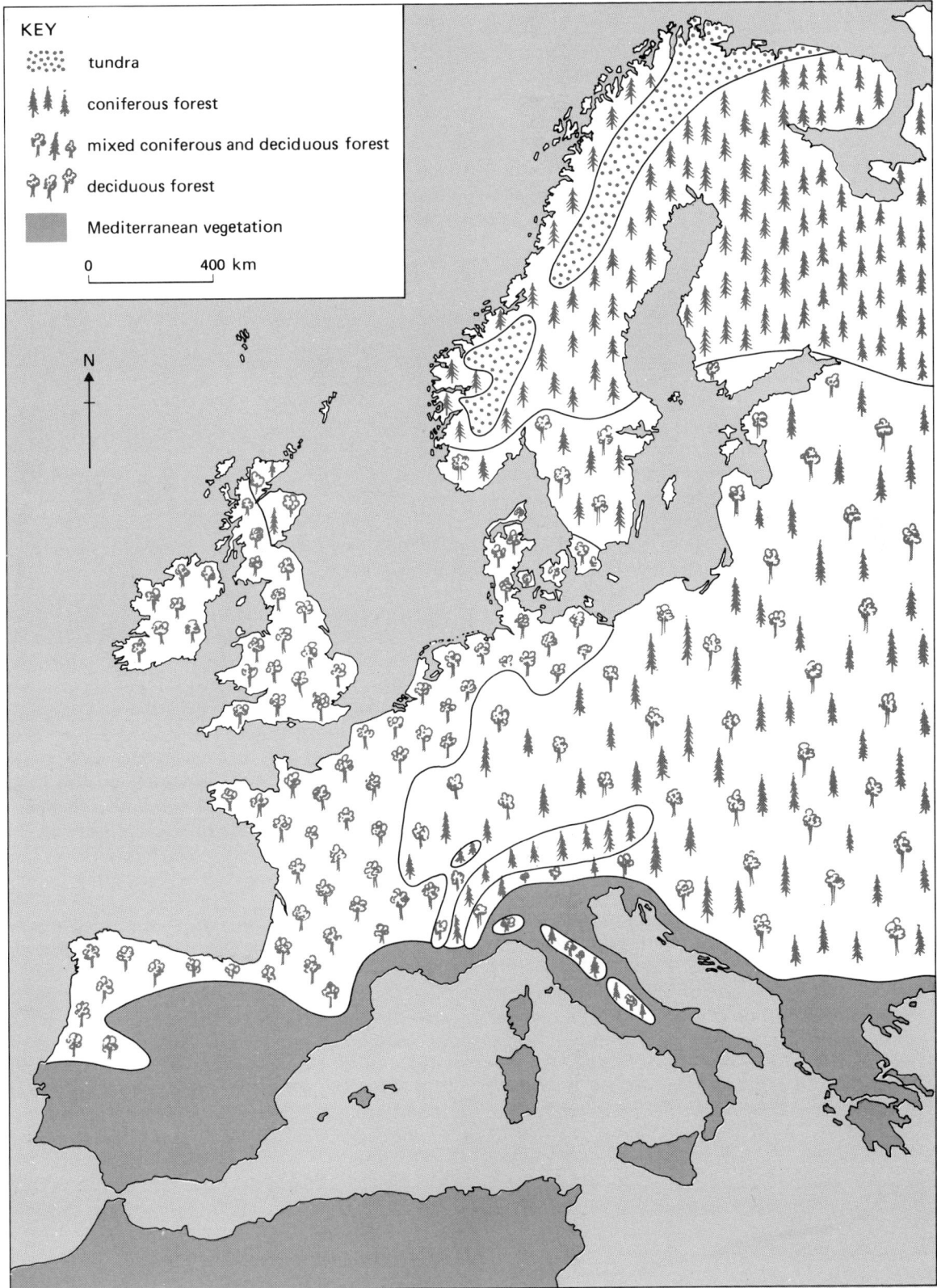

KEY

- tundra
- coniferous forest
- mixed coniferous and deciduous forest
- deciduous forest
- Mediterranean vegetation

0   400 km

N

31

can be considered truly natural. Most of the deciduous and mixed woodland areas of Europe have been cleared for agriculture, industry and settlement. The coniferous forest zones remain almost undisturbed in area but are being commercially exploited, and the structure and composition of the forests is now changing as a result of replanting programmes.

Tundra

In the high altitude and latitude areas of Europe, climatic and soil conditions prevent the development of a forest vegetation. However, in summer when there is almost continuous sunlight for two or three months the average daily temperatures rise above 6°C and hardy, low-growing shrubs and short flowering plants can flourish. Floods and waterlogged soil limit the vegetation cover. The sub-soil is often permanently frozen and only the top thaws in summer. In low lying areas the water cannot escape by seepage or run off and forms shallow pools and swamps. Where peat soils form, different groups of water-tolerant plants grow.

The tundra region is treeless and the typical vegetation consists of hardy grasses, berry-bearing plants, such as bilberry, dwarf birch, willow and alder and numerous kinds of moss and lichen.

In Northern Europe there is a wide transitional zone between the tundra and coniferous forest regions, characterized by the appearance of trees which gradually increase in height and density towards the south. At the same time, the low tundra vegetation dies out, being denied the heat and sunlight the taller forest vegetation can command.

Coniferous Forest

Coniferous forest in Europe covers a broad area between latitude 60°N and 68°N which continues into Asia. The minimum conditions required to support forest in these northern latitudes is that temperatures in the short three-month summer should be above 10°C. In the long, severe winters when the soil is frozen and growth ceases, the trees survive by gaining maximum benefit from the water taken in through the root system in summer. The needle-like leaves reduce the amount of water lost by transpiration in summer and store water by remaining on the tree through-

Figure 3.4 Forest in northern Sweden

out the year. The conifer is tolerant of a wide range of rainfall, existing equally in areas with 250 mm or 1250 mm a year. As it is shallow rooted it can also exist in thin or stony soils where its tolerance of dry situations is evident.

As a result of this ability to survive in difficult climatic and physical conditions, the conifer occurs in extensive stands, often covering hundreds of square km. Only where ground water is unable to drain away freely does the conifer give way to marsh plants. In Western Europe the dominant species are the Scots pine and Norway spruce. The number of species increases eastwards and fir and larch become more important. The deciduous silver birch also grows extensively in Northern Europe, but as its commercial value is less than pine and spruce, birch forest is progressively replaced with these more useful trees.

Mixed Deciduous and Coniferous Forest

A wedge of mixed forest covers much of Central Europe, extending from the North European Plain south to the Alpine ranges. This is not a transitional zone between the coniferous forest of the north and the deciduous forest of the south and west, although clearly a limited transitional area does exist. Rather it is the result of the great complexity of bed rock, soil, slope and drainage which exists in the area. Where local conditions are favourable, deciduous trees such as oak, ash, birch, chestnut and sycamore are found, but where the land is dry, steep or stony, large stands of conifers occur. The North European plain illustrates the variety of vegetation in this zone. On the damp boulder clay surfaces deciduous trees flourish, on the drier gravel and light clay areas conifers predominate, while on the light glacial sands heathland occurs.

The effect of man's interference with the natural vegetation is noticeable in north Germany, where the plains have been cleared and cultivated, but many of the infertile gravelly hills remain forested. Because of this interference the area retains only the coniferous forest and heathland of its original cover. Similarly, further south in the Alps the forest has been cleared from the valley floors, but conifers remain on the mountain sides.

Figure 3.5 An olive grove in southern Spain. The land has been overgrazed and the tree roots exposed. The fine soil particles have been removed by rain wash

Deciduous Forest

The area classified as true deciduous forest is limited to the western part of Europe. Local conditions are sufficiently consistent for deciduous forest to be the dominant vegetation cover, and only in parts of such high mountain areas as the Pyrenees and Northern Scotland do large areas of conifers occur.

Deciduous trees require six months with temperatures above 6°C and are well suited to the mild maritime climate of Western Europe. The trees lose their leaves in autumn and remain dormant during the winter before beginning their growth cycle when buds form in spring. A number of species such as oak, ash, elm and sycamore are common in these forests, but characteristic of the maritime environment is the beech. As on the Chiltern Hills of England, the tree occurs in large stands, adding an attractive feature to the natural landscape.

However, very little of the natural deciduous forest remains; over the past 2000 years, large areas have been progressively cleared for farmland and settlements. Inevitably, a

region which boasts a mild, wet climate with a six- or seven-month growing season has proved as attractive for farming as for forest growth. The only extensive deciduous forests which remain are in the less attractive farming areas which have been preserved for recreation and leisure pursuits, such as the sandy Fontainebleau Forest—south-east of Paris, and Epping Forest—north of London. Elsewhere, the density of deciduous trees in hedgerows and copses is rapidly being reduced as the demands of mechanization encourage farmers to enlarge fields by removing woodland boundaries. Only in the 'bocage' of Normandy and Brittany does the pastoral farming economy exist in what is still a wooded landscape.

Mediterranean Vegetation

The low scrub vegetation found over most of the Mediterranean region today is largely a result of the destruction of the original mixed deciduous and coniferous forest cover by man. In Calabria in southern Italy, where extensive forests were preserved for hunting, the original forest cover can be seen: oak, chestnut, beech and pine trees provide a thick cover to the hillslopes between 500 m and 1300 m. However, in other parts the forest areas are small in size and few in number.

The timber was used by man for fuel and for building material, and the forest clearings for grazing sheep and goats; the latter factor being mainly responsible for the destruction of the woodland. By grazing close to the ground these animals eat young seedling trees and bark, tear up and damage roots and prevent the forests regenerating themselves. A contributory factor, too, is the small number of tree species suited to the Mediterranean area and able to withstand the summer drought. Unfortunately, this process of woodland destruction by overgrazing continues, as shown in Fig. 3.5

The vegetation that has replaced the forest is low scrub and scattered trees, which have adapted to survive the dry conditions. Some leaves are small and hairy to reduce moisture loss by transpiration in dry periods, cuticles are thick and hard to provide a strong structure to the leaf and prevent collapse if the leaf withers with the heat. The waxy leaf surface of such evergreens as laurel and oleander reflect rather than absorb solar heat, so reducing the

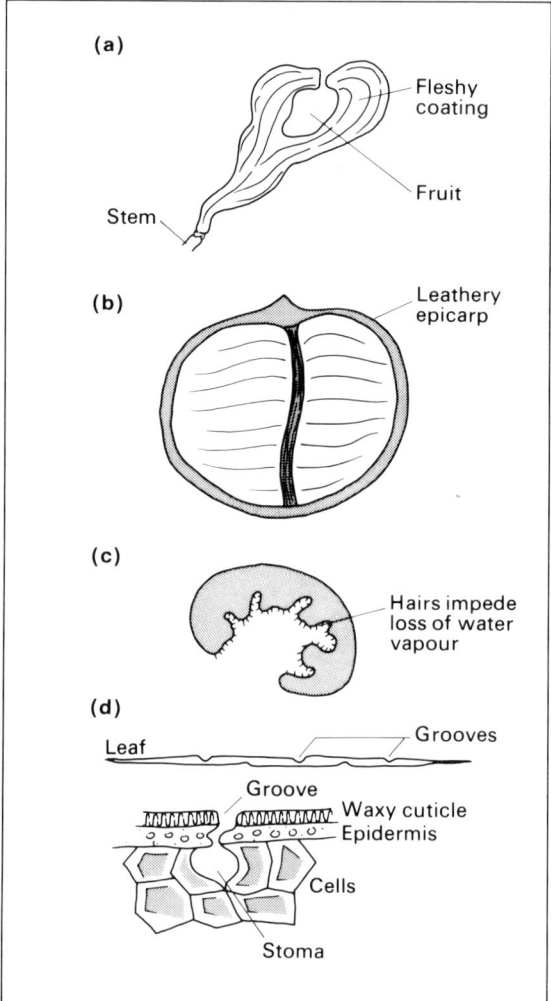

Figure 3.6(a–d) Some adaptations of drought-resistant plants (xerophytes).
(**a**) Succulent: storing water in leaf, stem or root, e.g., fig
(**b**) Wax covering to reduce evaporation, e.g., lemon
(**c**) Rolled leaves which open when water is available, e.g., lavender
(**d**) Enlargement of a groove. Stomata depressed into grooves in leaf to reduce evaporation loss e.g., pine

plant's temperature and its water loss by transpiration. Root systems are deep and widespread to draw as much water as possible into the plant system. Many plants are fleshy and trees thick-trunked to store water during the summer drought.

The olive tree and, in the wetter areas, the cork oak and pine, are the main tree species. The scrub cover known as 'maquis' in southern France, 'macchia' in Italy and

Figure 3.7 Garrigue on the foot hills of the Maritime Alps

'matorral' in Spain is characterized by thickets of oleander, laurel, broom, myrtle and thorn-bush growing up to about 3 m in height, with the occasional tree protruding through. In addition to water availability, variations in soil often lacking humus also cause changes in vegetation. The maquis cover usually develops on podzol soils derived from such rocks as sandstone, but in the limestone areas, which are numerous in Spain, southern France and Italy, a poor terra rosa soil develops which supports a thinner scrub cover known as 'garrigue'—a heather-like cover, including such herbs as thyme, rosemary and lavender. These plants exude an aromatic oil which prevents excessive water loss through transpiration.

The vegetation cover is at its richest in spring, when the ground is moist and the plants flower. This richness gradually fades during the summer and the land takes on a brown and parched appearance. Few of the plants are economically useful, with the exception of the vine and the olive; many of the cultivated plants, such as the citrus fruits and grains, have been imported into the Mediterranean area.

Mountain Vegetation

As climate is modified by increasing altitude, it follows that vegetation will similarly alter. Because of their northern latitude, the change is slight in the mountain areas of Scandinavia, but in the higher and more southerly Alps a wider range of vegetation zones occur. In all mountain areas the factors of slope and aspect also cause numerous local variations to the general pattern.

Questions

1. For each of the following areas—Denmark, north Norway, Sicily—(a) suggest the type of soil you would expect to find, and (b) briefly describe its characteristics and explain your choice.

2. Of the natural vegetation shown in Fig. 3.3, only the coniferous forest zones remain relatively unaltered by man. Attempt to explain the reasons for this.

3. In your local area, find or dig out a clear soil profile. Make an accurate scale drawing of the horizons you observe. Attempt to explain the influences (including man's) that have been at work in forming the soil.

4 The agricultural environment

The varied physical environment of Western Europe has encouraged many human occupations. The Scandinavian highlands and shield areas provide valuable industrial raw materials and water power; the North European Plain has intensive agricultural, industrial and commercial development, while the Mediterranean area of southern Europe, although lacking the level of economic development found in other parts of the continent, contributes a variety to the agriculture that would otherwise be lacking.

The variety within the economy of Western Europe can be attributed to the following factors.

1 The relatively gentle and accessible physical landscape which contrasts with other major continental areas—only 6% of the land area west of the Ural Mountains is over 1000 m.

2 The indented shape of the continent aids communication and encourages maritime and commercial activity.

3 The mild, damp climate allows many types of arable and pastoral farming.

4 The wide continental shelf off Western Europe is one of the world's most valuable fishing grounds.

5 The accessible timber and mineral resources.

6 The important sources of energy provided by coal, natural gas and water power.

7 The large population has provided a skilled work force to provide further economic growth.

Over the past century, Western Europe has become progressively more industrialized and urbanized. This has been beneficial in that it has provided a high material standard of living for the population; but the disadvantages can be seen in the increasingly crowded and polluted living conditions of the cities and the decreasing area available for farming and leisure pursuits. In such an environment the improved living conditions have not brought stability; many thousands of people, particularly from southern Europe, move to other European countries in search of work each year. Dissatisfaction with factory working conditions and the possible insecurity of some jobs have caused social unrest in several European countries. Such political problems are only likely to be solved at an international level, and the enlarged EEC may have an important role to play in this respect

Because of its variety of soils, mild climate and large area of productive land, Western Europe offers an excellent environment for farming. However, it is one of the most densely populated areas in the world, the density reaching over 400 people per square kilometre in the Netherlands, where there is great competition for land. The level, well-drained, accessible sites—which are equally attractive for factory, town or farm—are highly valued, and the farmer can only compete if he makes the most intensive use of his land and is given some protection by government controls upon land development. Figure 4.1, showing the recent increase in food output, illustrates the steady growth of farming in Western Europe. despite the loss of land to urban and industrial uses. The maintenance of a high level of agricultural production is essential to the economy of Western Europe, and the following factors help to explain how this is being achieved.

1 The Heavy Application of Chemical Fertilizers

Nitrogen, phosphorus and potassium are the main plant foods that are usually needed in greater quantities than soils are able to provide, and so it is these fertilizers which are widely used in Western Europe. Traditionally they have been obtained in their mineral form from sedimentary deposits and have had to be imported; but the rapid growth of the chemical industry during and since the Second World War has led to their production in a cheaper, synthetic form. The chief natural source of nitrates is northern Chile, but the increased cost of exploiting the inhospitable desert region, coupled with the growth of the European chemical industry, has caused this source of supply to decline in importance to the farmer. Today, the chief source is from chemical plants where nitrogen is taken from the atmosphere (e.g., Rjukan in Norway) or from coke-oven and refinery gases, which provide a source of soluble nitrogen in heavy industrial areas like the Ruhr coalfield. Phosphates are similarly costly to obtain in their natural form, the chief reserves being in North Africa, and the supply is now largely provided from basic slag, a product of steel making. Potash is more widely available, and large reserves exist near Hanover in West Germany and between Colmar and Mulhouse in eastern France.

The use of fertilizers is most intensive in the areas of highest population density—namely northern France, northern Germany and the Low Countries. Here fertilizers are not used solely to improve poor land, but to raise yields on good land to meet the demands of an urban population. The following statistics offer a comparison of the application of fertilizers in Belgium and Italy in 1972.

	kg per hectare of agricultural land	
	Italy	Belgium
Nitrogen	35	106
Phosphate	33	94
Potash	14	108

2 The Use of Marginal Farmland

The increasing demand for food products has made necessary the extension of cultivation into areas formerly considered to be of limited agricultural value. This extension to the area of productive farmland has been accompanied by improvements in the strains of crops and breeds of animals, producing types tolerant of more difficult environments. To further this process, government involvement has been increased to provide cash grants to farmers, the

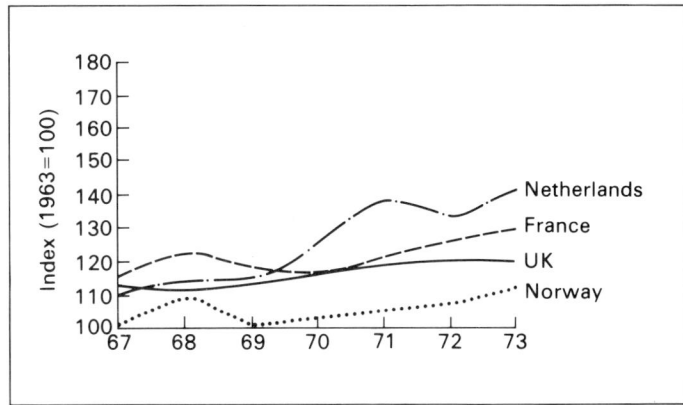

Figure 4.1 Agricultural output in selected countries 1967–73

financing of major land improvement schemes and research projects.

Outstanding examples of major extensions to the productive farmland of Western Europe are the reclamation of the shallow Zuider Zee in the Netherlands, the soil improvement programme for the infertile glacial outwash sands of western Jutland, the drainage of the Arno and Tiber marshlands in Italy, and the irrigation schemes in Languedoc and southern Spain. More modest changes include the extension of cultivation, grazing and forest in hill and mountain areas, and the use of traditional pasture regions for the higher cash returns of arable crops. The increasingly intensive use of the land has brought changes in the appearance of the countryside; there is a greater area of arable and forest land, and the increase in farm and field size has been accompanied by the removal of hedges and copses for the more efficient use of machinery and the extra land they provide.

3 The Development of Co-operative Organizations

The increasingly intensive and competitive nature of European agriculture over the past fifty years has brought greater co-operation between farmers both at a local and international level. Co-operatives serving the specialist needs of farming communities have spread into most parts of Western Europe. The example of the Danish dairy farming industry, where 90% of all milk produced is channelled through co-operative dairies, serves to illustrate the strength of the movement. The role

37

Figure 4.2 Irrigated farmland near Toledo in southern Spain (rainfall approx. 350 mm p.a.)

of the co-operative varies from country to country. In Denmark and in the Netherlands, co-operative organizations meet a great many of the farmer's needs, i.e., marketing of products, purchase of livestock, bulk purchases of feedstuffs, fertilizers and farm machinery, soil testing and technical advice, but in France a less comprehensive service with considerable regional variation is provided.

At an international level, the formation of the EEC in 1957 and the EFTA in 1960 produced free trading and the abolition of virtually all tariffs between member countries by 1969. The effect upon agriculture in the EEC has been to raise and rationalize production, with the aim of avoiding both overproduction and periodic shortage. The EEC is financed from a Common Fund built up by taxes levied on member countries according to their economic wealth; this fund has provided assistance to the poorer areas of the community and many agricultural developments in southern Italy have been financed in this way.

4 The Import of Supplementary Foodstuffs

With a population of 240 million in 1972 on a land area of 2.2 million km—an approximate density of 120 people per sq. km—it is clearly impossible for the West European farming community to meet all demands placed upon it. Agricultural imports consist of products which (a) cannot be grown in Western Europe, such as tropical fruits, vegetable oils and textile fibres, (b) meet a seasonal shortage, such as temperate fruits from southern hemisphere countries, and (c) supplement European output of grains, meat, wool, animal feedstuffs and market garden produce.

5 The High Level of Mechanization

The intensive use of machinery in West European farming is second only to North America, and the reasons for its wide application are similar. During the period 1956–72 the number of tractors in use in Western Europe increased almost fourfold, the most spectacular increases occurring in Spain and Italy. The greater speed and efficiency of mechanized farming is particularly valuable at such critical times in the farmer's year as sowing and harvesting. The cheapness of

	Number of tractors		
	Italy	Spain	West Germany
1956	124,436	22,443	383,852
1973	742,766	331,000	1,418,056

38

Figure 4.3 Mechanized harvesting in Denmark: sugar-beet tops are being cut for silage

machines when applied on a large scale reduces the size of the work force needed and the cost to the farmer in wages. Approximately 75% of West European farms are under 40 ha, and although sizes are increasing by amalgamation and purchase, most are run on a family basis with little hired labour except for harvesting. The reduced labour requirement that has resulted from mechanization has enabled the farmer to remain competitive with foreign foodstuffs, while releasing the labour force needed by industry. Industry itself has, of course, exerted an attractive influence upon the rural workforce, causing a steady migration to the highly paid jobs of the industrial regions. This movement is seen most vividly in Italy, where approximately 10 million people have moved in the post war period from the rural south to the industrial cities of the North Italian Plain.

The increased demand for agricultural machines—tractors, combine harvesters, pick-up balers, hay and grain driers—has been met by the highly developed West European engineering industry. These and other more specialized machines for use on small farms and in hilly terrain, have been developed at the large agricultural machinery plants in West Germany, France, Italy, Sweden, Denmark and the UK, supplemented by imported machines from the USA. The widespread use of machinery on the farms of Western Europe has been assisted by the general accessibility and gentleness of much of the terrain.

The agricultural land use in Western Europe is notable for its intensiveness and diversity. Some of the factors explaining the former have been given in the previous

Figure 4.4 A pedigree Charolais bull at an English live-stock show. The breed is very popular as a beef animal, particularly when crossed with other breeds such as Friesians. The Charolais has been introduced into the herds of 52 countries and its quick-fattening properties are very important, as the following comparison shows:

	Breed		Gain by Charolais	
	Charolais crosses	Hereford crosses	Wt	%
Mean daily liveweight gain (kg)	0·73	0·65	0·08	12·3
Liveweight at slaughter (kg)	454	421	33	7·8

section, but in examining the diversity others will emerge.

West European agriculture has undergone a period of change; the traditional regional patterns of livestock farming in the river plains and hill areas, and arable crop farming on the well-drained lower slopes, has been modified by the pressure of market forces. The growth in size and spending power of the urban population and the government programmes of assistance and improvement have greatly altered the use of land in the past twenty-five years. The range of crops grown has become more diverse with the use of irrigation and the development of strains suitable to West European conditions. Notable here has been the additional land given to grain for animal foodstuff. Maize, in particular, has shown spectacular increases: in France, output increased by over 300% between 1962 and 1972, allowing an export of 2·5 million tonnes in 1972, chiefly to other EEC countries. The improvement of livestock has been brought about by the elimination of such diseases as tuberculosis, the introduction of specialist breeding using artificial insemination, and the development of single purpose breeds, such as the Danish Landrace bacon pig and the French Charolais beef animal. Such improvements in the quality of crops and livestock have heralded changes in land use and the breakdown of traditional farming patterns. Although diverse in its land use, overall, Western Europe contains much specialist agriculture, the former mixed farm being less and less in evidence.

Natural conditions of climate, soil and terrain are favourable to farming and encourage the cultivation of a full range of temperate crops. The critical temperature below which few commercial plants will grow is 6°C, allowing growing seasons of up to seven months in southern Scandinavia and Denmark and twelve months in Italy, Spain and southern France.

Mild conditions allow outdoor grazing for much of the year if required, but cattle are increasingly being stall-fed. In addition to providing conditions which allow intensive all-year-round use of the land, the climate produces few extremes, such as floods, severe storms and drought—an annual problem to farmers in other parts of the world.

5 Studies of selected agricultural activities

Land use in selected West European countries					
	Total area	Percentage of total area			
		Agricultural land			Waste
Country	(,000 km)	Arable	Pasture	Forest	& urban areas
Denmark	43	62	7	11	20
France	547	33	26	26	15
Italy	301	38	32	20	10
Norway	324	2·5	0·5	26	71
Sweden	450	7	1	54	38
Switzerland	41	7	45	24	24
West Germany	248	33	22	28	17

1 Cereal Cultivation

Cereals are widely grown throughout Western Europe. Approximately 45% of the land devoted to agricultural use is in arable crops, only the high areas of central Europe and Scandinavia being unsuitable. There are wide variations between countries, as the above table shows.

The area used for arable crops and, in particular, cereals, has increased considerably over the past ten years, as the value of barley and maize as high-protein animal foodstuff has been appreciated. Consequently, an increase in area and output has been encouraged throughout Western Europe. The production of wheat and oats, however, has shown little change. Wheat is the chief bread grain, and as France produces a considerable surplus, the EEC countries are almost self-sufficient in this cereal. The statistics below illustrate the shift in cereal production from wheat and oats to barley and maize.

The distribution of the principal areas of cereal cultivation reflects the value of gently undulating land for the intensive production of these crops. The factors underlying the importance of the grain growing areas are as follows.

The Climate

The climate of Western Europe is widely suitable for the cultivation of wheat and barley, and while oats and rye are tolerant of the cooler conditions of northern Europe, maize can be grown in the warmer southern areas where the frost hazard is less. Newly developed strains of maize, which require a

Recent changes in cereal production in selected countries (in ,000 tonnes)								
	Denmark		France		West Germany		Spain	
	1962	1973	1962	1973	1962	1973	1962	1973
Wheat	644	540	14054	17828	4592	7134	4820	3966
Barley	3300	5490	6003	10844	3744	6622	2162	4402
Oats	683	458	2591	2203	1913	3045	495	425
Maize	—	—	1867	10620	43	573	920	2037

shorter growing season, have resulted in the spread of the crop northwards. The mild winters of Western Europe make it possible for the cereals to be planted in the autumn, and to start growth early. Sunny summer conditions for growth and ripening are important, interspersed with occasional falls of rain. Where the rainfall is inadequate irrigation is necessary, as in the Po valley of northern Italy and around Zaragoza and Valladolid in Spain. The greater control over yields given by the provision of water at important stages in the crop's growth has led to the widespread use of sprinkler irrigation.

The Soils

In the lowland plains of Western Europe the clay and loam soils are derived from alluvial and glacial deposits of recent origin. They offer a variety of soils which are usually water retentive, but relatively easy to work. Exceptions are the glacial outwash sands of the North German Plain and western Jutland, and the marine sands of south-west France, both surfaces being very difficult to farm to the same level of productivity as the surrounding lowlands. In such an area of intensive land use as Western Europe the natural soil fertility has to be supplemented by regular applications of natural or synthetic fertilizers. Nitrogen, phosphate and potash are the three basic plant foods and their quantity in the soil is steadily depleted when the land is under cultivation. The loss of nitrogen in the soil is the most serious. It is lost by leaching and mineralization when there is no plant cover, and within the crop when it is harvested. Records taken on experimental farms show that soil can lose 30% of its basic plant foods over a period of 20 years.

Soil fertility can also be maintained by crop rotation, cereals alternating with leguminous plants and leys. However, with the emphasis being placed upon grain production, farmers often grow grain for three or four years—the land being used for leys in the break year, mainly as a safeguard against crop diseases and weeds. The advanced chemical industry of Western Europe is able to supply large quantities of nitrate and phosphate fertilizers to the farmer; so the availability of fertilizer is not, as it is elsewhere in the world, a determining factor in land use. In New Zealand, the high cost of imported fertilizers has led to the

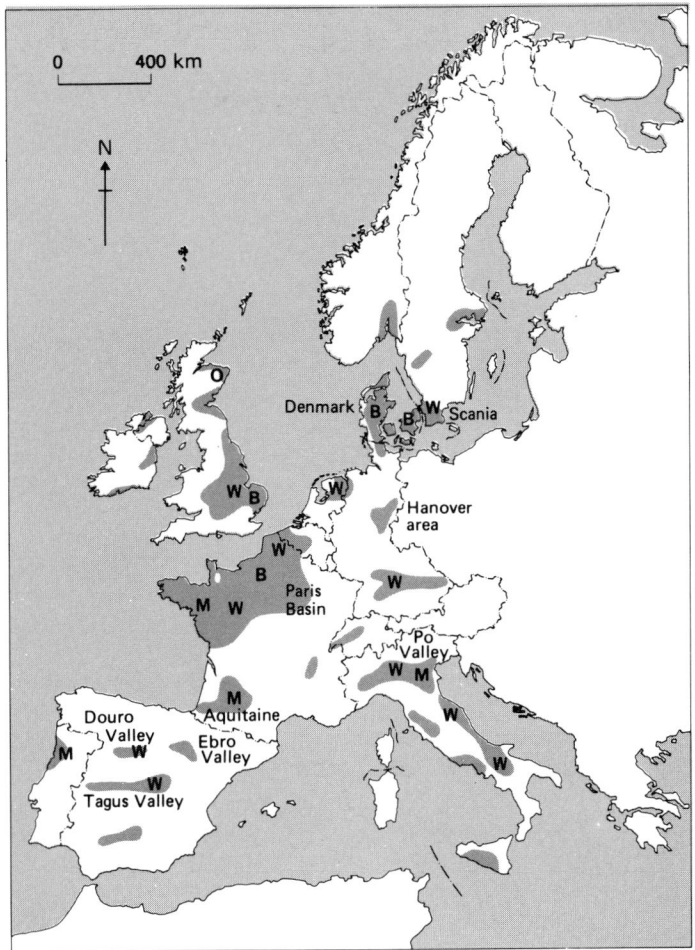

Figure 5.1 Major areas of grain cultivation
W—wheat; B—barley; M—maize; O—oats

widespread cultivation of nitrogen-fixing legumes in rotation to repair the nitrogen loss.

With the soil maintained at a high level of productivity, crop yields have increased significantly in recent years, as shown in the table below.

Crop yields in selected countries (100 kg/hectare)						
	Wheat		Barley		Maize	
	1958	1973	1958	1973	1958	1973
Denmark	36·2	44·1	34·5	37·6	—	—
France	20·8	45·0	21·8	38·9	28·4	54·7
Italy	20·3	24·8	13·2	22·5	30·2	56·3
Netherlands	36·2	52·6	38·5	42·5	40·6	56·0
UK	30·8	43·6	28·8	39·7	—	—
West Germany	28·3	44·5	27·5	39·6	29·3	54·1

Figure 5.2 Combine harvesters working on large, open fields

The Land

The gentle landscape of much of Western Europe offers good surfaces for the cultivation of grain with the extensive use of machinery. This is well illustrated in the North German Plain, the Netherlands and northern France. For the best results, crops should be cultivated in large units where the greatest cost benefits of mechanization can be achieved. The tendency is for farms to increase in size by purchase and amalgamation, but many farms are still too small to be able to afford the full range of machinery which would increase their productivity. In some areas the problem is overcome by farmers grouping together to form co-operatives. The greater use of machinery is a measure of the increased yield and efficiency of West European farming. Marginal areas in mountain districts of Norway and Switzerland have been brought under cultivation by the use of tractors, mowing machines, mobile milking units etc., to increase agricultural output further.

The Markets

Within the EEC, cereal production has steadily expanded through increased yields, which have averaged 100 kg per hectare for each year since 1958. By 1973 the community was producing 90% of its cereal requirements, although this included an overproduction of bread grains and a deficiency in animal foodstuffs. By establishing 'basic target prices' below which a buyer must accept the goods offered to him, the EEC has the power to use prices to regulate production and demand.

For example, if there is a surplus of bread grain, the 'basic target price' is set at a low level which will (a) encourage the purchase of the current surplus, and (b) discourage the farmer from cultivating the cereal next season.

It can be seen that European agriculture is not a free market system, being subject to EEC controls which aim to balance supply and demand while establishing prices which are fair to supplier and consumer alike. Within the EEC, France is the main agricultural nation: in 1971–2 the country produced 37% of the enlarged Community's cereal requirements, exporting a surplus of 6 million tonnes, chiefly to member countries.

Grain Production in the Paris Basin

The Paris Basin is one of the most intensively farmed regions in France; much of the land is

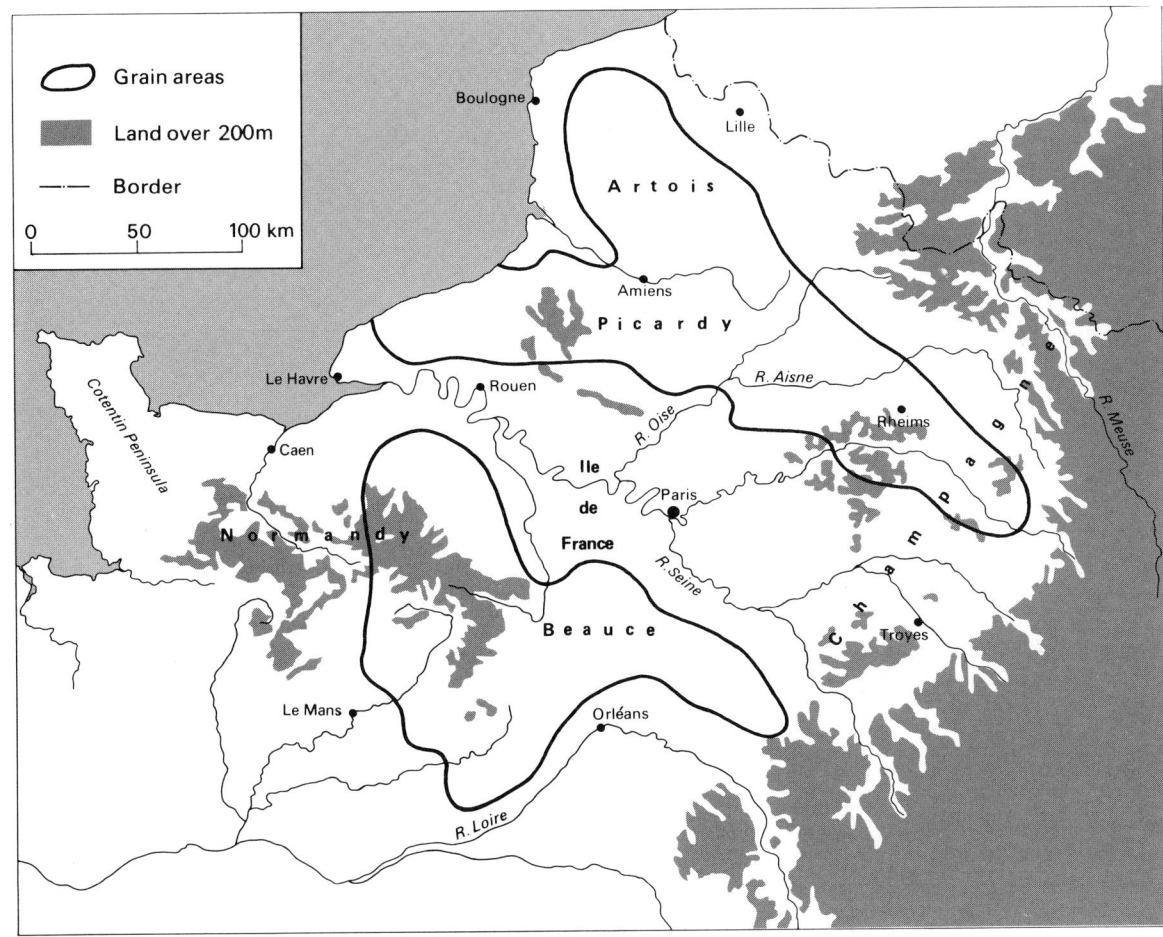

Figure 5.3 Principal grain-growing areas in the Paris Basin

devoted to cereal production and high yields of over 4500 kg per ha are achieved in wheat and barley. Within the region, the grain farms are located on the gentle rolling surfaces of Artois and Picardy in the north, and parts of Normandy and Beauce. The synclinal structure of the Paris Basin provides a variety of surfaces, soils and farming environments, and in the past each area or 'pays' tended to develop a type of farming that differed slightly from its neighbour, giving it a particular identity. This pattern is much less noticeable today, as the farmland and output of cereals has increased, and the landscape has taken on a more uniform appearance.

The climate is a maritime one with mild, damp conditions, as the following statistics illustrate. These support an 8–9 month growing season, and allow the autumn sowing of crops.

In the area around Rheims the climate has a slightly more continental character, and summer rainfall is often less effective, with the occasional heavy storm instead of the lighter but more frequent rainfall of the west. Consequently, drought can be a problem to the farmer, not to the extent of causing a complete failure, but resulting in lower than normal yields. The use of portable sprinkler irrigation systems has been an effective answer to this problem.

Station	Average January	Average July	Rainfall
Lille	3°C	18°C	30 mm
Rheims	2°C	20°C	25 mm
Paris	3°C	19°C	23 mm

Soils are usually light clay loams reaching 1 m in thickness on the rolling chalk plains of

45

Picardy. There are few stones in this area but patchy areas of 'clay with flints' occur around Rheims. Generally, cultivation is easy and encourages extensive mechanization. Regular top dressings of synthetic fertilizers—particularly nitrates—are applied, and chemicals are also used to check the spread of weeds and eliminate crop diseases. Autumn ploughing, which allows winter frost to penetrate the soil, also checks the spread of weeds.

The size of farm holdings in France is higher than in any other continental EEC country (37% are over 20 ha, compared with 15% over 20 ha for the EEC in 1972) and those in the Paris Basin are the largest in France: 60% of the farms are over 50 ha, some ranging up to 400 ha in size. The growth in farm size has been recent, but it is not complete and many small family-run market gardens and dairy farms exist alongside the large 200–400 ha grain farms. It is in this part of France that there are fewest co-operative organizations (Groupements Agricoles d'Exploitation en Commun), indicating the importance of the large self-sufficient farm. The development of the large, mechanized grain farm can be explained by two main factors.

1 The intensive use of machinery is necessary to avoid costly delays caused by bad weather, and to meet peak demands.

2 The competition for labour with the nearby industrial areas of Lille and Paris caused wages to rise, and farmers reduced their total labour costs by employing fewer men and using more machines.

The loss of the farm labour force to the towns encouraged mechanization which, in turn, encouraged the development of larger farm units, and also directed the farmer towards grain, which places the least demand on labour of all farm systems. The farming community benefits from its close proximity to the industrial areas of Lille and Paris in the provision of mains electricity, good road and rail links for bulk movement, and well-developed social services, such as education. In this respect the farming communities of the Paris Basin are much more advanced than in the rest of the country.

Crops are usually grown on a three year rotation: *Year 1*, wheat; *Year 2*, barley; *Year 3*, cash roots (i.e., sugar beet and potatoes) or fodder crops (i.e., hay, and maize for silage). On the specialist grain farms sugar beet and potatoes, with their demand on labour for thinning, weeding and harvesting, have given way to fodder crops. In the search for increased output hedges and fences have been dispensed with, one crop being grown right up to another. When extra manpower is needed, particularly at harvest time, migrant Spanish or Italian labourers are usually employed.

The wheat is principally bread grain and is used in the Paris and Lille areas, while also being available for export to Belgium, the Netherlands and West Germany. Barley, too, is exported and used extensively as an animal foodstuff and in the brewing industry of Lille, Roubaix and Paris.

2 Dairy Farming

The surface and climate of Western Europe is as suitable for cattle grazing as it is for arable farming, and in many areas the two activities are practised together. The development of the specialist grain farm has been recorded in the previous section, and similar specialization has occurred in the dairy farming industry of Denmark and the Netherlands.

The mild, damp climate enables the dairy farmer to graze his cattle out of doors for most of the year. Traditionally, the lower valley pastures have been used for grazing, while providing two hay crops each year to be stored for use as fodder during winter. The hay crop was supplemented by a small area devoted to root fodder crops. This pattern of the small family-run mixed farm keeping dairy cattle and cultivating fodder crops still dominates the mountain areas of Scandinavia and central Europe, but on the lowlands of France, the Low Countries, Denmark and West Germany the dairy farm increasingly has the appearance of an arable farm, with the bulk of the land devoted to fodder crops and the animals stall-fed for most of the year. Imported maize and soya beans supplement home-produced feed. In areas where open grazing is still practised, the grazing area is often controlled by tethering the animals or by electric fences; this has the advantages of:

(a) controlling the intake of grass available;
(b) preventing the animals from wandering and trampling new grass;
(c) enabling the fairly even application of manure.

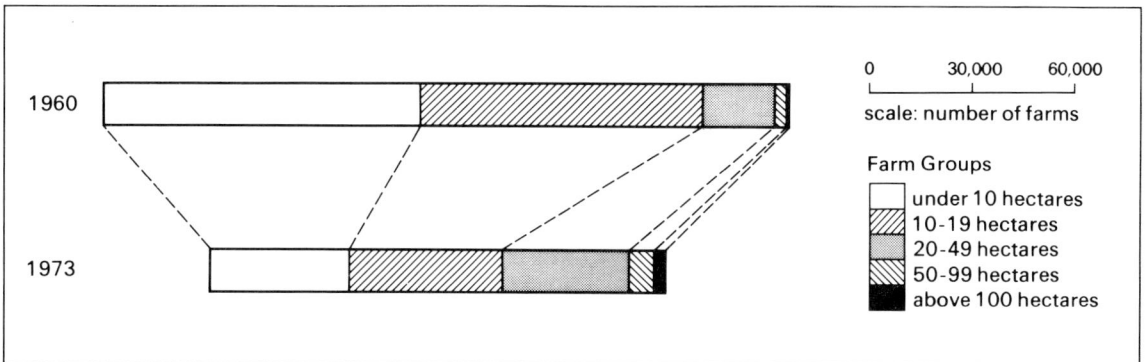

Figure 5.4 Graph illustrating the change in farm size in Denmark

The trend towards stall-fed dairy cattle has enabled the land to support a greater number of animals and the farm to achieve a high milk yield. Consequently, the major dairy farming countries use a high proportion of their land for arable crops; in 1973 over 80% of the cultivated land in Denmark was used in this way. At the same time, farms have increased in size and machinery has been used on a larger scale. As with other branches of agriculture, the size of the workforce has declined, due to the attraction of highly paid jobs in nearby towns and to the introduction of machinery into what has been a labour-intensive sector of farming. The widespread use of milking machines has been a very significant factor in reducing the workforce on dairy farms.

The distribution of dairy farming in Western Europe is closely related to the demand for milk and dairy produce in the densely populated industrial and urban areas. Milk is an easily perishable commodity and it is usually produced near to the area of demand. Good transport facilities, particularly by road, are essential for the rapid movement of liquid milk to dairies and bottling plants in the towns and cities. Switzerland, south-west Norway and central France, which are remote from any large markets, tend to concentrate upon the production of less perishable items, such as butter, cheese, chocolate and condensed milk. The major dairy farming countries of Denmark, the Netherlands and France have surplus quantities of butter and cheese which are distributed within Western Europe. The production of butter and cheese provides dairy waste (skim milk, i.e., milk remaining after the cream has been skimmed off for

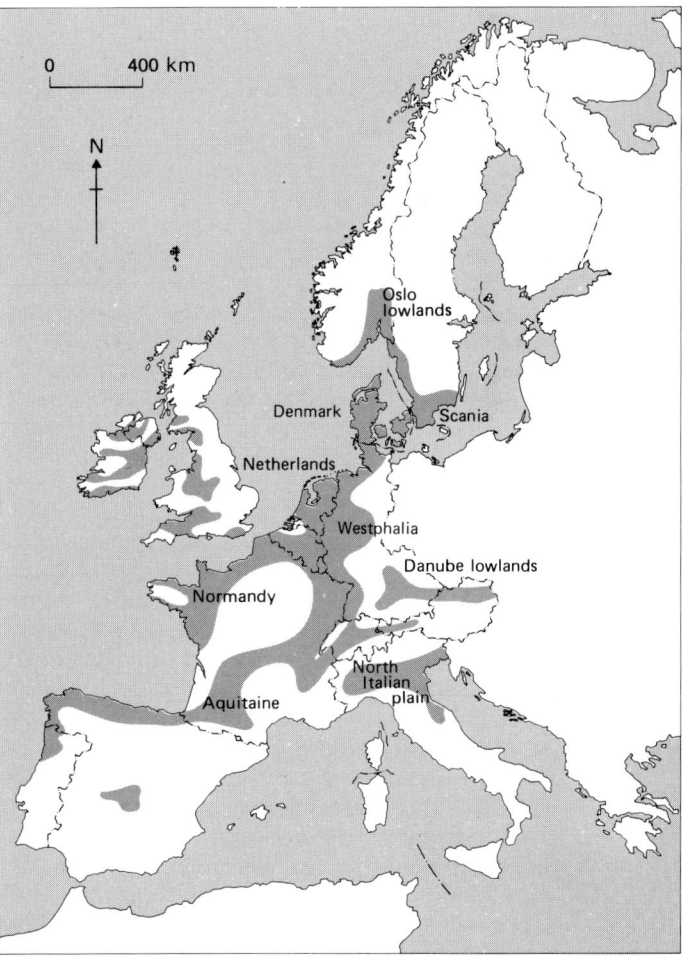

Figure 5.5 Chief areas of dairy farming

47

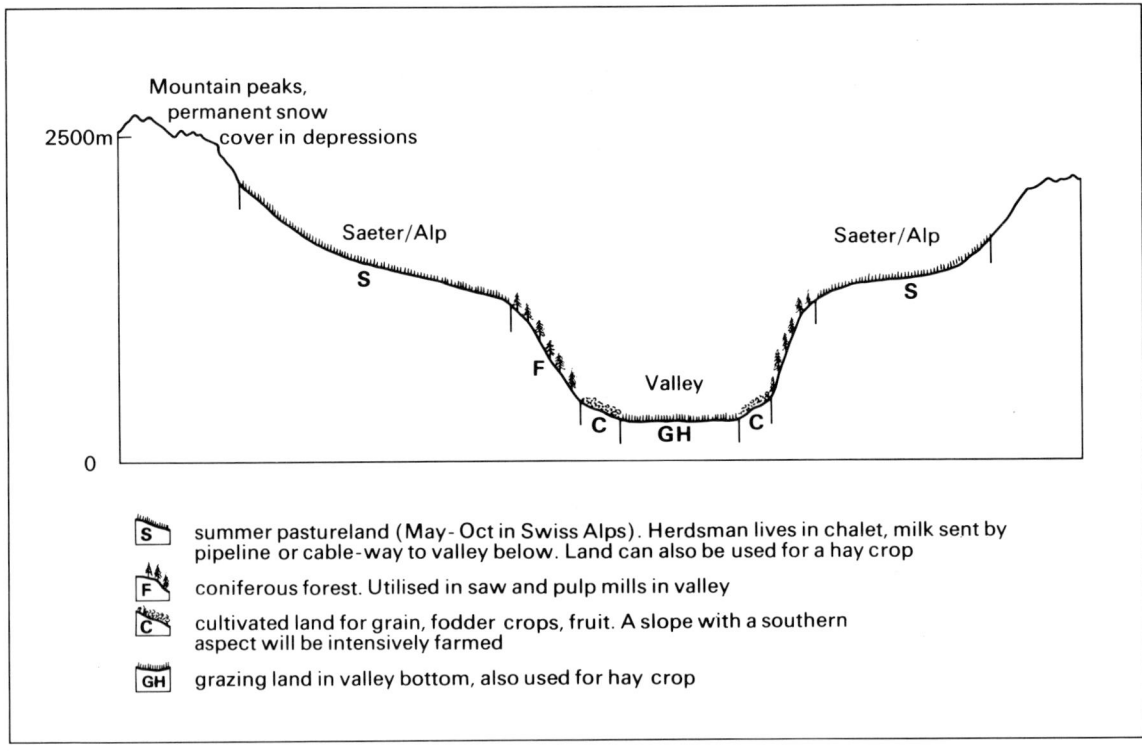

S — summer pastureland (May- Oct in Swiss Alps). Herdsman lives in chalet, milk sent by pipeline or cable-way to valley below. Land can also be used for a hay crop

F — coniferous forest. Utilised in saw and pulp mills in valley

C — cultivated land for grain, fodder crops, fruit. A slope with a southern aspect will be intensively farmed

GH — grazing land in valley bottom, also used for hay crop

Figure 5.6 Land-use zones in an Alpine area

butter and cheese manufacture, and cheese waste) which is dried and used to rear and fatten cattle and pigs as a secondary activity of many dairy farms. The demand for liquid milk and cream is a fairly stable one throughout the year, and a regular yield from the dairy cattle is essential. To achieve this, controlled stall-feeding is desirable, as the milk output from open-grazed cattle falls when temperatures are low, and the food intake is converted into heat energy rather than milk. The breed of cattle used is important too; the Friesian gives a high milk yield while the Normandy and Danish Red produce less milk. The latter, however, has the high butterfat content needed for the manufacture of dairy products. At various research centres, by processes of selective breeding, cattle with both a high milk and butterfat yield are being developed.

In the mountain areas of Norway and Switzerland, dairy farming is practised with the aid of *transhumance*. The steep environment provides limited flat land for cultivation, and the mountain pastures exposed by the spring thaw are used to supplement the grazing land or are used for a hay crop. The lower valley land is used to cultivate fodder crops for winter feed.

Three particular problems are common in these damp mountain areas.

1 the difficulty of drying hay, which can be seen in summer drying on racks in the fields;

2 the distance from markets, which is countered by a concentration upon products less perishable than liquid milk;

3 the shortage of labour, caused by the migration of people to the towns, has led to an increasing number of upper pastures being unused.

In the Mediterranean countries of Spain and Italy summer drought limits the development of specialist dairy farming areas. Production is concentrated upon liquid milk near the towns, with small centres producing butter and cheese—largely for home consumption.

During the 1960's, the EEC countries over-produced dairy products and 'a mountain of butter' was referred to as being in store in France. After 1969 this trend was reversed by using the mechanism of a low target price for dairy products, which has encouraged some diary farmers to turn their resources to meat production, in which the EEC countries have had a deficiency.

48

Dairy Farming in Denmark

Denmark is a small country with a population of 5.03 million in 1973. Two thirds of her agricultural production is exported, and in livestock products alone she is able to meet the needs of 16 million people. The concentration upon dairy farming dates back to the second half of the nineteenth century when cheap grain began to be exported into Europe from North America, and the producing countries of Europe found they were unable to compete. Denmark's arable land was gradually converted to pasture with many small family-run dairy farms. No large nearby market for liquid milk was available, so production was based upon high quality butter, cheese and bacon for export to the industrial areas of Germany and the United Kingdom. The factors which made the change to dairy farming possible and explain its development will now be considered.

The Land

Denmark consists of the Jutland peninsula, the large islands of Fyn and Zealand, and numerous small islands. This fragmented area is part of the North European Plain, its surface covered with a variety of sand, gravel and clay deposits laid down by the Scandinavian ice sheets. The gently-undulating surface rises above 150 metres at places along the morainic ridge near Vejle in Jutland, but throughout it presents a landscape that is ideal for arable and pasture alike. Of the land area, 69% is put to agricultural use—the highest figure of any European country; and only on the outwash plains of west Jutland, where moor, marsh and sand dune areas occur, does the land have limited agricultural value. The boulder clay surface of east Jutland and the islands provides a water-retentive loam soil which is virtually stone-free on the islands. On the poor sandy heaths of west Jutland areas of land have been reclaimed by deep ploughing (mixing surface sand with underlying clay) and regular applications of lime, marl and synthetic fertilizers. The marshy areas near the coast have been drained and empoldered on the Dutch pattern, to make additional land available for cultivation.

The Climate

The temperature and rainfall conditions illus-

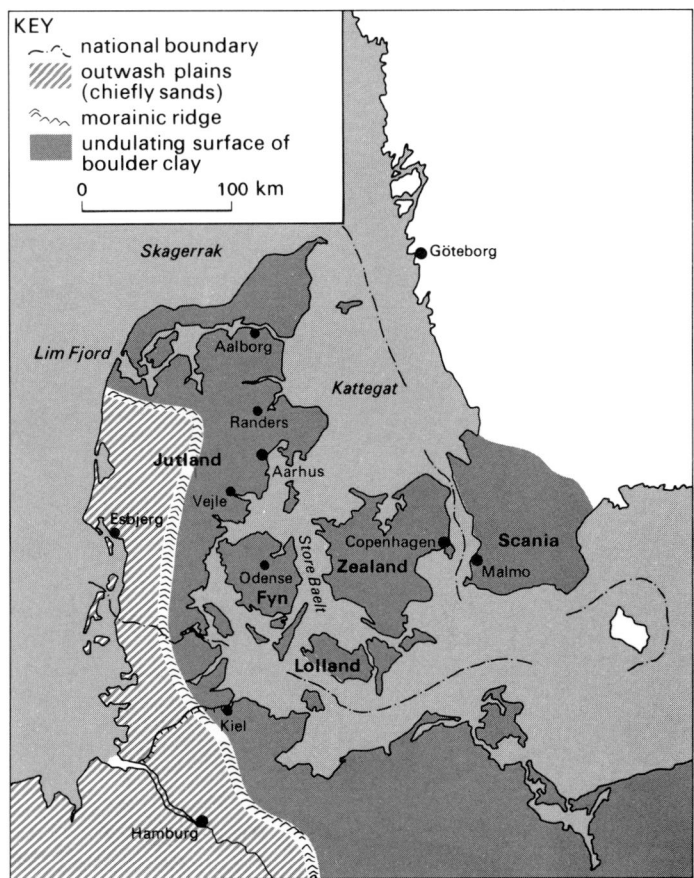

Figure 5.7 The principal landscape zones in Denmark

trated below favour open grazing and allow a 7–8 month growing season for grain and fodder crops.

Station	Height	Average January	Average July	Total Rainfall
Copenhagen	5 m	0°C	18°C	490 mm

The small size and low altitude of the country mean that there are only slight variations from the climate experienced in Copenhagen. In the west, rainfall is slightly higher (686 mm) and temperatures a little less extreme (ranging from 2°C to 17°C), while in the southern islands of Lolland and Falster, shelter and a southern position produce a higher incidence of sunshine, encouraging fruit and market garden crops as well as dairy farming.

The climate is very suitable for grain production; the frosty winters break up the soil

49

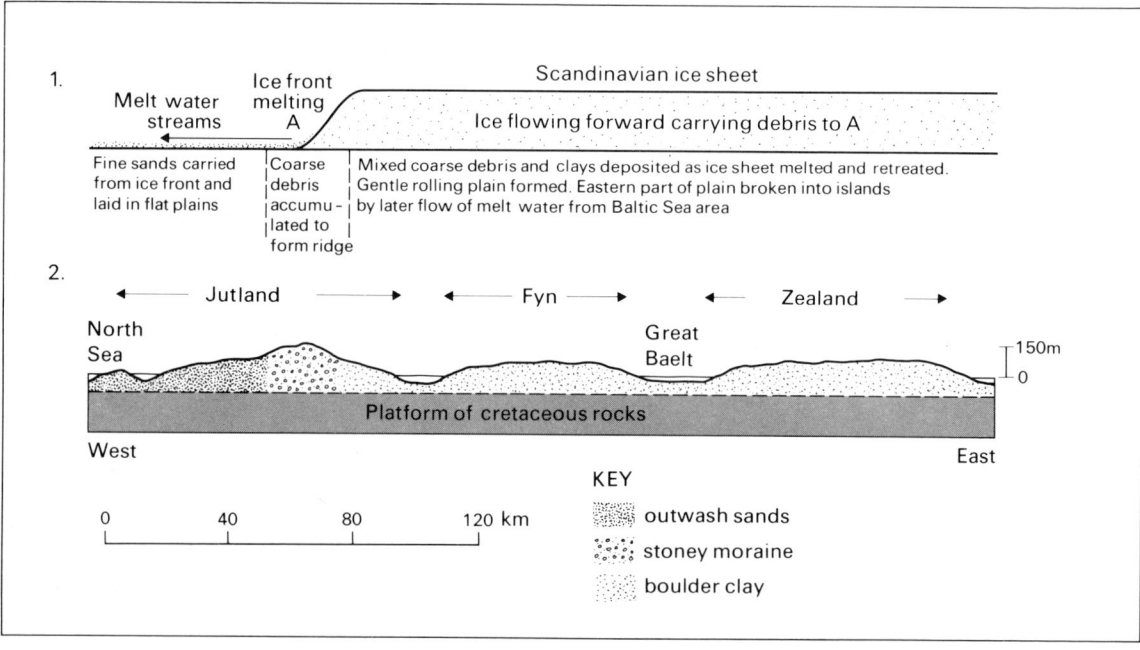

Figure 5.8 Section across Denmark showing the landscape and its formation

and help to kill weeds while the low rainfall produces the relatively dry, cloud-free conditions that are needed in summer. Exposure to the prevailing westerly wind, which frequently sweeps unimpeded across the low lying countryside, is a problem farmers have to face. The removal of hedges and most of the original deciduous forest means that there are few natural barriers, and fields of grain are unprotected from the wind. Increasingly, plantations of coniferous trees are being established, particularly on land of low agricultural potential, like the sand dunes of west Jutland. The largest areas occur in Jutland, but plantations of conifers are familiar features of most Danish landscapes.

The Farming System

In 1950 the average Danish farm was 15 ha in size, but by 1973 it had increased by amalgamation and purchase to 23 ha. When one considers the variety and cost of the machinery required for arable cultivation, together with the advantages of large open fields, it is clear that considerable ingenuity has been necessary for Danish farming to reach its present high level of efficiency. By working together, the Danish farmers have reduced the costs of working small farm units.

In 1960 there were more than 500 private- and publicly-owned co-operative dairies, having an average of 150 members each and handling 90% of Denmark's milk production. Most large villages and towns had a dairy serving the needs of local farmers, but many have now closed and operations are instead centred upon a few large units. The excellent road system has helped to make this level of centralization possible, and faster collection from farms has been achieved by the elimination of churns and the compulsory installation of hygenic stainless steel tanks to which the road tankers connect. The dairy at Ringsted is intended to handle almost the entire milk production of Zealand. The dairies sell milk, butter, cheese, yoghurt and dried milk—some of the latter being used for animal feed. Co-operative members receive an annual share of the profits, according to their milk contribution. To reduce production costs, the bulk purchase and distribution of animal feedstuffs, fertilizer and seed is also undertaken by co-operatives. Farm machinery is either purchased singly or jointly by farmers, or hired from machinery contracting depots—the extensive use of machinery is very important in keeping labour costs down.

The dairy has to maintain a very high

Plan of Carousel

Figure 5.9 An 8-point Rotary Carousel rotates in 4–12 minutes and one man can milk 100 cows. During rotation the animals are milked, fed and observed by the stockman

standard of hygiene and quality control and its operations are regularly inspected and certified by government officials. The bulk of the butter and cheese products are exported, and the supervision is sufficiently good for an individual product to be traced back to the producing dairy and farm.

A Danish farmer is usually a member of several co-operatives for marketing his produce. There are co-operative abbatoirs producing bacon and meat for canning factories, and co-operatives to process and market cereals, sugar beet, broiler chickens, eggs, etc. In all cases the tendency is to replace the small local unit by the large, centrally-situated factory; although abbatoirs have always drawn from a wide area with a large membership to ensure a regular supply of livestock. The abbatoir at Nykopping (Falster) slaughters 1200 pigs each day.

Approximately 90% of Danish butter, cheese and bacon products come from co-operative enterprises. It is not only in the marketing of farm produce that the principle of co-operation has been established. Co-operation exists in many walks of Danish life, including banking, insurance and house building, and in such industries as baking, cement and fishing and in retail shopping.

In addition to co-operation between farmers, the high productivity of dairy farming in Denmark can be attributed to the strong support given by the government to the following.
(a) *The control of quality.* All attested produce bears the stamp of Lurmark, which is a guarantee of quality; this has been shown on all butter, cheese and bacon exports since 1906.
(b) *The encouragement of highly selective breeding* for cattle and pigs. The Danish Red

Figure 5.10 Tethered Danish Red dairy cattle

Figure 5.11 Containers of Danish bacon awaiting export to Britain at Esbjerg

and Holstein breeds provide a good milk yield with a high butterfat content, while the Landrace pig was the direct result of the state approving specialist breeding centres (the first of which was established in 1893) to develop an animal suitable for meeting the requirements of the British bacon market.

(c) *An involvement with research,* which includes financial support for the Royal Veterinary and Agricultural College in Copenhagen and numerous other establishments. Research is carried out into such varied subjects as fertilizers, weed-killers, animal diseases, high-yielding crop strains, packaging and marketing.

The Export Market

Only the urban area of Copenhagen, measuring 5000 sq. km and containing two million people (more than one-third of the country's total population) constitutes a large urban market. In the eastern half of Zealand many of the farms and dairies are organized to meet the liquid milk demands, but elsewhere in the country production is geared primarily towards export.

West Germany and Great Britain are Denmark's chief customers, the former for cheese and meat products, and the latter for butter, cheese, bacon and poultry. Denmark's link with Britain was strengthened by their membership of the EFTA, and over the past ten years an increasing proportion of Denmark's trade has been in this direction. The principal transportation of dairy produce is by road and rail from Jutland and Fyn to the port of Esbjerg, where refrigerated containers are loaded for transport to the English ports of Hull, Harwich, Felixstowe and Tilbury. Produce from Zealand and the southern islands is exported through Copenhagen. Exports to West Germany chiefly travel by road and ferry to Hamburg, which acts as a distribution centre for Danish farm produce.

These markets are very competitive, the Danish product facing competition from home produced goods, Commonwealth imports in Britain, and French and Dutch imports. The Danish share of the market has only been maintained by establishing the highest quality of produce and packaging, and by forceful sales promotion through various advertising media.

In 1973 foodstuffs accounted for 29% of the total exports of Denmark, whereas in 1960 the figure had been over 50%. This does not indicate a decline in the quantity of agricultural exports, but rather a large increase in the exports of manufacturing industry, particularly ships, machinery and textiles.

The early development of the dairying industry to supply an export market was a reflection of the lack of industrial raw materials within the country. The development of bulk carriers for cheap sea transport has made this factor less important; instead, such factors as site, position and good labour relations have become significant. The industrial growth in Denmark since 1965 has had three effects upon dairy farming:
(a) a loss of 100,000 ha of farmland to industrial and urban growth has required further increases in yield;
(b) an increase in the home market for liquid milk and dairy produce;
(c) a reduced agricultural labour force as the following table shows.

	Agricultural Exports	Agricultural Production	Industrial Exports	% of population employed in Agriculture
1966	£398 m	£515 m	£430 m	12·5%
1969	£405 m	£567 m	£649 m	10·0%
1972	£532 m	£758 m	£1024 m	9·5%

Although dairy farming will continue to occupy a major place in the Danish economy, it seems unlikely that it will again dominate the exports of Denmark as it did in the post-war period up to 1965.

3 The Cultivation of Root Crops (Potatoes, Sugar Beet)

The cultivation of root crops, whether for cash sale or for animal fodder, is normally undertaken on heavily fertilized land in rotation with cereals. The principal cash crops—potatoes and sugar beet—are widely grown in Europe, but they both require specialist conditions for good yields.

Yields for 1973/4 (in 100 kg/hectare)					
	Belgium	France	Italy	Netherlands	West Germany
Sugar Beet	49·2	41·5	38·3	47·7	45·1
Potatoes	28·2	23·1	16·2	36·8	28·5

Potatoes can produce more food per hectare than any of the cereals, and a long, cool, moist growing-season, with temperatures ranging from 7°C to 18°C, is ideal. High temperatures or high humidity will result in reduced yields. Western Europe, with its mild maritime climate, has perfect conditions for cultivation, and the potato is extensively used for human consumption, animal fodder, and for starch distillation. Growing seed potatoes is a speciality along Western Europe coastal areas, where high quality stock can be produced free of the wind-borne aphid diseases which affect inland areas below 180 metres in height.

The areas important for sugar beet cultivation are similar to those for potatoes; a mild, moist, growing-season again being necessary. A special requirement for sugar beet is an autumn which is either dry or has cool nights

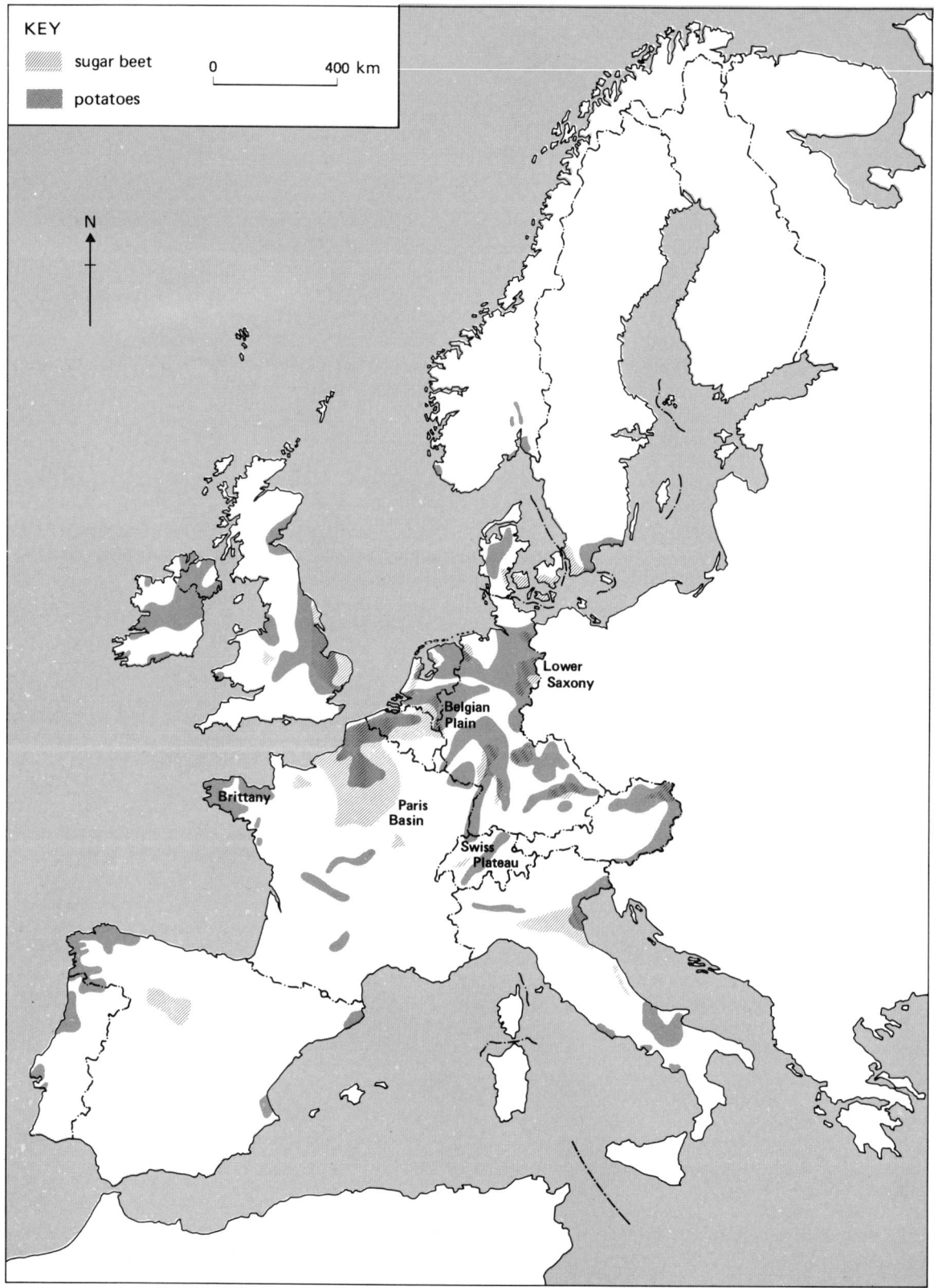

Figure 5.12 (*left*) The main areas for the production of potatoes and sugar-beet

to check top growth and encourage sugar accumulation in the root. The crop is usually harvested over the period September–April, according to a timetable drawn up in advance by the local sugar factory to ensure a continuous and regular supply of beet. At the beginning of each season the farmer is given a quota of sugar beet to grow; if he exceeds this quantity he is paid at a reduced rate for the excess. As with potatoes, it is difficult to completely mechanize the harvest process; casual labourers are usually employed to collect the crop after the tops have been cut and the beet lifted by machine. None of the plant is wasted, the sugar beet tops and residue being used for animal fodder. Yields have increased by more than 50% and the European beet crop is now produced at costs similar to those for sugar cane.

The Loess Soil Zone of Lower Saxony

Along the northern edge of the Central German Hills is an area of loess soils. These deposits were carried south from the debris left by the melting Scandinavian ice sheets by strong winds sweeping off the glaciers. Loess provides an excellent soil which is light and loamy for cultivation and allows the free drainage of moisture; it is particularly suitable for sugar beet.

On the plains of the rivers Aller and Weser, separated by the wooded Leine Hills, farms grow wheat, rye, barley, sugar beet and potatoes. They are mostly above 20 ha in size, and keep dairy cattle and pigs. The stock are fed on grain and roots, while the liquid milk and meat is supplied to the nearby towns of Hanover, Bremen and Braunschweig. The sugar beet is transported by road to local sugar refineries near Hanover, Braunschweig, Helmstedt and Hildesheim. The supply is regulated to meet the demands of the factory, the farmer being told at the beginning of the season when he must lift his beet and send it to the factory. Sugar beet is a bulky product costly to transport, so the refineries are usually sited in the midst of the farms supplying the raw material.

4   Commercial Market Gardening

The cultivation of easily perishable fruit,

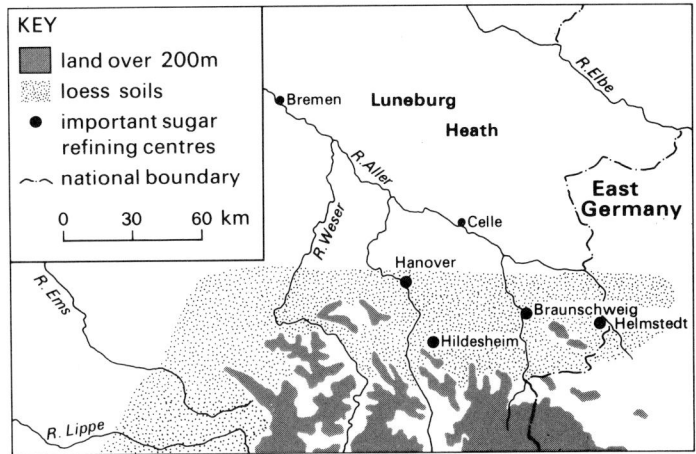

Figure 5.13 The lower Saxony area

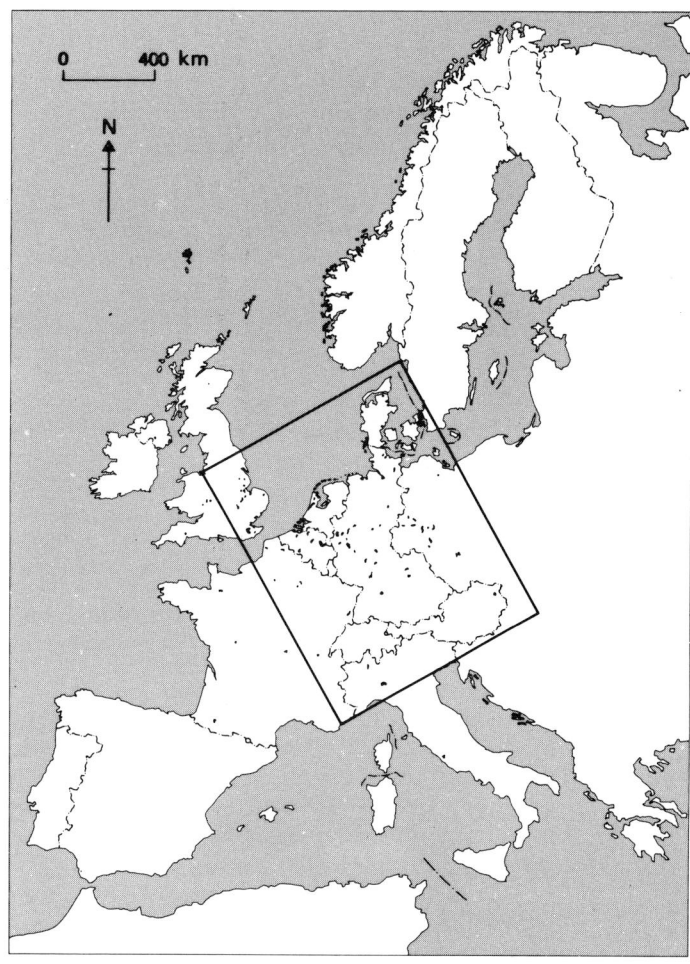

Figure 5.14 The main areas of commercial market gardening. The area in the box contains 60% of the population of Western Europe

55

Figure 5.15 Strawberries being picked on the slopes of the Sorfjord, Hardanger, south-west Norway. At latitude 60°N the fields must have a southern aspect to give a satisfactory yield.

With reference to the photograph:
(a) draw a simple section across the fjord, and mark the position of the strawberry field;
(b) describe how the sheets of polythene are being used, and explain their purpose;
(c) describe the problems of farming in the fjord country of Norway

flowers and vegetables is chiefly restricted to the main areas of dense population. It is concentrated around the industrial areas of the Rhineland, Belgium and the Netherlands, and near great cities like Paris, Copenhagen and Hamburg, where a large and high-earning population creates demand for market garden produce. Market garden produce yields a high cash return per hectare cultivated, but nearness to the urban areas usually means that land prices are high and there is great dependence on reliable transport links and market outlets. In addition, the activity is labour and capital intensive, and production costs are high. With so much emphasis upon economic factors, the natural factors of climate, soil and drainage are of less significance in determining the distribution of market gardening. Where soil or drainage difficulties exist they can be countered by fertilization and the construction of water control systems, such as drainage ditches and irrigation works. The cost of such improvements is relatively small in view of the small units of cultivation and the already capital-intensive character of the activity. Most market gardens are under 2 ha in size, but usually farmers group themselves into co-operative organizations.

The chief items grown are salad crops, vegetables and flowers, and several crops are usually taken from the same plot each year. In the producing centres of the North European Plain, cool climatic conditions limit the outdoor growing season and much cultivation is done in heated glasshouses. The cultivation of plants on polythene sheets has the advantage of reducing the loss of heat and moisture to the atmosphere, and is a technique now widely used. The use of polythene and a southerly aspect enables strawberries to be grown as far north as latitude 60°North in Norway. The aim of the grower is to produce a heavy crop early in the season when a high price can be commanded and many early-maturing, disease-free strains have been developed.

Most European output is geared to a local market, but in the Netherlands over 50% of all market garden produce is for export, chiefly to West Germany and the United Kingdom. This requires particularly efficient transport facilities and specialist, attractive packaging—much of the produce being frozen. Western coastal areas with a very mild winter climate can specialize in the outdoor production of early crops for sale in March and April. Two of the most important of these areas are the west and south coasts of Brittany. The average January temperature at Brest is 7°C, which is warmer than either Bordeaux or Marseilles; and the light loam soils of the coastline warm

quickly in spring to encourage early growth. The chief vegetables are early potatoes, cauliflowers, peas, beans, onions and artichokes, which are sent to Paris and other EEC markets.

Market Gardening in the Netherlands

The Netherlands, a small, densely populated country, had few important industrial raw materials until the recent discovery of natural gas in Groningen. As in Denmark, the economy was built upon commerce and agriculture. The agriculture is intensive, with specialization

Figure 5.16 Glasshouses in the Westland district of the Netherlands. They were formerly used for the cultivation of fruit and vegetables but as competition within the EEC has increased, many growers have turned to the production of indoor plants and flowers.

With reference to the photograph:
(a) draw a plan of the area; mark and label on it a drainage canal, a dyke, the sand dunes and beaches, the area of glasshouses, the site of a village, and a main road;
(b) explain why the land is so flat;
(c) explain the purpose of the tall chimneys among the glasshouses

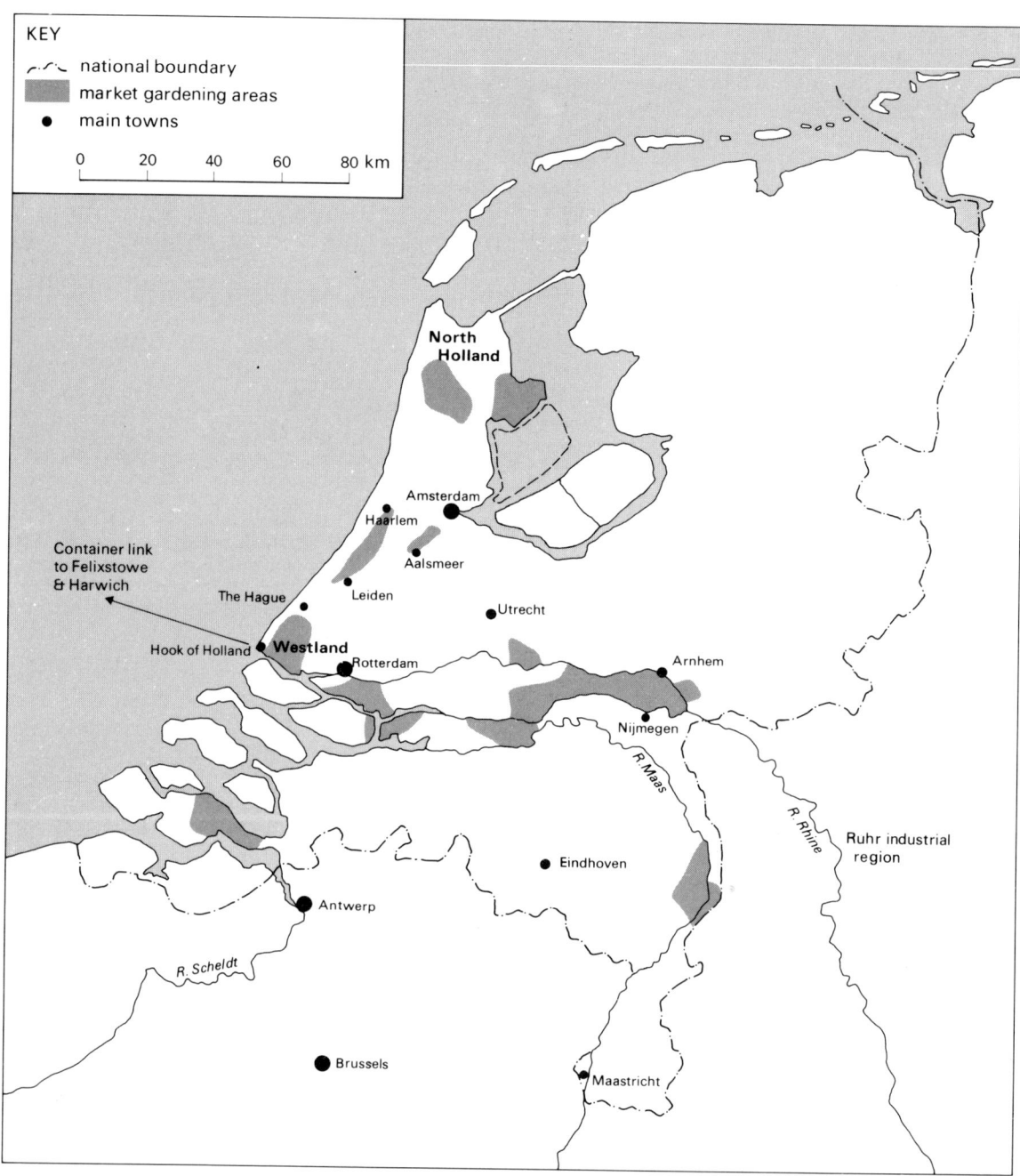

KEY

⌐‿⌐ national boundary

▓ market gardening areas

● main towns

0   20   40   60   80 km

North Holland

Amsterdam

Haarlem

Aalsmeer

Container link to Felixstowe & Harwich

The Hague

Leiden

Utrecht

Hook of Holland Westland

Rotterdam

Arnhem

Nijmegen

R. Maas

R. Rhine

Ruhr industrial region

Eindhoven

Antwerp

R. Scheldt

Brussels

Maastricht

Figure 5.17 (*above*) The distribution of market gardening areas in the Netherlands

Figure 5.18 (*opposite*) The distribution of areas important for the cultivation of apples, vines and oranges

in market garden crops and dairying, which require a large labour force, to meet the demands of her industrial neighbours, West Germany and the United Kingdom. The position of the Netherlands is ideal for export to these countries, utilizing the short North Sea cross-ing to England, and the developed water, rail and road links with the industrial Rhineland.

The distribution of the market garden area is chiefly in the low-lying western section of the country, where the light clay and peat soils area is sheltered by coastal dunes, and along

58

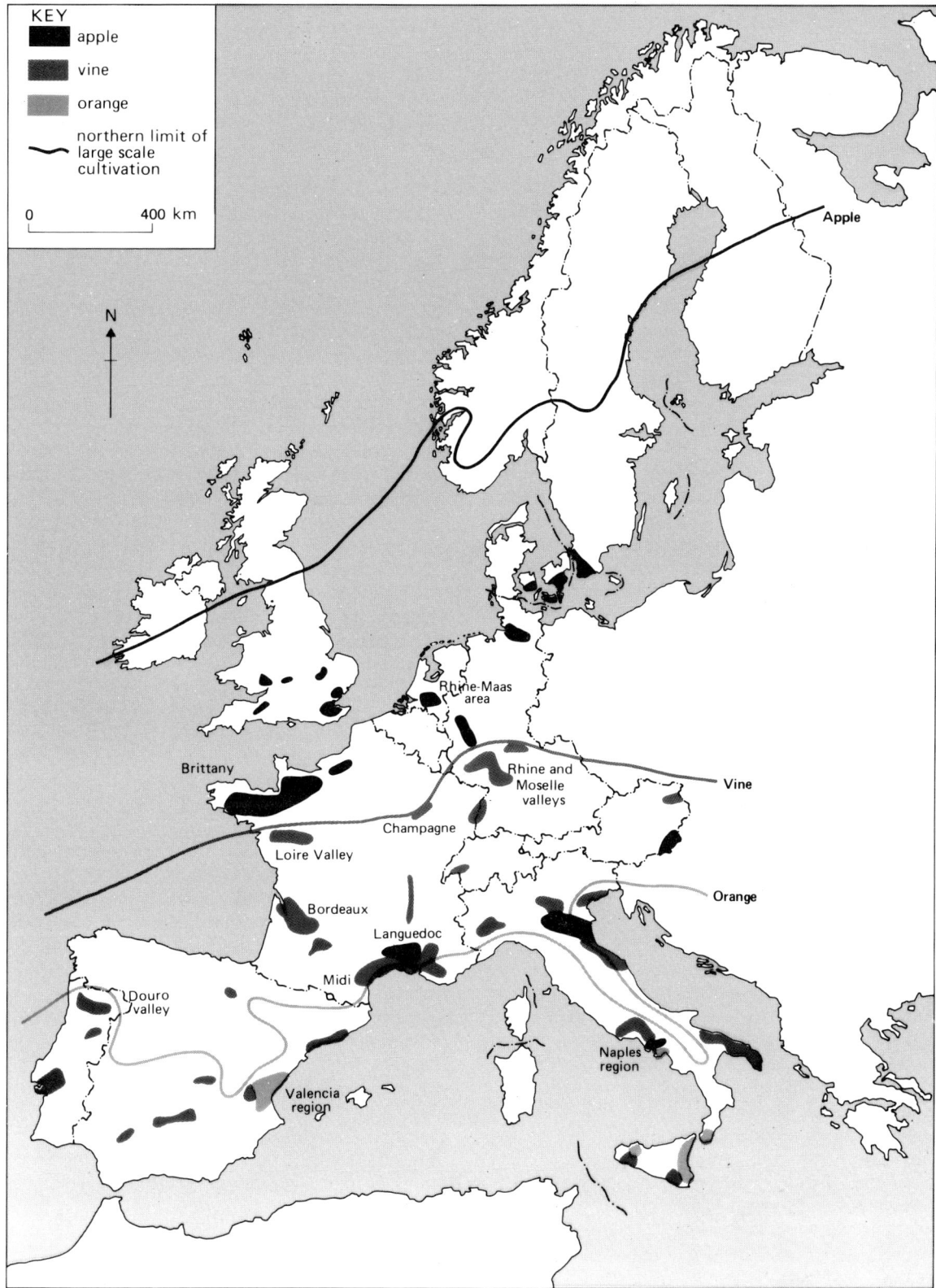

KEY

apple

vine

orange

northern limit of
large scale
cultivation

0   400 km

N

Apple

Brittany

Rhine-Maas
area

Rhine and
Moselle
valleys

Vine

Champagne

Loire Valley

Orange

Bordeaux

Languedoc

Midi

Douro
valley

Naples
region

Valencia
region

the Rhine-Maas plain. The size of farms averages 4 hectares. In the older polder region many drainage canals break up the farmland, and communication between fields has to be by boat. In the Westland area, the concentration is upon salad crops, vegetables and soft fruits, with over 2,400 ha under glass, in both heated and cold frames. In the Haarlem area and in North Holland there is a specialization in bulb and vegetable production, while around Aalsmeer the production of cut flowers, pot plants, nursery stock and horticultural seeds is predominant. In the Rhine-Maas area vegetables, soft fruits, apples and pears are most important. To achieve the highest possible yields the land is heavily fertilized; four or five salad and vegetable crops per year are raised and considerable inter-cropping is done.

Approximately one-third of the Dutch output is exported in fresh, frozen or dried form. In addition to the conventional movement of produce by sea to England and road and rail to West Germany, increasing quantities of high value fruits and exotic flowers are exported to all parts of the world from Schiphol Airport, Amsterdam.

5 Fruit Production

The distribution of the main fruit growing areas is more restricted than other crops and involves small specialist areas. The reason for the limited distribution is climate; most fruit trees are perennial plants and require suitable conditions throughout the year, whereas quick-maturing strains of annual plants, such as wheat and maize, can be grown outside their normal habitat. In the cooler areas of Europe, apples, pears and plums are the main fruits, while in the warmer southern half of the continent, citrus fruits, apricots, peaches, olives and vines predominate. Some fruit is grown on most farms, but the commercial production of fruit is a highly specialized activity.

Frost, poor drainage and strong winds are the chief hazards to cultivation, and crops are frequently cultivated on the light free-draining soils of lower hill slopes. The vine is very tolerant of dry conditions and is frequently grown on high slopes above the damper valleys; in Europe it is rarely irrigated, unlike viticulture in California and other parts of the world. In the Rhône valley, where the cool

Mistral wind can have severe effects on spring blossom and retard growth, peach and apricot trees are protected by tall cypress hedges. Many European fruit farms are family-run and are under 4 ha in size.

Fruit cultivation is difficult to mechanize and the farms employ a lot of labour relative to their size; planting, weeding, spraying and pruning are jobs which can be contained, but extra labour is usually required for picking. Many migrant pickers come from Spain and Italy, where the late citrus fruit harvest from November to April enables them to travel north to France, West Germany and the Low Countries for the summer harvest of deciduous fruit. Most fruits are prone to attack by pests and diseases, and heavy applications of chemical sprays are made to ensure a high crop yield. However, spraying is costly and often destroys much of the natural fauna of an area; also, as insects can develop an immunity to chemical sprays, the desirability of the process is questionable.

Fresh fruit is easily perishable and special refrigerated storage and transport facilities are needed. Increasing quantities of fruit are now dried, canned, frozen and pulped into juices, and the factories doing this work are usually found in the specialist fruit growing areas. However, Western Europe is not self-sufficient in temperate fruit production and the summer demand for many fruits, including apples and oranges, is largely met by southern hemisphere producers such as South Africa and Australia.

Citrus Fruit in the Valencia Area of Spain

The cultivation of citrus fruits is well suited to the Mediterranean climate, although irrigation is usually needed to counter the low and unreliable rainfall. The orange is the most important (Valencia Province supplies 44% of Spanish output) and is harvested between November and April; ripe fruit can remain on the tree for several weeks so picking can be spread over a lengthy period and regulated to meet demand. Lemons are usually picked green, and are allowed to ripen indoors; unlike oranges, the bulk of the crop is not sold fresh but is used for juices and flavourings.

The Valencia area is the most intensively farmed area in south-east Spain. The rivers entering the lowlands are longer and have a more reliable flow. Cultivation is in a zone of

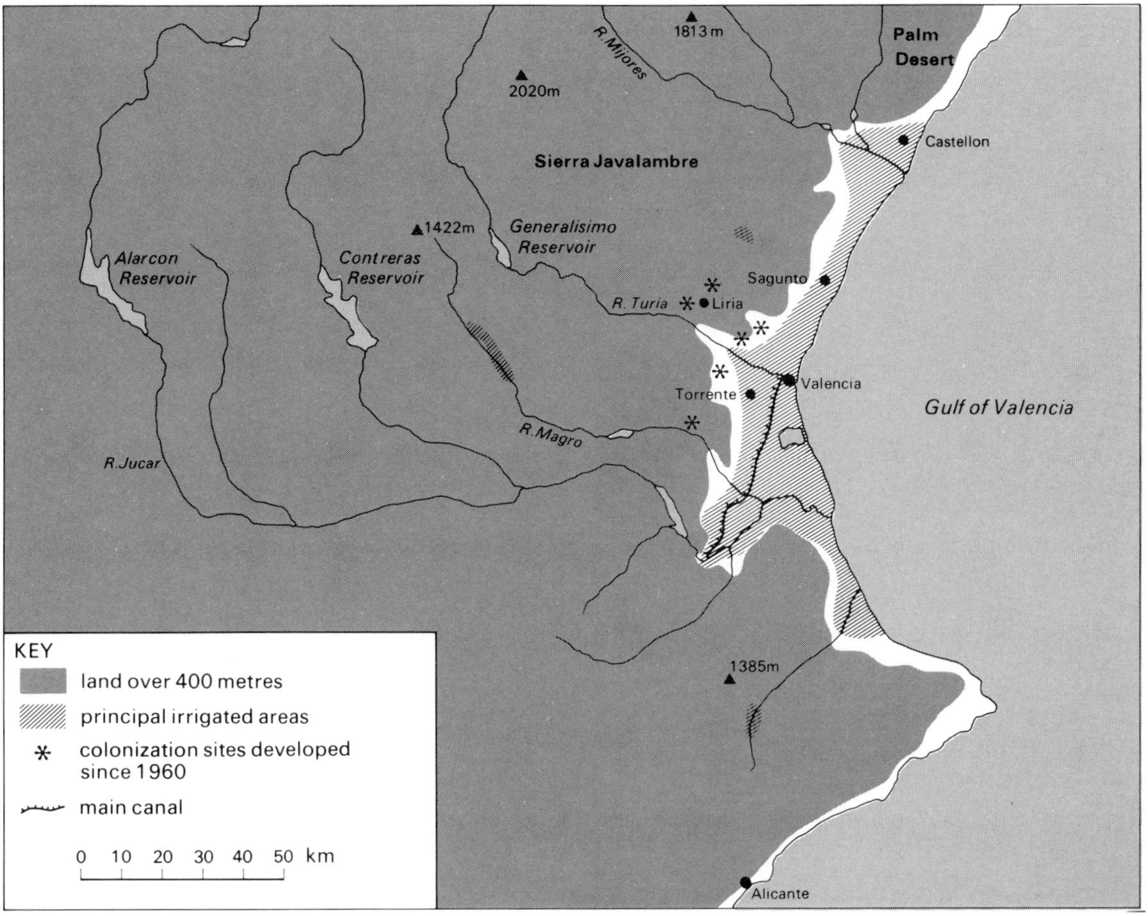

Figure 5.19 map with the following labels:

1813 m

Palm Desert

2020m

Sierra Javalambre

R. Mijores

● Castellon

▲1422m

Generalisimo Reservoir

Alarcon Reservoir

Contreras Reservoir

✳ Sagunto ●

R. Turia ✳ ● Liria

✳ ✳

✳

Torrente ✳ ● Valencia

R. Magro

✳

Gulf of Valencia

R. Jucar

1385m ▲

Alicante

KEY

land over 400 metres

principal irrigated areas

✳ colonization sites developed since 1960

main canal

0 10 20 30 40 50 km

Figure 5.19 (*above*) Irrigated areas in the Valencia lowlands

Figure 5.20 Prefabricated concrete irrigation channel

small intensively cultivated plots or 'huertas', occupying a broad area a few kilometres inland and stretching over 80 km along the coast. Water is brought by channels and aqueducts from the River Jucar which has a series of major dams in its upper section, used for irrigation purposes and hydro-electric power generation. The flooding of sections of the valleys of the Juca and Turia has displaced many families from their farms and villages. In 1960 the State purchased 573 ha of poor quality land in six areas west of Valencia on which three new villages and 176 houses have been built. The land is irrigated with water from deep wells which have been sunk into the porous sub soil, and distributed through a network of pipes and channels. The land is divided into units of under 5 ha in size, and is chiefly used for crops of oranges, potatoes and

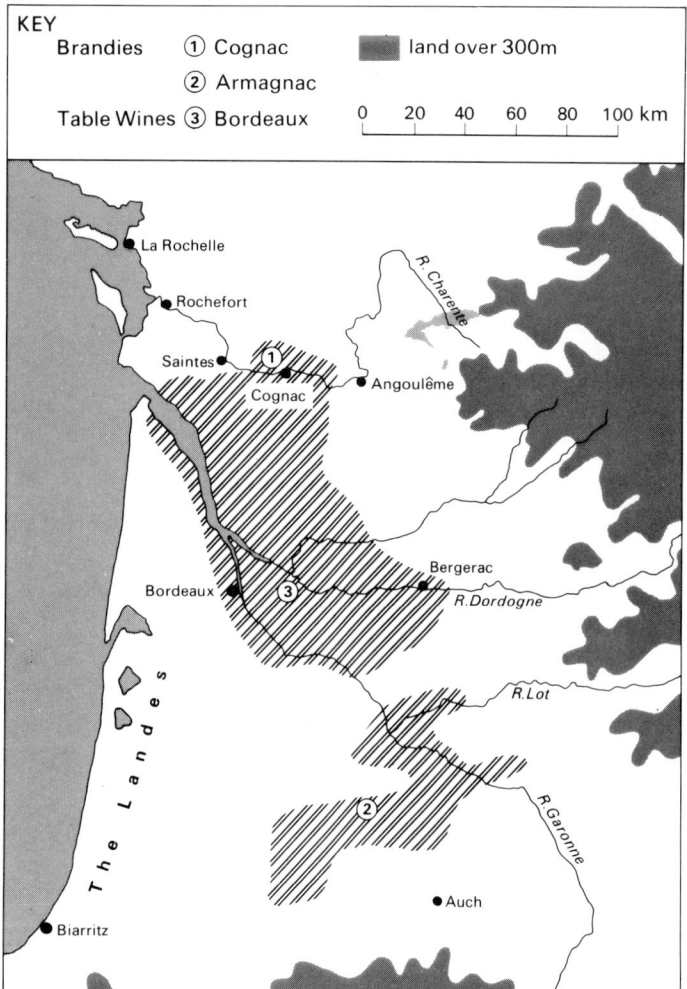

Station	Average January	Average July	Rainfall
Bordeaux. Height 7 m	7°C	20°C	826 mm 450 mm fall in the October-March period)

KEY

Brandies   ① Cognac   land over 300m

           ② Armagnac

Table Wines ③ Bordeaux   0   20   40   60   80   100 km

Figure 5.21 The chief wine-producing areas in south-west France

vegetables—only 6% is used for fodder crops of maize and alfalfa.

The heavily cultivated light alluvial soils of the coast plain stand out in marked contrast to the barren hill country behind the Valencia lowlands. The bulk of the orange crop is exported from Valencia by sea to the North European markets during the winter period from November to May.

Vine Cultivation in South-West France

The warm sunny summers, mild winters and moderate rainfall of this region provide excellent conditions for the production of high quality vines, and approximately 25% of the total French production comes from this area. The vine is very sensitive to the local conditions of temperature, rainfall, sunshine, soils and aspect, and these variations explain the range and variety of wines produced in the area. On the eastern side of the river Garonne and in the Dordogne valley, the soils are light clays, while on the west, flanking the Gironde estuary, they are derived from river gravels. Here the rich vineyards of the Médoc are sheltered from onshore winds by the pine forests of the Landes. However, atmospheric pollution from the oil refineries on the estuary at Pauillac is causing concern to the growers.

The vines are grown on small 'estates' or chateaux usually under 2 ha in size; the quantity grown is controlled by a system of quotas operated under the authority of the Ministry of Agriculture. The growers supply the grapes to the wine producers in their area, some of the most famous wines being Médoc, St. Emilion, Graves and Sauternes. The production of wine employs a large labour force and this is one of the most densely populated farming areas in France.

The wines from the region are chiefly quality wines rather than 'vin ordinaire' and are exported in large quantities to the United Kingdom and USA from the port of Bordeaux. Cognac and Armagnac brandies are distilled from local wines in the Charente valley and Gascony areas and matured in casks traditionally made from Limousin oak. Production is dominated by the firms of Martell, Courvoisier, Hennessy and Hine, who receive wine from local producers. Bordeaux exports brandy from both areas, while La Rochelle handles some export from the Cognac area.

Although the overall area under the vine in France has declined in the past ten years and output has fallen from 75 million hectolitres in 1970 to 60 million hectolitres in 1974, this reduction has principally been in the Midi region of southern France; the Bordeaux area has undergone little change.

6   Sheep Rearing

Sheep are more widely distributed throughout the world than any other farm livestock,

Figure 5.22(a–c) Vine cultivation at Pauillac, Bordeaux.

(**a**) (*above*) Vines growing in free-draining gravel soil

(**b**) (*below*) Vineyards

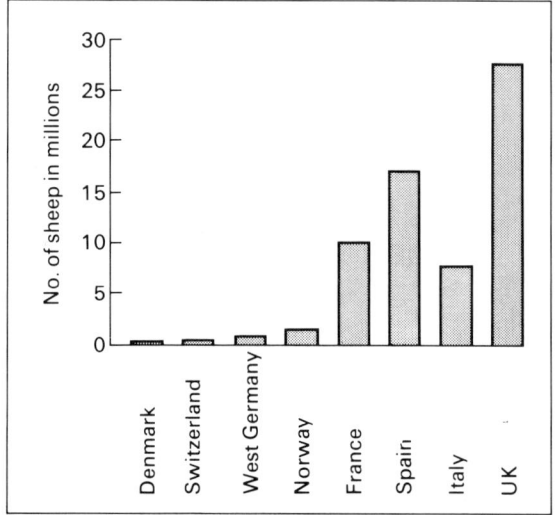

Figure 5.22 (c) Grapes arriving at a chateau for processing

reflecting their tolerance of mountain and arid areas alike. Only in the highest parts of Scandinavia and the Alps, which are snow covered for most of the year and almost completely lacking in vegetation, are sheep not found. Sheep are sure-footed and can graze areas inaccessible to other livestock, and the narrow jaw and cleft upperlip allows the animal to graze close to the ground and to search out vegetation from between rocks and boulders.

In the damp, richer, grazing areas of Western Europe sheep are primarily kept for their meat, and in the drier southern areas for their wool. The United Kingdom has the largest sheep population in Europe; most of the animals being cross-bred to ensure both a reasonable wool and meat yield. In continental Europe, mutton and lamb are less popular meats, and sheep farms similar to those in Britain are rare, the fine wool-producing Merino being the commonest breed kept. The main sheep rearing areas are in Italy, Spain and Southern France, where the dry landscapes would otherwise have little economic

Figure 5.23 Comparison of the number of sheep kept in selected countries in 1973

64

value. In these marginal areas, the quality of the grazing will often vary from season to season and from year to year, just as the rainfall varies both in its quantity and reliability. Most southern Europe farms are under 20 ha in size, and do not support vast flocks of sheep like their larger counterparts in Australia. When the lowland pasture becomes inadequate, as it does in the late summer months in southern Europe, the farmer has three alternatives:

(a) to reduce the size of his flock;
(b) to grow or buy supplementary fodder, such as hay or roots;
(c) to move the animals to better pastures nearby.

The movement of animals to moist, higher pastures in summer is still a feature of the farming practice in these areas.

Sheep Rearing in the Meseta of Central Spain

The climate graph for Madrid (Fig. 5.25) illustrates the heat and dryness of summer, and shows how difficult farming is in the central part of Spain. Many farms are under 20 ha in size and the keeping of livestock plays an important part in the mixed farm economy. Difficulty in obtaining water limits the cultivation, and only a small area is used for wheat, barley, fruit and vegetable crops. Where cereals are grown without irrigation, yields are usually unreliable. Most of the farm land is given over to rough grazing, and the cultivated area (without irrigation) is organized on a four year rotation, using a dry farming technique. The land is left fallow or rough grazed to accumulate and store water in the ground before a crop is cultivated in the fourth year. For example: *Year 1:* rough grazing for sheep on cereal stubble; *Year 2:* rough grazing for sheep; *Year 3:* land left fallow; *Year 4:* cultivation of cereal crop.

The farmer must resist the temptation to overstock his grazing land, particularly after a good year, as overgrazing can result in the destruction of vegetation as sheep and goats destroy root systems in their search for food. This is the pattern of farming in the dry limestone country of the high Sierras and in the sheltered Ebro valley region, where the peasant farm exists as an almost self-sufficient unit—wool sales often providing the only cash income. Land improvement by the provision

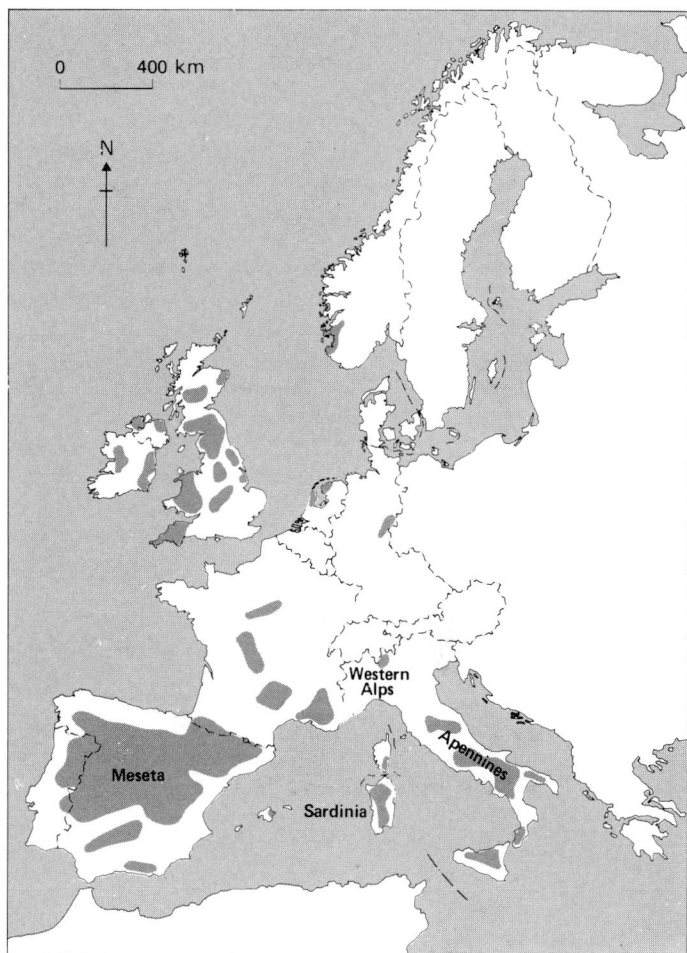

Figure 5.24 The chief sheep-rearing areas

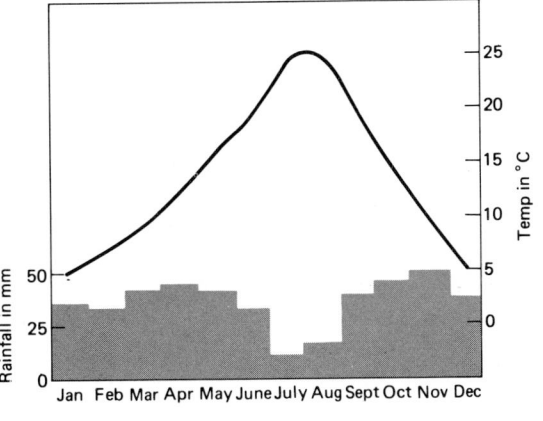

Figure 5.25 Climate graph for Madrid (height 655 m)

of irrigation water is handicapped by a lack of capital and the conservatism of the individual farmer, who often mistrusts government-sponsored schemes.

As government schemes of irrigation and colonization take place, the land is improved to produce high-yielding food crops, while the number of sheep decline (see table below). The decline in wool sales is also related to the increased use of synthetic fibres as an alternative textile.

	1965	1973	% Change
No. of sheep	20,855,000	17,191,000	17·5
Wool production (in tonnes)	36,000	31,000	13·8

The chief wool-producing region in the Meseta is Estremadura—the hilly area between the Tagus and Guadiana valleys—where 60% of the land is in large estates of over 200 ha. Most of this wool is sent to textile mills at Salamanca and Seville. The main centres of the Spanish woollen textile industry are located near large centres of population, notably Barcelona, but also at the northern Meseta towns of Burgos, Leon and Zaragossa, which are within easy reach of the industrial cities of the north coast.

Questions

1. With reference to the table showing cereal production on page 42:

(a) of the grains listed, state which *two* show the highest overall percentage increase in the period 1962–73;

(b) suggest reasons to explain this increase;

(c) name the countries which show a decline in wheat output and attempt to explain this trend;

(d) explain why maize production has shown a marked expansion.

2. With reference to Figs 4.2 and 5.2, (a) describe the landscape and type of farming shown in each photograph and (b) account for the use made of the land in each region.

3. Choose *one* commodity from each of the following pairs: wheat or maize, milk or lamb, citrus fruit or apples. For each commodity chosen:

(a) name the location of a producing area in Europe and one elsewhere in the world;

(b) give a reasoned account of the similarities and differences in the growing conditions and methods employed for the areas named in (a).

4. With reference to the climate graph of Madrid (Fig. 5·25), answer the following questions:

(a) describe the main features of the climate;

(b) explain the principal causes of this climate;

(c) describe the natural vegetation of the area;

(d) explain why it is difficult to pursue any form of agriculture other than pastoral farming.

5. (a) Name an important area of production for each of the following: early vegetables, fruit, arable crops.

(b) Under the headings of relief, climate, soils and markets, describe the conditions which favour production in the areas named.

6. Copy out and complete the table below.

	NAME		
Commodity	(A) One country exporting to Western Europe	(B) A West European area using the commodity	(C) A port where the commodity is imported for the area named in (B)
Beef			
Wool			
Maize			
Tropical fruits			
Temperate fruits			
Vegetable oils			
Cotton			

6 The forestry industries

The natural vegetation illustrated in Fig. 3.3 shows that Europe is largely covered with two broad bands of forest. The coniferous forest requires a minimum growing season of three months at temperatures above 10°C and covers most of the land north of latitude 60°N, except for high, steep or swampy areas. Where these conditions prevail in the mountain regions of central Europe the conifer replaces the deciduous tree. Deciduous forest requires milder conditions, where the seasonal temperature ranges between 4° and 18°C, and the rainfall is above 500 mm; it is mainly concentrated in the zone between latitude 45° and 60°N. There is a wide transitional area where trees of both species occur, while extensive tracts of the more commercially valuable conifer have been planted within the deciduous zone. Conifers are tolerant of low rainfall and dry soils and have been introduced into poor, sandy areas, notably the Landes in south-west France, the dune coast of the Netherlands and Jutland and the heathlands of northern Germany. The original evergreen deciduous forest of the Mediterranean region has been largely cleared or destroyed by overgrazing to leave only a low scrub growth. Among the few areas of natural forest are parts of the Apennines in Italy and the Sierra Nevada in Spain. The cork oak, yielding a layer of bark every seven years, is one of the few trees cultivated and is important in southern Portugal, Sardinia and southern Italy.

The two forest areas are contrasted in their exploitation; the coniferous forests provide an essential resource for softwood constructional timber and paper, whereas most of the broadleaved deciduous forests have been cleared for farming and settlement. Very little replanting of deciduous trees is done, but the conifer is carefully cropped and most European countries have afforestation policies aimed at conserving their resources of softwood forest. Western Europe is not self-sufficient in its timber requirements, and large quantities of softwood products are imported from the USSR and Canada.

The table below illustrates the main forest resources in Western Europe.

Main forest resources of Western Europe

	% of total land area in forest	Reserves of timber (in m m³)	
		Deciduous	Coniferous
Austria	38	47	432
France	26	525	453
Italy	20	152	144
Norway	26	76	357
Sweden	54	319	1770
Switzerland	24	45	185
West Germany	28	334	656

Forestry in Sweden

Although Sweden contains only 0·6% of the world's timber resources, the accessibility and commercial value of the forests enable her to take an important share of the world export market, as the following figures show.

	Sawn wood	Wood pulp*	Paper	Plywood, board products
Sweden's percentage of world export trade	13%	23%	12%	24%

* Includes (a) Mechanical pulp (20%)—wood fibres contain impurities (lignin) and paper will turn yellow; chiefly used for newsprint, cardboard, (b) Chemical pulp (80%)—chemical process removes lignin and bleaches fibres to produce high quality paper.

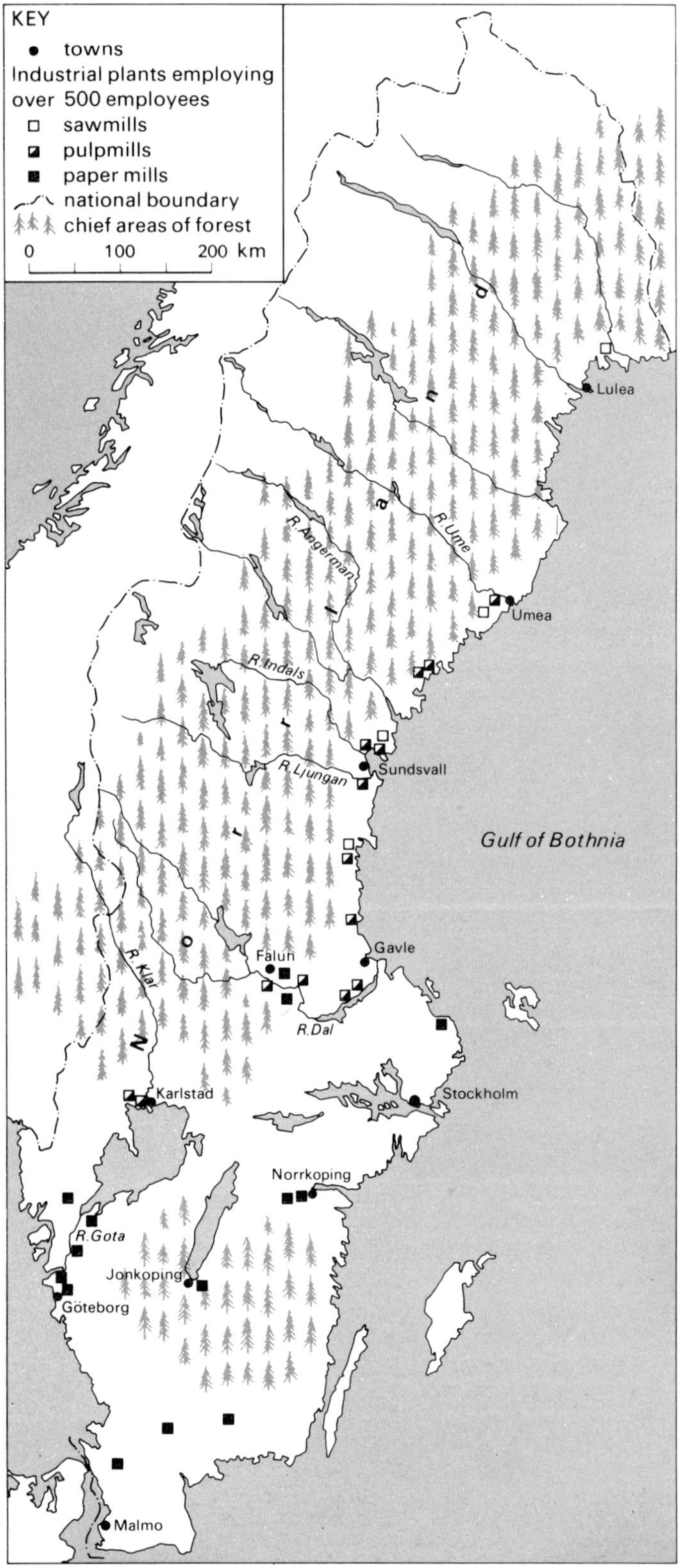

KEY

- towns

Industrial plants employing over 500 employees

- □ sawmills
- ◪ pulpmills
- ■ paper mills
- ⌒⌒ national boundary
- 🌲🌲 chief areas of forest

0   100   200 km

Lulea

R Angerman

R Ume

Umea

R Indals

R Ljungan

Sundsvall

Gulf of Bothnia

Falun

Gavle

R. Klar

R.Dal

Karlstad

Stockholm

Norrkoping

R.Gota

Jonkoping

Göteborg

Malmo

Figure 6.1 (*left*) The location of forest areas and chief timber-processing plants in Sweden

The forests cover approximately half of the country and are chiefly conifers, dominating the landscape of the area north of the river Dal. The main species, spruce and pine, occur in extensive stands and make up over 80% of the total forest reserves, and are extremely important for pulp and sawn timber respectively. The only hardwood of significance, the birch, occupies 10% of the forest area and, formerly used for fuel and charcoal production, it is now increasingly used for pulp manufacture. The larch is important in the Smaland area and supplies the wood for the match industry of Jonkoping. The forests are carefully conserved, sufficient trees being replanted each year to make good the loss from felling. The best conditions for tree growth are found in southern and central Sweden, where the annual growth rate is two or three times greater than in the north. The area under forest, particularly in central Sweden, is increasing as

Figure 6.2(a–d) The forest industries of Norrland.

(**a**) (*above*) After cutting by power saw the trees are gathered for limbing

(**b**) (*opposite, above*) The trees are mechanically stripped of their limbs and left in bunches for collection

(**c**) (*opposite, below*) The logs are either transported directly to the mills, or to river and rail terminals, such as the rail terminal at Tova, where they are stored before being carried to the mills in bulk

Figure 6.2(d) Log booms moored alongside the Tunadal sawmill after being towed from the river terminal by tug

hill farms working difficult land are sold to large forestry corporations who plant conifers. The forests are chiefly state owned in the north and privately owned in central and southern Sweden. Almost half of the privately owned forests are worked by corporations who often own saw and pulp mills; the remainder is under the ownership of individual farmers who usually lease their forest area to one of the large local organizations.

The exploitation of Sweden's forests has been chiefly along the Gulf of Bothnia coast and the major river valleys of Norrland. River valleys, such as the Ume, Angerman, Indals, Ljungan and Dal, have provided access routes into the forests, hydro-electric power for saw and pulp mills and a means of transporting the logs. Consequently, many small saw mills were established to meet local needs. The number, however, is declining as production is concentrated upon fewer, but larger, plants; between

1958 and 1974 the number of saw mills declined from over 7000 to approximately 3000, but timber production has still increased during this period. The establishment of pulp mills came as a later phase in the forest exploitation, and their location has been chiefly at such tidewater sites as Umeå, Sundsvall, Hudiksvall and Gävle, where facilities for sea transport are available. Increased world demand for paper, pulp and newsprint led to a rise of 14% in Swedish output in 1973. The integration of the saw and pulp mills at tidewater sites has also been a recent feature of an industry aiming to reduce the high wastage of saw mills.† The advantages of sites in Norrland can be summarized as follows:

---

† Up to 40% of a tree used only for board timber is wasted in the form of off-cuts and sawdust. These can be used for pulp and for plywood and blockboard at integrated plants.

70

Figure 6.3 The Ortviken pulp mill at Sundsvall. The mill is sited near the mouth of the river Indals, and receives most of its logs by river floatway. The mill specializes in the production of newsprint and has an annual capacity of 340,000 tonnes.

With reference to the photograph, answer the following questions.

(a) The mill is built on the narrow coast plain. Describe (i) the physical landscape, and (ii) the distribution of settlement in the area inland.

(b) In which direction do you think the camera was pointing when the photograph was taken?
(c) In which direction was the prevailing wind blowing?
(d) The two main chimneys of the mill are over 60 m high. Why is this?
(e) Compare Figs 11.10 and 11.11 with Fig. 6.3 and list the differences you notice in the landscape of the two areas

1 use of the rivers as floatways during the period March to October;

2 the availability of cheap hydro-electricity from such rivers as the Indals, where there are 14 large low-head dams between Lake Störsjon and the Gulf of Bothnia;

3 nearness to vast areas of coniferous forest;

4 cheap sea transport for the movement of timber in bulk from Bothnian ports. (Ice can close the ports from Gavle northwards, for up to five months of each year.)

However, climatic difficulties and the distance from Western European markets, coupled with the improved road communications and reduced electricity costs in southern Sweden, has led to an expansion in the timber processing industries outside Norrland, particularly paper making in the Göteborg and Norrköping areas. Here facilities for export are not limited by ice in winter, and the markets in West Germany, the United Kingdom and other West European countries, which take 80% of Sweden's timber products, can be served more reliably.

Until recently, the timber resources of Norrland have been extracted chiefly during the winter months by a largely part-time labour force drawn from the farming communities. As the felling and transport of timber has become more mechanized and less dependent upon seasonal transport along the river floatways, a more permanent labour force has been recruited, without the close link with farming. The increased use of mechanized transport has led to the construction of many new forest roads and a decline in the use of river and lake floatways.

	Total used length of floatways (km)	Maintenance costs & investment in forestry roads (million kroner)
1968	9831	156·3
1972	3984	211·3

As the opportunities for working on both the farm in summer and in the forests in winter have dwindled, many farmers have had to decide whether to continue farming or take up forestry permanently. The need to recruit a permanent labour force, and the difficulty of achieving this in Norrland, helps to explain the more marked growth of such finishing industries as paper, printing and furniture in southern and central Sweden.

Questions
1. The statistics of Sweden's timber exports on page 67 show that while the country contains only 0·6% of the world's forest resources, it is one of the world's major exporters of timber products. What factors explain this situation?

2. With reference to Fig. 6.1, describe the distribution of: (a) saw mills; (b) pulp mills; (c) paper mills.

7 The fishing industry

The north-east Atlantic is one of the world's major fishing areas, and Britain, France, Norway, Denmark and Spain all have well-developed fishing industries. The reasons for the importance of this activity are summarized below.

1 *The seas of the shallow continental shelf off Western Europe are rich in the tiny marine organisms called plankton, which form the chief food for fish.* The distribution of the plankton is variable, but it is most highly concentrated in a zone extending from the North Sea to Iceland. In this area the shallow seas allow the sunlight to penetrate into the waters, maintaining a suitable temperature for plankton growth. Also, the frequent winter storms set up turbulence in the shallow water to disturb the seabed sediments and release important nutrients, notably phosphates and nitrates, needed by the plankton. These essential minerals are often in short supply in deeper waters. The main period of plankton growth occurs in the warmer conditions of spring, and shoals of pelagic and demersal fish gather to make this the principal fishing season.

2 *The drowned ice-free coastline with its numerous rias, fjords and sheltering off-shore islands, has provided many excellent sites for ports.* It is a characteristic of the industry that there are a great many small ports engaged in fishing, and the move towards a few large centres having a full range of service facilities and processing plants has only recently begun. Among the large fishing ports landing over 100,000 tonnes of fish annually are Esbjerg, Bremerhaven, Hull, Ijmuiden, Boulogne and Vigo; over 500,000 tonnes were landed at Esbjerg in 1968.

3 *The inhospitable climate and mountainous terrain of north-west Europe has made farming difficult.* This has encouraged the development of a fishing industry along the whole length of Norway's 28,000 km coastline.

4 *The demand for fish from the densely populated industrial countries of Western Europe is considerable.* In 1973 the value of fish products (in $000,000) bought by the five main importing countries was as follows:

United Kingdom	Netherlands	West Germany	France	Belgium
323	58	286	339	126

5 *The modern fishing fleets carry a range of advanced equipment.* These include echo-sounders for measuring the depth of water and locating fish shoals, sonar equipment which can detect shoals up to 1 km from the vessel, and such navigational aids as radar and radio. In recent years vessels have increased in size and power; the modern stern-loading freezer trawler has a gross displacement of over 2000 tonnes, is highly mechanized and requires only a small crew. Such technical advances as these have enabled the industry to maintain its output in spite of dwindling stocks and increased costs.

A wide variety of fish are caught in the waters of the north-east Atlantic; in the North Sea, cod, herring and mackerel are the principal fish taken, and off Iceland, the Lofoten Islands and north Norway, cod and haddock are the main catch. Small vessels fish the inshore waters of the French and British coasts for shellfish, and the coasts of south-west Norway, the Channel and the Bay of Biscay for brisling, sprats and sardines.

The main methods used to catch fish on the open sea are trawling, drifting, and purse-seining.

Figure 7.1 A giant shoal of herring making good its escape when the net breaks under the weight of the fish (seine fishing)

Trawler Fishing

The trawler tows a cone-shaped net, at positions and depths regulated by floats and weights, to catch chiefly demersal fish such as cod, haddock, hake and sole, which live near the sea bed. It is the most highly organized section of the industry, fleets of trawlers often working together for a co-operative enterprise or a large processing company. The modern trawlers stay at sea for up to three weeks, and the catch is stored in a deep-frozen condition. The freezing plant is expensive to install and is increasingly being reserved for the new factory ships (up to 10,000 tonnes) which serve a fleet of smaller trawlers. In the factory ship the catch can be processed, ready for sale immediately the ship returns to port.

Drifter Fishing

Pelagic fish such as herring and mackerel which inhabit surface waters are caught by this method. The ship plays out nets which are suspended vertically through the water and held in position by weights and floats. The vessel and net then drift freely with the current into the shoals of fish. The drifter is usually under 200 tonnes in size, and is used to fish coastal waters, staying at sea for short periods of two or three days.

Seine Fishing

This method is also used to catch pelagic fish in coastal waters and has replaced the drifter in many areas. The vessel, usually of about 300 tonnes, suspends a purse-shaped net between itself and a fixed buoy or accompanying vessel. The shoal is encircled and the net drawn in, trapping the fish in the enclosing net.

When landed, the catch is processed in a variety of ways. A small proportion is sold fresh, but the majority of the catch for human consumption is processed into fish fillets, frozen and packaged for sale. Small quantities of cod are dried and salted, herrings are smoked, and sardines, pilchards and tuna, canned. The remainder of the catch is pulped and dried for use as a high-protein animal foodstuff, or used for a variety of minor products like fertilizer, glue and cod-liver oil. Thus the fishing industry directly supports a wide range of shore-based processing industries. In addition, industries indirectly related to fishing include shipbuilding and repair, rope and net manufacture and the production of packaging materials. Although fishing is relatively less important in the economy of Western Europe today, many ports, such as Hammerfest in Norway, Skagen in Denmark and Eskifjordhur in Iceland, are still dominated by this one activity.

The chief problem facing the industry at present is the conservation of the fishing stock in the north-east Atlantic. The area is being overfished and there is little effective control over its exploitation. Although yields are being maintained this is the result of increasingly efficient fishing techniques, and stocks are dwindling. Attempts to regulate fishing through international organizations stipulating closed seasons, closed areas of the sea and regulations on mesh size, have had only limited success, as not all countries fishing the area recognize these controls. The result for countries with particularly important fishing interests has been to establish national fishing limits within which they can operate an effective conservation policy.

From the early nineteenth century until recently, a 5 km limit (the range of cannon shot) was generally accepted. The pressure on fish resources and claims to submarine mineral rights has led to the establishment of wider limits, and in 1964 a 20 km limit was formalized by all West European countries. The EEC countries having limited offshore resources agreed in 1970 to open all waters within the 20 km limit to fishing fleets of member countries. However, the entry of Britain, Denmark and Ireland, with relatively rich resources, may lead to a revision. Iceland, in the meanwhile, with 30% of its working population engaged in some aspect of fishing, is attempting to extend territorial waters to a distance of 320 km from the coast.

A problem of growing concern is the dumping of toxic waste into the North Sea from the industrial centres along the coasts and major rivers of Europe. In inshore areas the natural dillution of waste is slower than in the open seas, and there have been cases of dangerous minerals, notably mercury, building up to critical levels in the tissues of fish. When one considers the additional pollution hazard of spillage from the North Sea oil and gas wells, the case for stricter control is indisputable.

The Norwegian Fishing Industry

With the rich offshore fishing grounds and a difficult mountainous interior, fishing is an important activity along the whole length of the Norwegian coastline. In the north, fishing is often the only main means of livelihood, and in the Tromso area over 50% of the employed population are engaged in fishing or fish processing. In winter and spring, cod and various other demersal fish move into the coastal waters north of Kristiansund in search of food and spawning grounds. This period is the peak of the northern fishing season and vast quantities are taken from particular favoured areas, like the waters around the Lofoten Islands. Off southern Norway in the North Sea and Skaggerak the catch is chiefly of herring and mackerel and the main fishing period extends from February to October. The herring fisheries are centred upon Bergen, Ålesund, Haugesund and Kristiansund, but as the catch has declined dramatically in the past few years due to over-fishing, fleets from these ports are beginning to fish in more distant waters.

Herring catch (in tonnes)			
1967	1969	1971	1973
1,214,837	188,699	236,500	146,200

Off south-west Norway, there is a specialization in catching brisling (sprats) and the smaller members of the herring family, sardines and pilchards, which are canned at Stavanger.

The fish processing plants are widely distributed along the Norwegian coast. The largest plants are for meal and oil, and in 1973 74% of the total catch was used in this way. An increasing proportion of the catch is being frozen and packaged as ready-for-sale fillets at

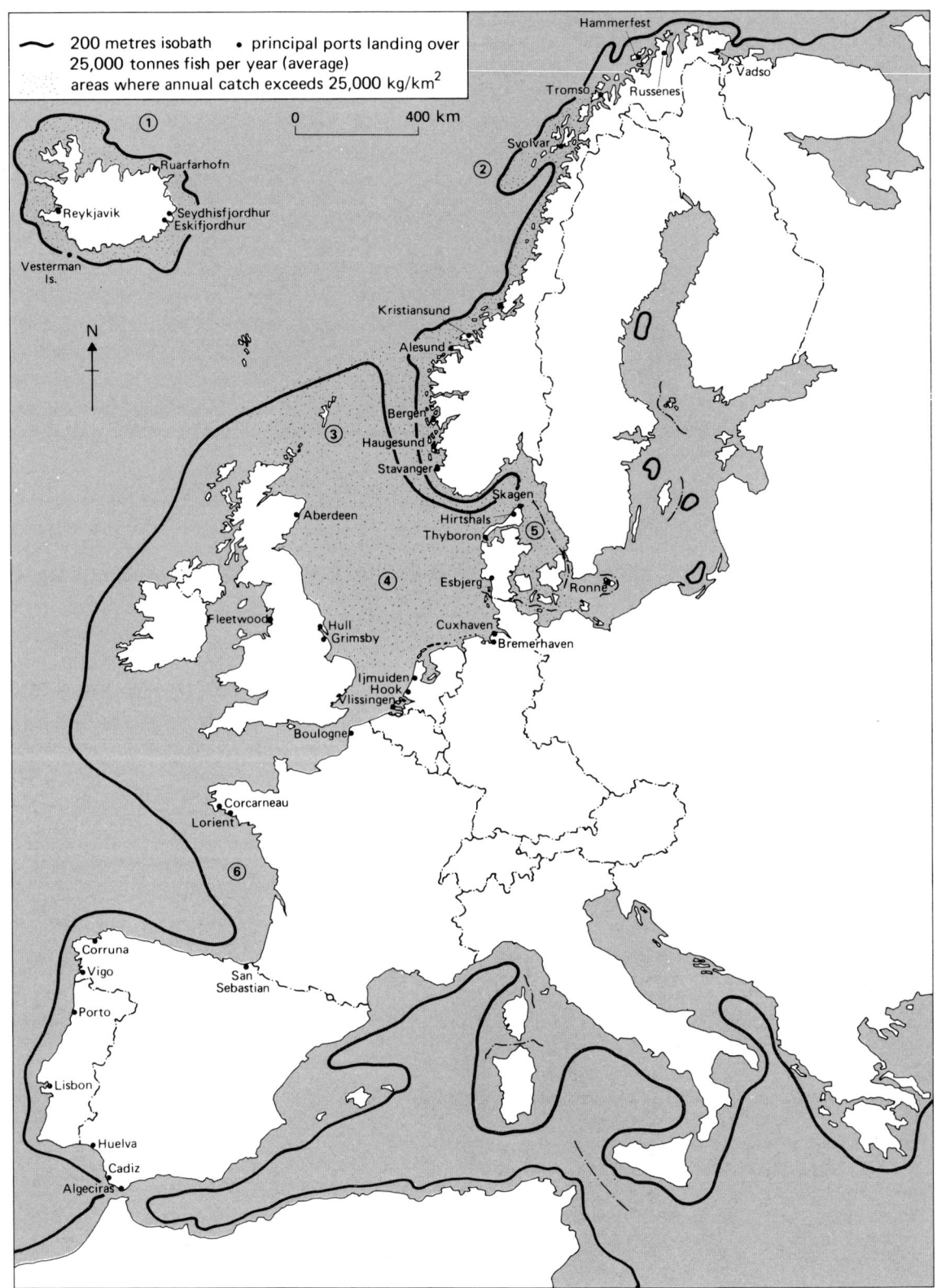

200 metres isobath • principal ports landing over
25,000 tonnes fish per year (average)
areas where annual catch exceeds 25,000 kg/km²

0   400 km

①

Hammerfest
Tromso   Russenes   Vadso
Svolvar   ②
Ruarfarhofn
Reykjavik   Seydhisfjordhur
Eskifjordhur
Vesterman
Is.

N

Kristiansund
Alesund
Bergen   ③
Haugesund
Stavanger
Skagen
Aberdeen   Hirtshals   ⑤
Thyboron
④   Esbjerg
Fleetwood   Ronne
Hull   Cuxhaven
Grimsby   Bremerhaven
Ijmuiden
Hook
Vlissingen
Boulogne

Corcarneau
Lorient
⑥

Corruna
Vigo   San
Sebastian
Porto

Lisbon

Huelva
Cadiz
Algeciras

Figure 7.2 (*opposite*) Fishing grounds and major fishing ports. The main species of fish are taken from the following areas (**1–6**):
1 Iceland—cod, herring; **2** Lofoten Islands—cod, saithe; **3** North Sea (northern)—herring, mackeral; **4** North Sea (southern)—herring; **5** Baltic Sea approaches—herring, mackerel; **6** Bay of Biscay—haddock, pilchard

large plants such as the one at Hammerfest. Traditionally, much of the cod catch has been dried and salted (klipfish) or dried (stockfish); the drying process is illustrated in Fig. 7.4. The market for dried and salted fish is chiefly in Scandinavia, but there are large exports to Italy and Brazil. In 1974, fish products comprised 10% of Norway's exports, the principal markets being the USA and UK for frozen and canned fish products and fish meal.

Like all fishing nations, Norway is very concerned with the depletion of stocks in the north-east Atlantic. The decline in the herring catch has led to the Norwegian fleets equipping themselves with more stern trawlers and factory trawlers suitable for deep water fishing, rather than small vessels for the seasonal inshore fisheries. The decline of the whaling industry, in which the Norwegians were pioneers, also reflects the severe depletion of resources in the North Atlantic and Antarctic Oceans.

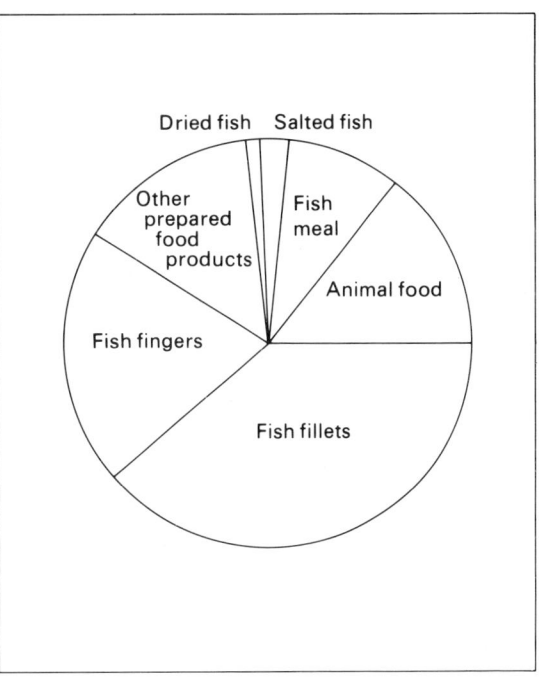

Figure 7.3(a) (*above*) Categories of fish products produced by Nestlé-Findus factory, Hammerfest. Total output: 21,750 tonnes (1974)

Figure 7.3(b) (*below*) Nestlé-Findus fish processing plant, Hammerfest

Figure 7.4 Cod drying on racks at Henningsvoer, near Svolvar, in the Lofoten Islands

Questions

1. Study the following table of the fish catch of the five leading West European fishing nations, and answer the questions below.

	1961	1963	1965	1967	1969	1971	1973
Norway	1523	1387	2307	3268	2481	3074	2974
Spain	988	1125	1341	1435	1486	1505	1570
Denmark	637	847	840	1070	1275	1400	1464
UK	892	960	1047	1026	1083	1107	1144
France	750	742	767	820	746	741	797

(Figures in ,000 tonnes)

(*a*) Draw a graph of the above figures and comment on the general trend shown in the annual fish catches.

(*b*) Suggest reasons for the variation in the tonnage landed by the Norwegian fleet.

(*c*) List *five* ways in which the European fish catch is utilized.

2. (*a*) What are the main reasons favouring the concentration of the fishing fleets at a few large ports?

(*b*) Name *five* leading West European fishing ports.

3. Write a reasoned account of the factors which have led to the development of the Norwegian fishing industry.

4. The following statistics refer to the Norwegian fishing industry. Suggest reasons to explain why the value of the catch has increased while the proportion of total exports has declined.

	1970	1974
Exports of fish products (in million kroner)	1776	2930
Fish products as a proportion of total exports	13%	10%

8 Energy resources

Before the recession of 1974/5, demand for energy in Western Europe was increasing at an annual rate of approximately 6%. Although this trend was reversed and energy consumption fell by 2·3% between 1973–4, an enormous annual demand of 1250 million tonnes of oil equivalent has to be met from oil, natural gas, solid fuel, water power and nuclear sources. The importance of these types of energy source varies from country to country, as the statistics for 1974 (*below*) illustrate.

The relative importance of the different types of energy has altered considerably since the 1950's. The growth in demand outstripped production from home-produced energy sources, notably coal and lignite, and to meet the deficit all Western European countries began to import large quantities of crude oil, chiefly from Middle Eastern countries. The imported oil was cheaper than the home-produced coal, which was being extracted from coalfields where geological conditions were becoming progressively more difficult after a hundred years of continuous mining. By 1960, imported oil occupied a dominant position in the energy market, and some countries, notably the UK, turned to nuclear power as a new home-based energy source which offered a long-term alternative to their dependence on imported oil. However, the development of the large natural gasfield at Slochteren in the Netherlands, with further discoveries offshore in the North Sea, has enabled Western Europe to become a little less dependent on imported energy supplies. The following statistics show how the energy market has been shared since 1950.

	Coal & lignite	Crude petroleum	Natural gas	Water power	Nuclear power
1950	87%	12%	—	1%	—
1958	71%	25%	1%	3%	—
1961	58%	36%	3%	3%	—
1969	37%	53%	6%	4%	—
1971	29%	60%	7%	4%	—
1974	21%	57%	12%	8%	2%

In addition to natural gas from the North Sea, Libya, Algeria and the USSR are supplying liquified gas in increasing quantities and there are plans to link the North African gasfields by pipeline with Italy. The most dramatic recent development has been the

Consumption of energy (in million tonnes of oil equivalent)						
Country	Coal & lignite	Crude petroleum	Natural gas	Water power	Nuclear power	Total
West Germany	82·9	134·4	32·1	5·0	2·7	257·1
United Kingdom	68·9	105·8	30·8	1·3	7·3	214·1
France	27·0	120·1	17·0	12·6	3·0	179·7
Italy	9·2	100·7	15·9	11·0	0·9	137·7
Scandinavia	7·3	51·1	—	36·7	0·4	95·5
Netherlands	3·3	35·4	32·9	—	0·8	72·4
Spain	12·3	38·2	1·0	8·2	1·9	61·6
Belgium and Luxemburg	11·6	27·5	10·0	0·1	—	49·2
Other Western Europe countries	39·4	86·0	6·4	25·4	1·5	158·7
Total	261·9	699·2	146·1	100·3	18·5	1226·0

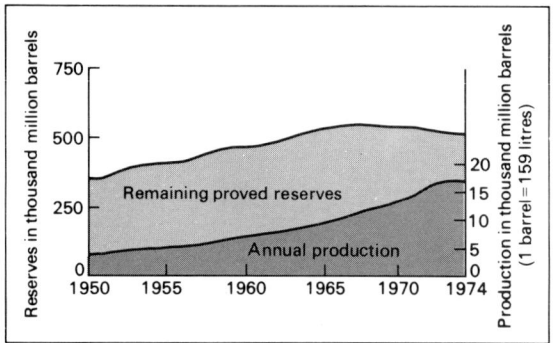

Figure 8.1 A comparison of proved oil reserves and production in the world (USSR, Eastern Europe and China)

discovery of oil in the North Sea, which was first brought ashore in 1972 by tanker from the Ekofisk field. It seems likely that in the future Western Europe will gradually reduce its dependence on imported fuels and rely increasingly upon home-based resources of coal, natural gas and oil.

In spite of solid fuels losing so much of the energy market to oil and natural gas, the large increase in world oil prices in 1973/4 has brought about a modest revival. The relationship between world oil reserves and production is shown in Fig. 8.1. It is probable that the long-term trend of production outstripping discovery will continue and that large quantities of fuel other than oil will be needed to produce energy. In these conditions, scarce, and therefore costly, oil will find coal a keen competitor, and the coal mining industry which suffered a large cut in production in the 1960's and early 1970's may revive.

Crude Oil

Although oil has been known to exist in 'traps' in the sedimentary rocks of the North German Plain since its discovery at Pechelbronn in 1870, yields have never been sufficient to meet European requirements. Small oil deposits are still worked in the Hamburg and Hanover areas, but the first substantial developments were after 1950 in the area between the Ems and Weser valleys in north Germany and at Schoonebeek and Ijsselmonde in the Netherlands. These workings supply 7% of West Germany's requirement for crude oil and 4% of Dutch needs. Clearly, as these producing sites are the major

ones in Western Europe, almost complete dependence has had to be placed upon imports from outside Europe.

The growth of oil refining away from the Middle Eastern oilfields has occurred chiefly since 1950, when the demand for fuel oil rapidly increased as it began to replace coal as the main industrial and domestic fuel. A further factor which encouraged the oil refining industry to develop near its markets rather than at the producing oilfield was the political instability of the Middle Eastern area. Incidents like the nationalization of the oil companies' assets in Iraq in 1951, the closure of the Suez Canal in 1956 and frequent damage to pipelines all influenced the massive recent growth of oil refining in Western Europe.

Following the discovery of natural gas at Slochteren in 1959 a succession of gas and oil finds have been made, particularly offshore in the North Sea. Estimates of the reserves of oil in the area vary considerably, but it is anticipated that by 1980 the North Sea fields will be providing at least 150 million tonnes of oil per year, which is approximately 10% of Western Europe's expected energy requirement. The North Sea waters are mainly shared by the UK and Norway and it is these two countries which are likely to benefit most from the discoveries. The principal oilfields being developed in the North Sea basin are Ekofisk, Frigg and Statfjord in Norwegian waters, and Forties and Brent-Ninian in British waters. For Western Europe as a whole, great dependence will still be placed upon imported oil, particularly on the 'heavier' crude oils from the Middle East, which are needed to give the correct balance at the refineries.

Exploitation of the North Sea resources posed a number of problems not met before on land-based or the shallow-water drillings of the Persian Gulf and Gulf of Mexico.

1 This was the first major open sea operation undertaken by the oil companies, and large new rigs with a displacement of over 10,000 tonnes and costing several million pounds were needed. In the summer of 1972, 24 rigs and drillships were at work and by 1974 this number had increased to 50. The North Sea required new types of drilling rig,

Figure 8.2 (*opposite*) Oilfields and principal crude oil pipelines of Western Europe

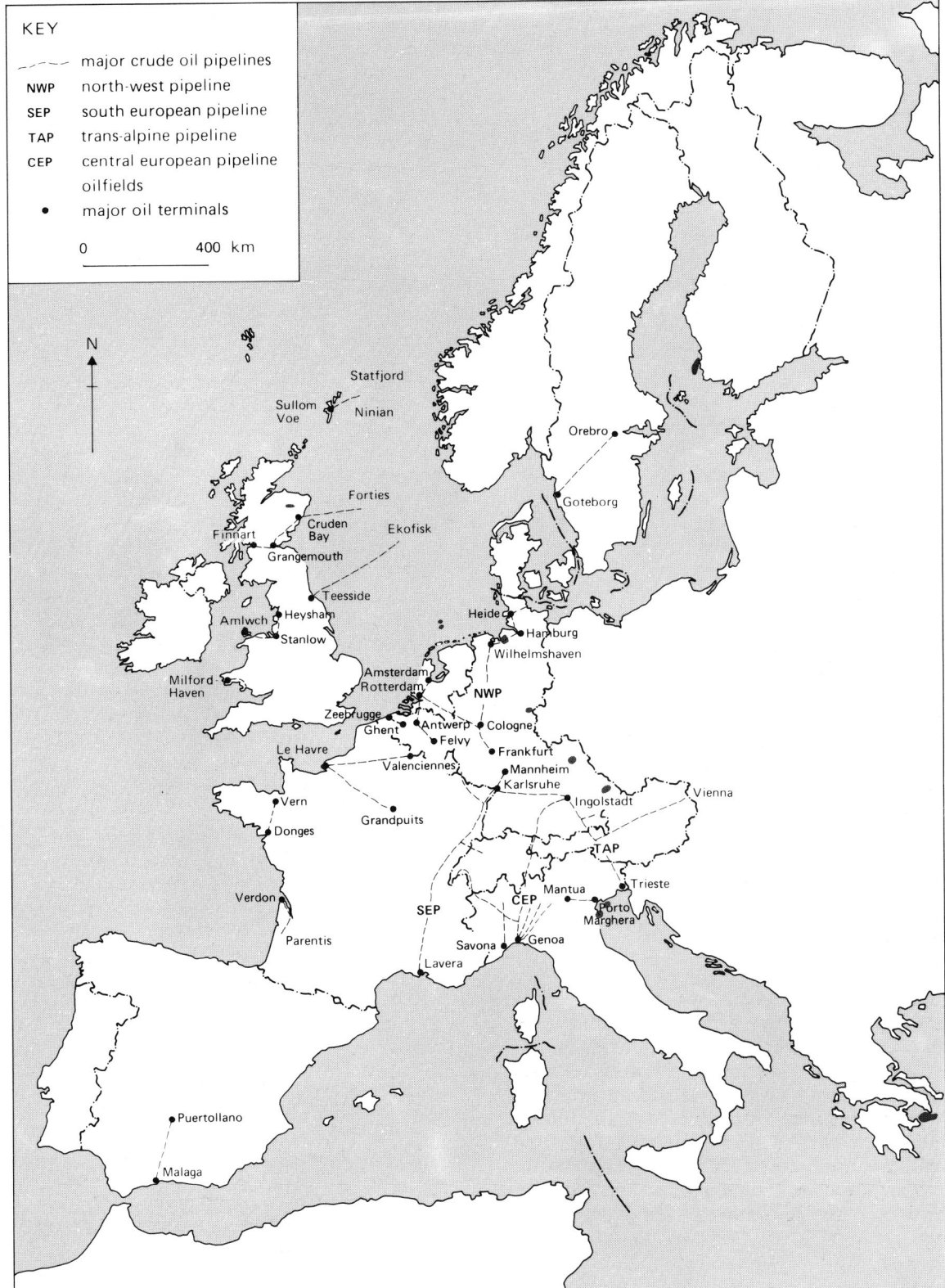

KEY

_ · _ · _	major crude oil pipelines
NWP	north-west pipeline
SEP	south european pipeline
TAP	trans-alpine pipeline
CEP	central european pipeline
	oilfields
●	major oil terminals

0   400 km

N

Statfjord

Sullom
Voe   Ninian

Forties

Cruden
Bay   Ekofisk

Finnart

Grangemouth

Teesside

Amlwch   Heysham
          Stanlow

Heide

Hamburg

Wilhelmshaven

Milford
Haven

Amsterdam
Rotterdam   NWP

Zeebrugge   Cologne
     Ghent   Antwerp
          Felvy   Frankfurt

Le Havre
          Valenciennes   Mannheim
                          Karlsruhe

Vern   Ingolstadt   Vienna

Donges   Grandpuits

                              TAP

Verdon   Mantua   Trieste

          SEP   CEP
               Savona   Porto
                        Marghera
Parentis   Genoa
          Lavera

Orebro

Goteborg

Puertollano

Malaga

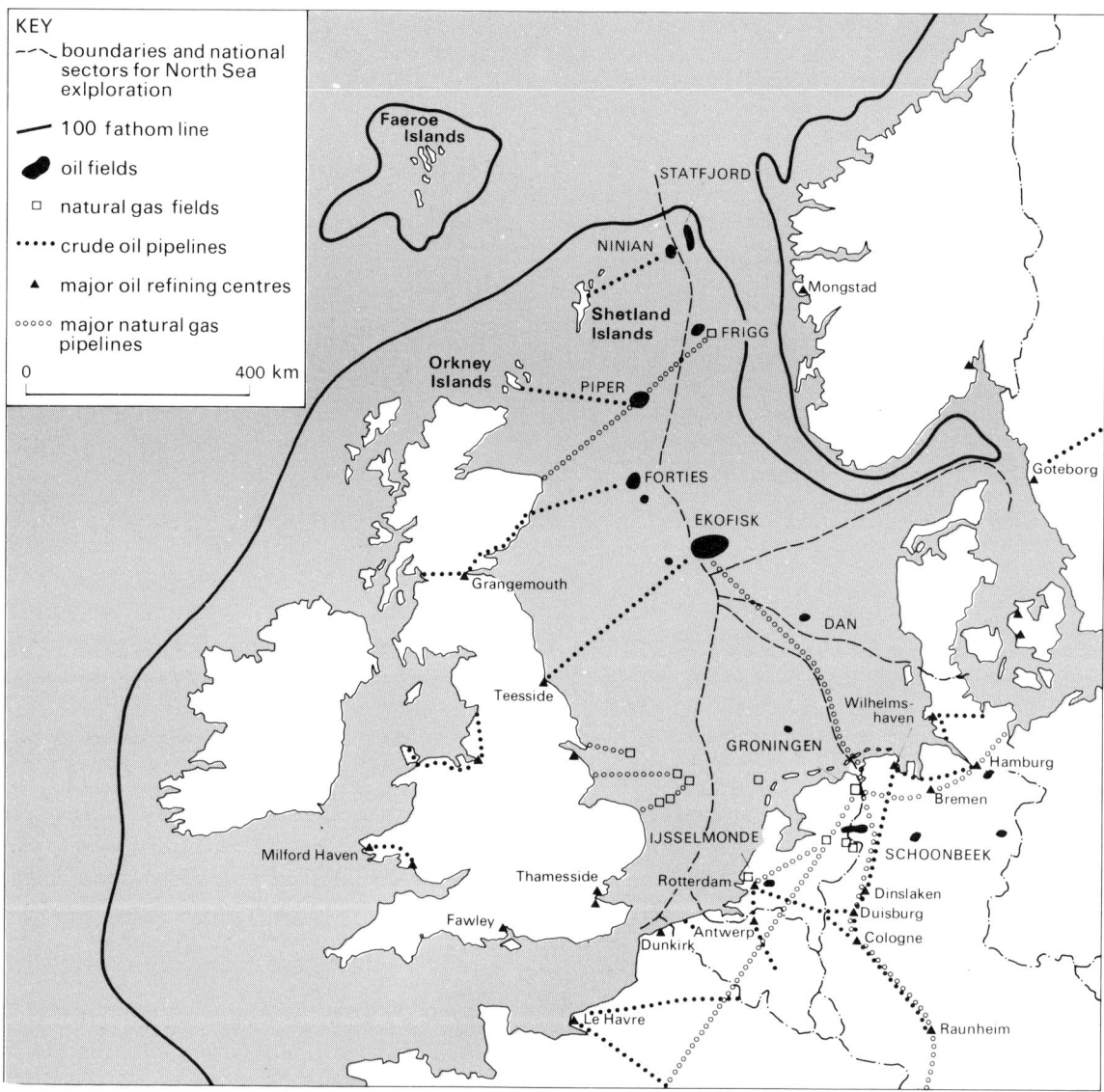

Figure 8.3 Oil and natural gas development in north-west Europe

and delays occurred waiting for these to be built or brought from other parts of the world. In addition to the drilling equipment, permanent production platforms, storage tanks and pipelines have had to be constructed and laid in position. The West European shipbuilding industry has received the stimulus of new orders for this equipment; yards at Teesside, Stavanger and Hamburg specializing in the construction and servicing of oil rigs.

2 The difficult weather conditions in the North Sea can be measured by the fact that no weather forecast for the area can be expected to hold good for more than 10 hours. High waves up to 20 m and strong winds constitute supply problems for ship and helicopter alike, and delays of a fortnight or more have been experienced. Fog, reducing visibility to less than one kilometre, occurs between twenty-five and thirty days each year, while winter ice has meant the installation of costly de-icing equipment. Weather conditions constitute a greater problem for the permanently fixed production rig than for the more mobile exploration rig.

Figure 8.4(a) The semi-submersible drilling platform can be moved from site to site, and is used down to a depth of 300 m

Figure 8.4(c) The floating drill ship has four propellers thrusting forward, rear and sideways, enabling it to hold accurate station over a drilling site

Figure 8.4(b) The fixed platform is mounted on concrete poles driven into the sea bed and is used down to a depth of 30 m deep

3 Although a shallow continental shelf, the bed of the North Sea contains some irregularities which make pipeline laying difficult. The most notable example is the 100-km wide, 300-m deep submarine trench off the south-west coast of Norway. It has been an important factor in deciding not to pipe Ekofisk oil to a refinery at Stavanger, and would similarly prevent oil from the Frigg and Statfjord fields being piped to the Mongstad refinery, north of Bergen, unless future technological advances make this possible. At present, the oil is stored in a vast tank and taken off by tanker from single buoy moorings. However, with gales and high seas being such a regular feature in winter, this is not a permanent solution, and an oil pipeline has been laid to a terminal at Teesside, and a gas pipeline to Emden.

Oil Refining at Rotterdam–Europoort

The refining of imported crude oil in Western Europe is concentrated at a number of major coastal sites, notably Rotterdam, Antwerp, Le Havre, Hamburg, Lavéra, Bordeaux and Genoa, and at inland sites along the major pipelines, of which the most important are Duisburg, Cologne-Wesseling, Frankfurt, Karlsruhe and Ingolstadt in West Germany, and Feyzin and Strasbourg in France. The consumption of crude oil in West Germany accounts for approximately 20% of the total used in Western Europe, and this explains the high concentration of refining in that country and at Rotterdam, which mainly serves the German market.

The reasons which explain the choice of Rotterdam as the premier European oil port are as follows.

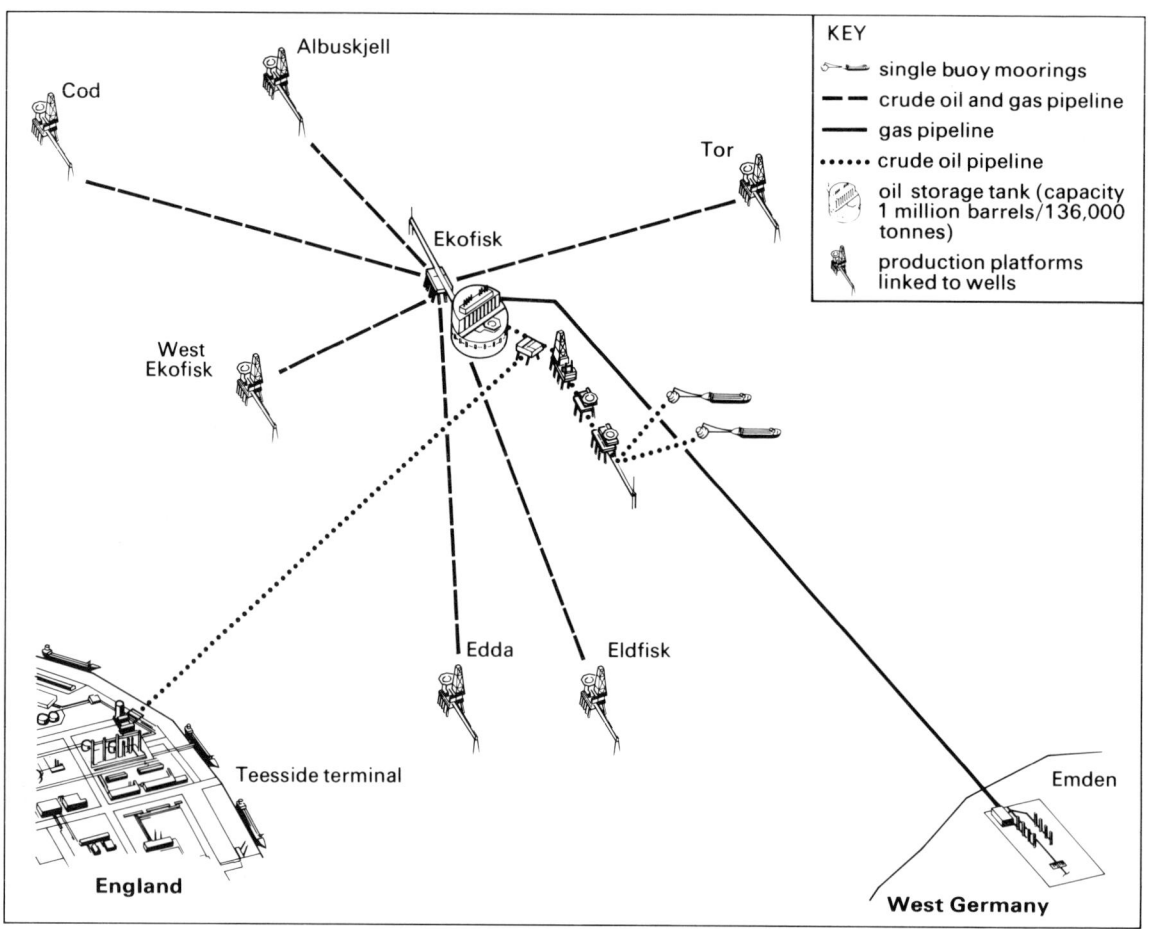

KEY

⟋⟍ single buoy moorings

— — crude oil and gas pipeline

——— gas pipeline

······· crude oil pipeline

🛢 oil storage tank (capacity 1 million barrels/136,000 tonnes)

⚒ production platforms linked to wells

Cod

Albuskjell

Tor

Ekofisk

West Ekofisk

Edda

Eldfisk

Teesside terminal

England

Emden

West Germany

Figure 8.5 The development of the Ekofisk and associated oil- and gasfields 1971–7. The producing area covers 70 km². Oil and gas are drawn from 3250 m below the seabed in waters 70 m deep

1 The proximity of Rotterdam to the densely populated areas of West Germany, linked by the natural waterway of the river Rhine. Barge transport for both crude oil and oil products has now largely been replaced by pipelines, but until 1960 it was the superior water communications of Rotterdam that gave it an advantage as an oil terminal over the less accessible north German ports of Hamburg and Bremen.

2 The New Waterway channel, completed in 1872 and enlarged since, provided a straight, deep route across the delta from Rotterdam to the Hook of Holland. The canal has a minimum depth of 12 m, enabling 100,000-tonne tankers to reach the docks at Pernis and Botlek, while the channel serving the Europoort dock has a minimum depth of 13·6 m, and can handle tankers up to 250,000 tonnes. The waters around the reclaimed site of Maasvlakte have a depth of 27 m and can handle vessels up to 370,000 tonnes. The deepening of the channel has been necessary for the port to keep abreast of the increasing size of vessels. Maasvlakte has been developed as a specialist oil and mineral ore storage area. A system of pipelines carries the crude oil to refineries between Maasvlakte and Rotterdam and to the Rhine valley and Antwerp. The closure of the Suez Canal, the depth of which had limited the size of tankers on the Middle East/Western Europe service to 96,000 tonnes, brought in the era of the super-tanker. By using very large tankers the oil companies have been able to make economies in cost

Figure 8.6(a) (*above*) A reinforced concrete oil-storage tank under construction at Stavanger. It has been sunk into the seabed at Ekofisk in 70 m of water. Storage capacity: 1 million barrels of oil (136,000 tonnes)

Figure 8.6(b) (*below*) A single-buoy mooring

Figure 8.6(c) (*right*) A pipe-laying barge working on the gas pipeline from Ekofisk to Emden

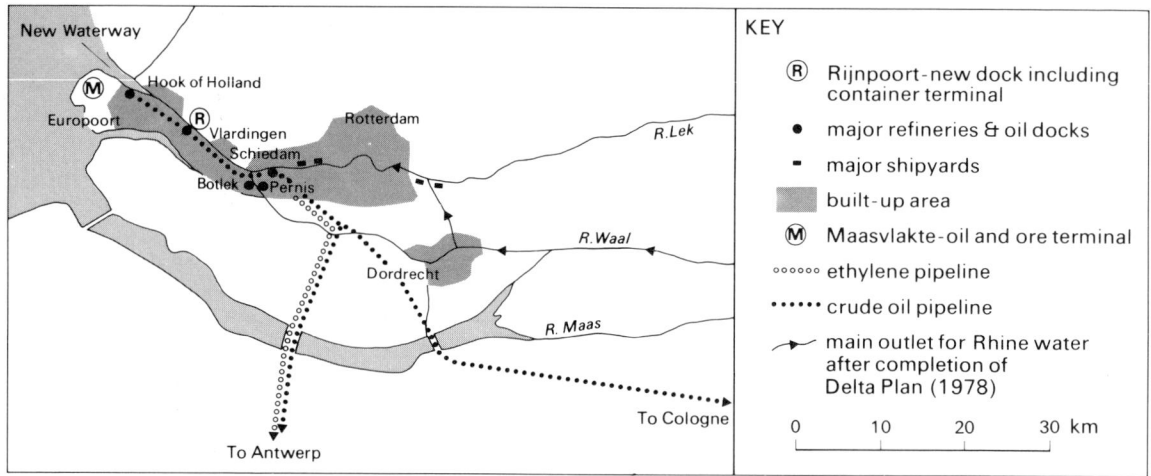

Figure 8.7 The Rotterdam–Europoort area

Figure 8.8 The oil refinery, storage tanks and tanker berths at the BP terminal, Europoort

which offset the expense of using the longer route to Europe around the Cape of Good Hope. The new oil terminals being built at Suez and Alexandria for 250,000-tonne tankers and the 320 km connecting pipeline across the isthmus are likely to bring back some of the Middle East/Western Europe crude-oil traffic to the Mediterranean in the 1980's.

Although tankers of up to 500,000 tonnes have been proposed, it is unlikely that they will enter West European coastal waters, and the difficulty of manoeuvering these giants in the English Channel would exclude them from Europoort.

3 The Dutch government has promoted the development of Europoort, through the inducement of development grants to the oil companies, and by financing dredging and land reclamation schemes. It has been public policy to encourage the oil refining industry in Rotterdam, particularly as one of the beneficiaries has been the 60% Dutch-owned Shell Company.

Rotterdam has grown from a small fishing port sited in the sheltered tidal creek of the river Rotte to become a major world port, handling 294 million tonnes of goods in 1973, 65% of which was crude oil and oil products. The major refineries are on the southern side of the New Waterway at Pernis, Botlek and Europoort. In addition to refining crude oil into a variety of petro-chemical products* which are distributed by barge and pipeline, increasing quantities of crude oil are received in Rotterdam for dispatch by pipeline to the refining centres of the Rhine valley and Antwerp. The role of the port as an oil terminal is at present developing more rapidly than oil refining. The slowing down in the growth of oil refining reflects the concern of the Dutch

---

* Fuels: petrol, diesel, fuel oil, paraffin. Chemical products: fertilizers, insecticides, detergents, plastics.

86

people with the pollution of their environment. Within the Rotterdam region vast areas of land have been disfigured by oil storage tanks and refining plant; water pollution has killed virtually all organic life in the Rhine, and atmospheric pollution, particularly by sulphur dioxide, is such that public warning systems have been installed in the residential areas. The strength of public feeling against pollution has caused the construction of an integrated steel plant on the newly drained site at Maasvlakte to be postponed.

In addition to oil, Rotterdam imports other bulk goods, notably iron ore, grain, coke and foodstuffs, the majority of it being transferred between West Germany and her trading partners. Large quantities of manufactured goods are exported and imported, increasingly in containers through the Rijnpoort terminal. Industries include the processing of imported raw materials, notably vegetable oils, from West Africa and the East Indies at Vlaardingen for margarine, soap and cooking fats; shipbuilding at Schiedam; engineering, metal working, organic chemicals and food processing at Rotterdam.

Natural Gas

The statistics in the table below show the important role of natural gas as an energy source. Its use on a wide scale in Europe followed the Dutch discoveries at Slochteren in the province of Groningen in 1959, and the technological advance which made it possible to liquify† the gas for sea transport by tanker from the distant North African fields. Before, the gas was usually burnt off at the well head of oil drillings; for only in the USA were large deposits conveniently situated near markets to

† Liquification: reduction of volume of methane gas to $\frac{1}{600}$th (natural gas).

justify a pipeline grid being built. In Europe limited networks were laid down to serve the industrial cities of northern Italy and south-west France from gasfields at Ravenna and Lacq respectively.

The advantages of natural gas are its cleanliness, ease of transportation, value as a fuel and chemical feedstock, and its relative cheapness when compared with rival fuels. Unlike the North American natural gas deposits, those from the Netherlands lack the higher hydro-carbons (ethane, propane and butane) needed for the production of chemicals. The gas is used primarily as an industrial and domestic fuel and for thermal electricity generation. The known reserves in Western Europe are chiefly associated with the sedimentary structures of the North European Plain and the offshore waters of the continental shelf; they are believed to be sufficient to last for at least 24 years from 1975, with an annual consumption rate estimated at 165,000 million cubic metres.

The pattern of consumption is based upon the Netherlands gasfields, and a grid network is in the process of being completed, which will export approximately half of the Dutch output to Belgium, France, West Germany, Switzerland and Italy. In contrast, the output of the other West European areas is expected to be almost wholly used within the producing countries. An increasing amount of gas to supplement production is expected to be drawn from the USSR by pipeline and from North Africa in liquified natural gas carriers. The USSR natural gas fields in the Caucasus, Ukraine and southern Urals are connected by a grid of gas pipelines to Eastern Europe and link with Austria near Vienna, connecting with the West German system in Bavaria. The principal North African gasfields are at Hassi R'Mel in Algeria and near Dahra in Libya.

Major natural gas consuming countries 1973				
Country	Production (in T. cal)	Import (in T. cal)	Sources of import	% of total energy consumed
Netherlands	597,500	—	—	31
Austria	21,900	15,000	USSR	15
Belgium	450	81,500	Netherlands	10
UK	272,500	7,400	North Africa	10
Italy	140,200	18,300	North Africa	9
West Germany	154,270	117,500	Netherlands	8
France	70,200	84,900	Netherlands, N. Africa	7

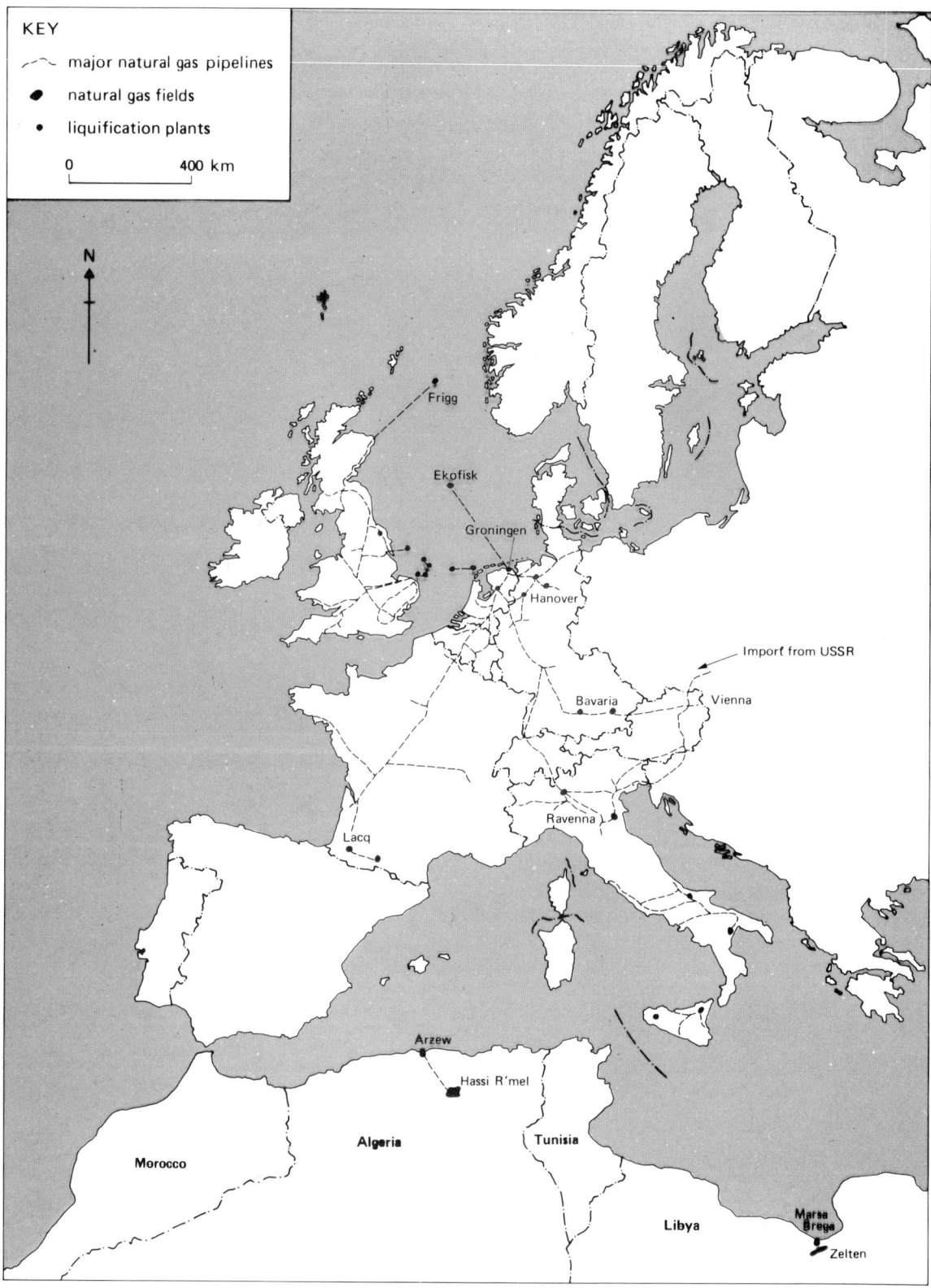

KEY

--- major natural gas pipelines

● natural gas fields

• liquification plants

0   400 km

N

Frigg

Ekofisk

Groningen

Hanover

Import from USSR

Bavaria   Vienna

Ravenna

Lacq

Arzew

Hassi R'mel

Morocco   Algeria   Tunisia

Libya

Marsa Brega

Zelten

Figure 8.9 (*opposite*) The major natural gasfields and pipelines

Figure 8.10 (*right*) Diagrammatic section showing the types of structure which may contain natural gas

From the Algerian fields pipelines run to liquification plants at Arzew and Skikda, from where the gas is shipped in specialist carriers to Le Havre and Fos in France, Barcelona in Spain, and Canvey Island in the United Kingdom, while Libyan gas is shipped chiefly to Spain and southern Italy. Plans are advanced for pipelines to be laid across the Straits of Gibraltar to Spain and across the Sicilian Channel and Straits of Messina to Italy.

Coal and Lignite

In spite of having reserves of over 400,000 million tonnes, the coal mining industry of Western Europe is in decline. Until the 1950's coal supplied 80% of the energy market, but its share fell to approximately 30% in 1970 with a recovery to 37% in 1974 as a result of the increase in world oil prices and a fall in total energy demand. The cause of this decline is

Figure 8.11 (*below*) Natural gas wells at Slochteren. The exploitation of this resource has done little damage to the rural landscape

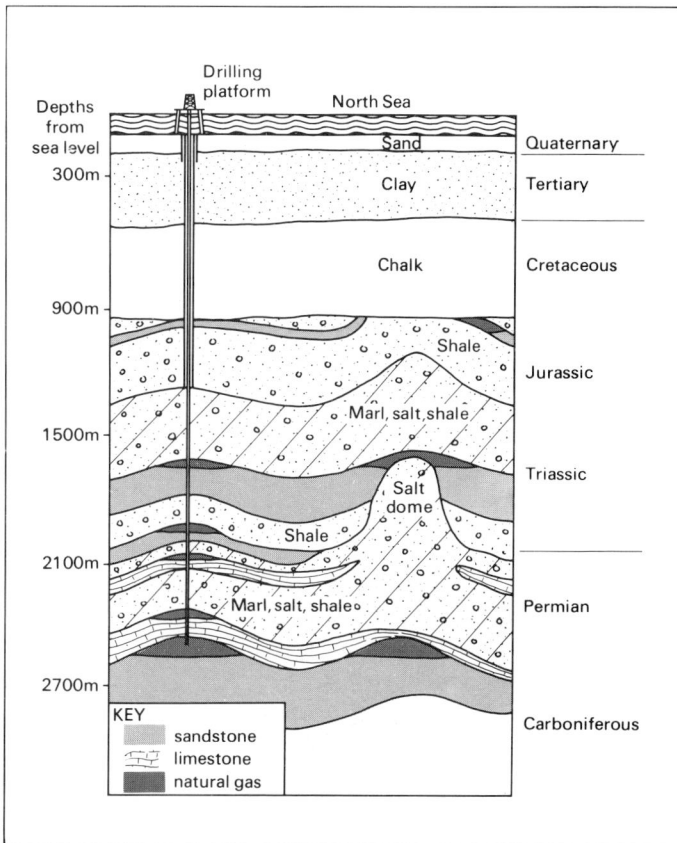

89

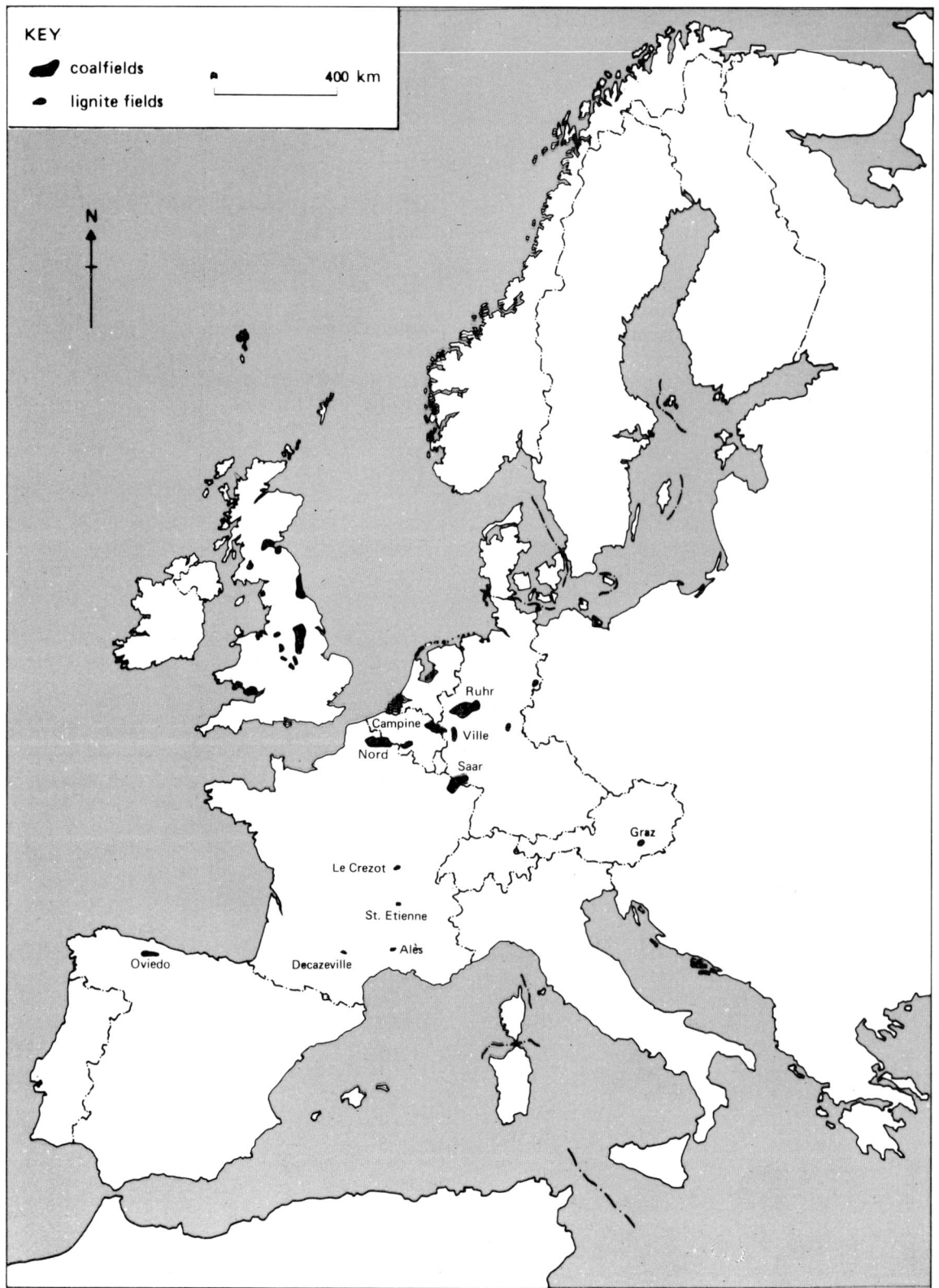

Ruhr

Campine

Ville

Nord

Saar

Graz

Le Crezot

St. Etienne

Alès

Oviedo

Decazeville

KEY

coalfields

lignite fields

400 km

N

Figure 8.12 (*opposite*) Coalfields and lignite fields

high production costs resulting from costly deep-mining conditions and the large labour force employed by the industry. Oil and natural gas have benefitted from these difficulties to capture the major share of the European energy market.

The position of coal can now be assessed fairly clearly. West Germany and the United Kingdom are the only major coal mining countries in Western Europe, production from the French, Belgian and Dutch mines having been greatly reduced. The demand for coal as a domestic and industrial fuel will remain small, and its utilization for electricity generation will be gradually reduced, while the requirement for metallurgical coke in steel making is expected to show a modest increase. However, in view of the heavy demand for energy, it is probable that the decline in coal mining will be arrested, proving that some mine closures were premature—as the 30 million tonnes of coal imported into the West European countries in 1970 suggests. In the USA, oil companies are buying coal mines and are spending considerable sums on research into coal liquification, which will make the fuel more convenient to transport and to use as a chemical feedstock.

The low grade bituminous fuel, lignite, has never been heavily exploited in Europe as better quality coal has been available. Mining occurs where the lignite is near the surface and can be excavated with large machines employing little manpower. It is uneconomic to transport over a distance, and is mainly used near the workings to fuel thermal electric power stations.

The main coal basins lie along the southern edge of the North European Plain. In the Ruhr, Sambre-Meuse valley and in the Nord region of France the coal has supplied fuel and power for a wide range of metal and chemical industries. In Chapter 9, one of these areas, the Rhine-Ruhr region, is studied in detail.

Hydro-Electricity

The potential capacity of hydro-electric power in Western Europe is 164 million kWh, of which approximately 40% has been developed to supply 8% of the energy requirement. It is the major form of energy in the Scandinavian peninsula and in south-central Europe where adequate alternative energy sources are lacking. In order to develop electrical energy from running water, a good head of water is necessary. In *high-head* developments, pipes carry a mountain stream of water to the turbines of the power station below. In lower valley areas a *low-head* development is built with a dam to raise the level of water in the reservoir and give a suitable gradient onto the turbines, which are often built within the dam wall. In the low-head power station the impounded reservoir provides a reliable and consistent supply of water and a far larger volume than the high-head plant.

Most of the developed hydro-electric power sites are in mountainous areas where high-head sites are in abundance and where the flooding necessary to support a low-head power station is least likely to cause opposition. As electricity cannot be successfully transmitted over 500 km without a loss in voltage the utilization of many hydro-electricity developments is limited to the immediate environment of the plant. The recent development of major low-head sites has been in conjunction with irrigation, flood protection and navigation schemes; in Europe this is well illustrated on the river Rhône. Electricity generated by running water is relatively cheap at the power station, and industries consuming large quantities of electricity have been attracted to these sites, in spite of their remoteness.

The factors which influence the choice of a site for hydro-electric power development can be summarized as follows.

1 *Precipitation.* A reliable and evenly distributed precipitation is ideal. If severe winters reduce surface run-off, pump storage‡ at off-peak periods may be needed to maintain the water supply.

2 *Relief.* A head of water is provided either from the fall of water off a steep hillside or from a high level reservoir impounded by a dam. Steep slopes or wide, steep-sided valley sites for dam construction are necessary. In the case of high-head developments natural storage lakes, often eroded by glaciers, can be

‡ As winter water shortage coincides with peak seasonal demand, in some plants electricity is used at night to pump water from a reservoir alongside the power station up to the one supplying it from above.

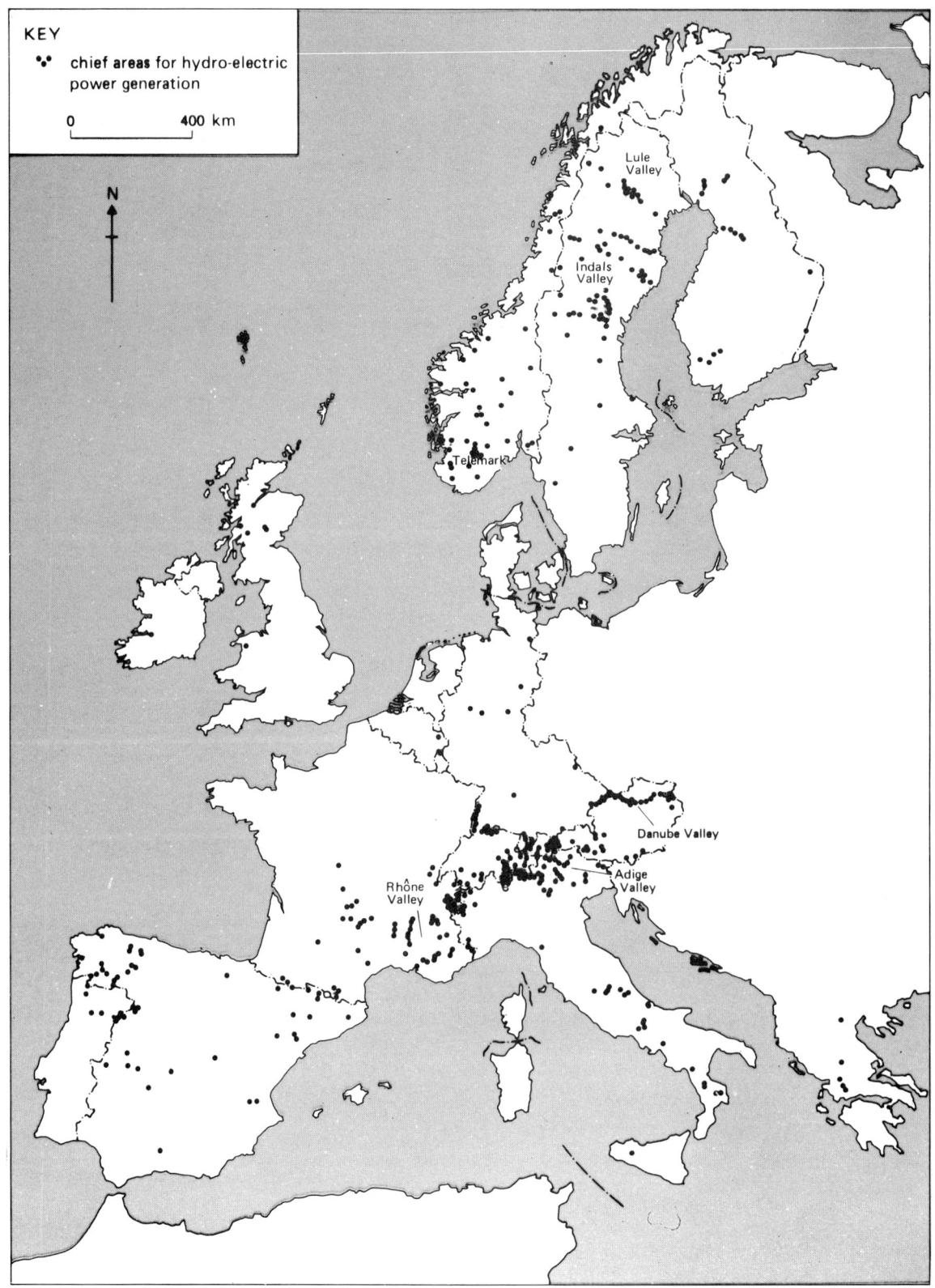

Figure 8.13 (*opposite*) The chief sites of hydro-electric power generation

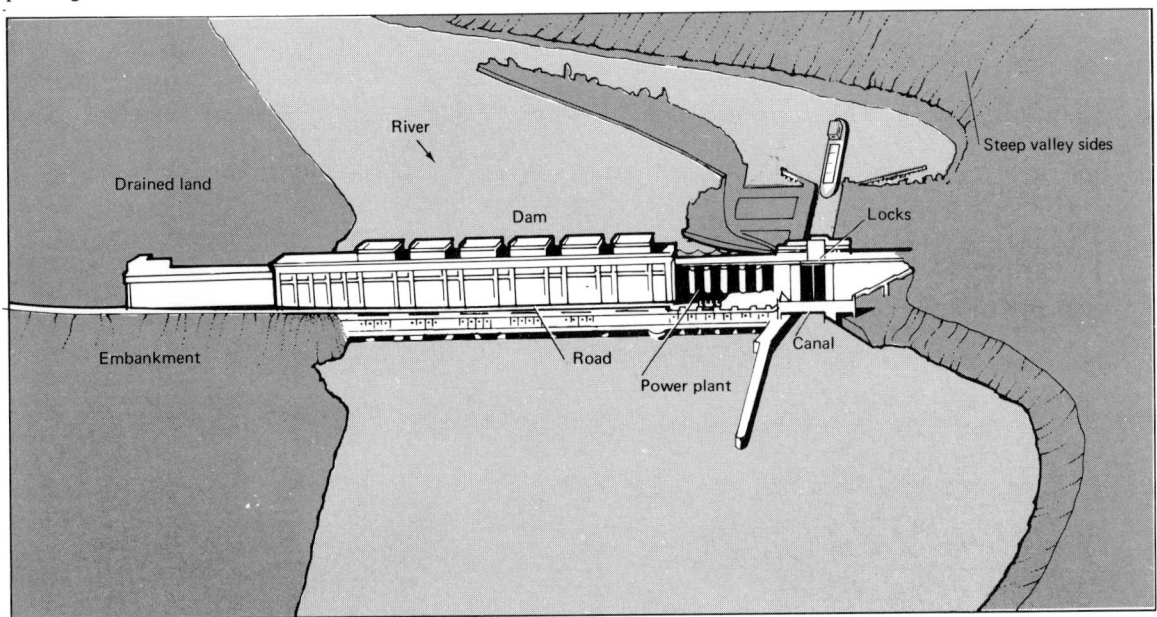

Figure 8.14(a) Low-head power site, e.g., river Rhône, south-east France

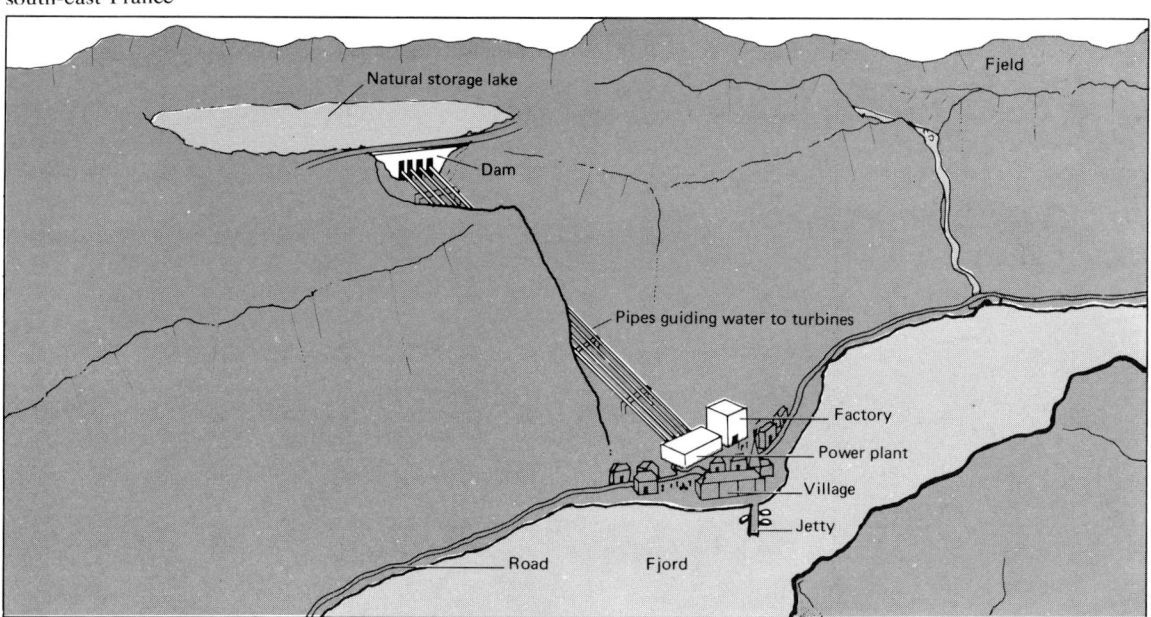

Figure 8.14(b) High-head power site, e.g., south-west Norway

utilized. A flat, accessible site for the power plant and possible factories and houses is important.

   3 *Demand*. Ideally, a local demand is required in order to reduce high transmission costs from thinly populated mountain regions to distant industrial areas.

   To illustrate the uses of hydro-electricity, the following studies in Norway and south-east France contrast the utilization of

93

Figure 8.15 A high-head h.e.p. plant at Bolzano, northern Italy

relatively small high-head resources with the all-round development of a major river.

Hydro-Electric Power Development in Norway

Of all West European countries, Norway relies most upon hydro-electricity for its major source of electrical energy; in 1974, 99% of its electricity was generated by this means. Development in the post-war period increased electricity output sixfold between 1946—1974. This can be explained in terms of the excellent natural conditions which exist, and the absence of any major alternative home-produced fuel. The heavily glaciated highland landscape offers natural storage lakes and steep valley and fjord sides, while all-year-round access from the sea helps to counter the difficulty of transport inland. The mild, damp climate of Norway ensures a reliable precipitation, but a large water storage capacity in lakes and reservoirs is usually needed to meet the peak winter demand, a time when surface run-off from the snow covered surfaces of the fjeld is at a minimum.

The deep fjords of south-west Norway have numerous developed power sites supporting local metallurgical and chemical industries, but these are not often connected into the national grid network. Examples of important industrial centres which have developed in this area using hydro-electricity are the aluminium smelters at Hoyanger and Ardal in the Sogne Fjord and at Husnes and Tyssedal in the Hardanger Fjord. Special steels are made at Alvik and nitrates at Rjukan, while at Odda, zinc is refined and calcium carbide and acetylene manufactured.

Although the Norwegian economy has depended almost exclusively upon hydro-electricity in the past, it seems likely that the dominance of this form of electric energy generation will be reduced in the future. The reasons are as follows.

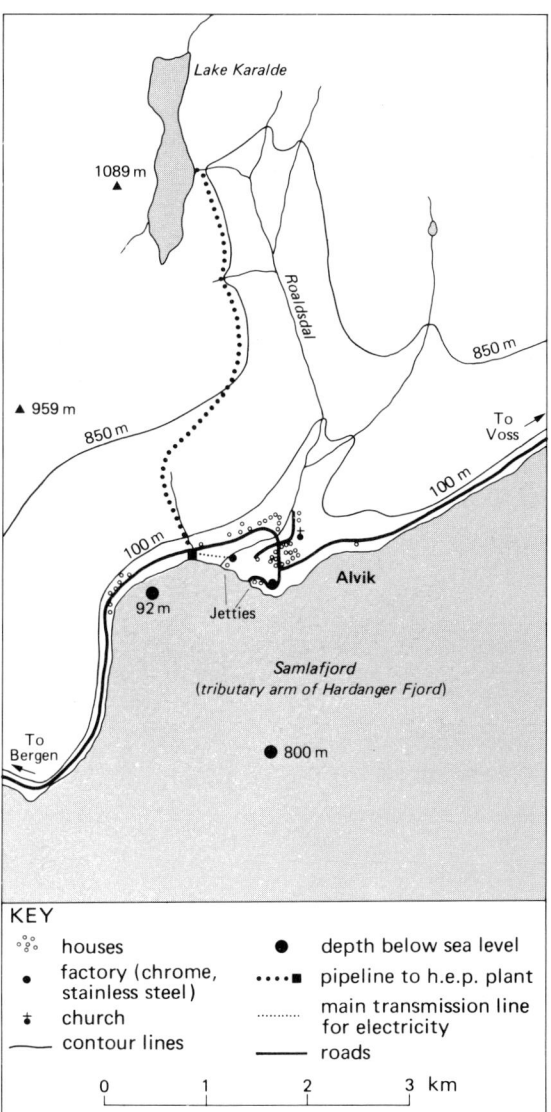

KEY

houses	● depth below sea level
● factory (chrome, stainless steel)	••••■ pipeline to h.e.p. plant
church	⋯⋯ main transmission line for electricity
contour lines	roads

0   1   2   3 km

Figure 8.16 High-head h.e.p. plant at Alvik, south-west Norway

1 Sixty per cent of the total capacity had been harnessed by 1974, and the remaining sites are in remote areas where the cost of development is high.

2 The cost of some alternative fuels has fallen and technical improvements have made the generation of thermal electricity more efficient and economical; so the cost and efficiency advantage of hydro-electric power stations is less. With electricity from other fuels costing less, industrial sites near hydro-electric power plants in remote areas are less acceptable.

3 The weakness of hydro-electricity is its dependence on natural conditions of precipitation and run-off, which can prove unreliable, and do not easily provide increased output to meet increased demand.

With the advantages that hydro-electric power has enjoyed in Norway becoming less, it is likely that the country will introduce thermal stations to complement hydro ones, and to make good the danger of electricity shortages in winter. The discovery of oil in the Norwegian sector of the North Sea will provide an alternative home-produced fuel for this purpose, although nuclear energy may play an important role too.

The River Rhône

The river falls 333 m in the 522 km from Lake Geneva to the Mediterranean Sea and receives two major tributaries, the Isère and Durance, from the Maritime Alps. The value of this system for power, transport and water supply had long been realized, but the problems posed by rapids and periodic flooding in a well-populated area meant that any integrated development programme for the river would be technically difficult and costly. However, partly inspired by the success of the integrated development scheme on the river Tennessee in the USA, work, begun on a piecemeal scale, blossomed into a full programme for harnessing this difficult river.

The first phase in the development was the construction of the low-head dam at Genissiat, which provided a large output of electricity at a relatively low cost. The project, delayed during wartime, was completed in 1948—much of the electricity being transmitted direct to the Paris region. The aim of the private company financing the Genissiat project was that the sale of electricity would provide funds for the further development of the river, but the nationalization of electricity in 1946 made available grants from the state and enabled subsequent schemes to go ahead more rapidly.

The second major development completed in 1952 was the Bollene power station and 31 kilometre canal constructed between Donzère and Mondragon. Here the shallow river had a fast flow on a steep incline and this fall was utilized for power and navigation by the construction of an embankment to impound the river in a narrow 10 km reservoir, which

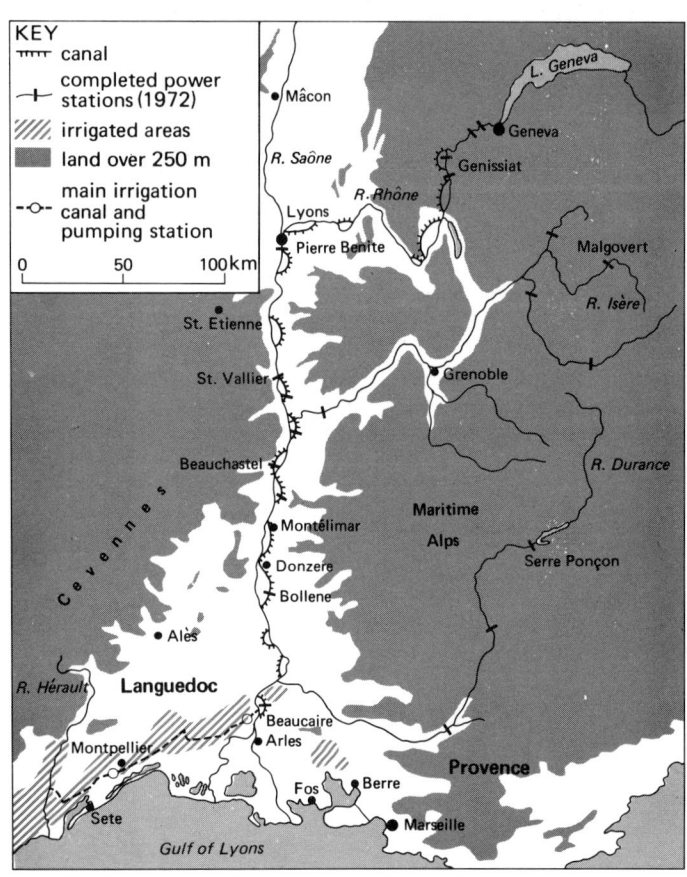

Figure 8.17 (*above*) Industrial sites alongside the Sorfjord at Odda (foreground) and Tyssedal in Norway. Settlement is limited to the small areas of level ground and road communication follows the ledge along the side of the fjord

Figure 8.18 (*left*) The development of the river Rhône

raised the river level by 5 m and eliminated the shallows. The electricity from Bollene is incorporated in the national grid, but much is used to power the nearby atomic energy isotope separation plant at Pierrelatte. Among subsequent developments, those at Montelimar (1953–7), Pierre Benite (1956–66) Beauchastel (1957–68), Vallabregues (1966–70) and Saint Vallier (1969–72) have similarly included power dams and the construction of a navigable channel for 1330-tonne power barges.

In addition to providing power and a navigable channel from Marseilles to Lyons, the French government has begun to develop the region industrially and agriculturally to provide an economic growth area that will relieve the overcrowding in metropolitan Paris. To this end, docks have been reconstructed at Lyons and new ports established at Valence, Montelimar, Avignon, Beaucaire and Arles. In this zone, new industries include the large

Feyzin oil refinery near Lyons, fed by crude oil from Lavera along the South European Pipeline, and metallurgical, engineering, chemical and cement works supplied with raw materials in bulk along the navigable waterway.

In the south the area between Marseilles and the Gulf de Fos is developing into a major deepwater industrial complex. The oil refining industry at Marseilles, Berre and Lavera has extended to the port at Fos, where steel and cement industries and a new container port are being established. Other established industries in the area include the Aerospatiale aircraft plant at Marignane, alumina production at Gardanne, and textile and food processing industries. To meet the increased industrialization, communications have been improved by the complete electrification of the railways of the south-east, the construction of new motorways along the coast and north to Lyons, and the expansion of Marignane airport.

Figure 8.19 The Pierre Benite power station and locks on the river Rhône. Port Edouard Herriot (1934–73) and the city of Lyons are also shown.

With reference to the photograph:

(a) draw a plan of the river course and waterways from the foreground to the centre of Lyons in the background. Mark on the plan the h.e.p. station, the locks, the dock basins, two industrial areas, the railway marshalling yards, a dual carriageway road, and an area of tall apartment and office blocks.

(b) The area around the power station in this photograph is densely populated, whilst that around the power station shown in Fig. 8.22 has remained rural. Suggest reasons to explain this contrast

Figure 8.20 Small fruit farms and vineyards near Draguignan in Provence. The land has no ditch irrigation system, but sprinklers are occasionally used

Figure 8.21 (*opposite*) Nuclear power stations

One of the most dramatic changes resulting from the development of the river Rhône has been the provision of irrigation in an area suffering an annual summer drought. Several of the power schemes include irrigation projects, but the major development is the 135 km canal diverting Rhône water from Beaucaire through Languedoc to connect with rivers like the Hérault, draining off the Cevennes. Agriculture in Languedoc has traditionally been dominated by small farms cultivating Mediterranean crops such as vines and olives, but the provision of a reliable supply of water has introduced a wider range of high-yielding fruit and market garden crops. Accompanying the changes in land use, farmers have been encouraged to co-operate and amalgamate their farms into larger units, and new wholesale markets and canning factories have been built at Montpellier and Nîmes.

Nuclear Power

At present, nuclear power supplies approximately 2% of Western Europe's energy, but clearly this proportion will increase as world reserves of the hydro-carbon fuels, coal, oil and natural gas, decline. The idea of a uranium-fuelled boiler for power generation was first developed in the 1930's, but it required the wartime military research, directed towards producing an atomic bomb, to bring it to reality. The present high cost of nuclear power is due to the technically difficult process of enriching the uranium fuel for the reactor, and solving the problem of cooling the reactor by water or carbonic gas. The costs of mining and preparing the low grade uranium ore and operating the power station are small when compared with the development costs of designing fuel enrichment factories and technically efficient reactors. Most European countries have embarked upon nuclear programmes, usually purchasing the enriched uranium fuel from the USA under an agreement made with Euratom§.

Rocks containing uranium have a wide distribution in the world, and any deposit of over 1000 tonnes with more than 0·5% uranium is considered workable. The rock occurs both as an ore and pitchblende, and because of its solubility it is also found precipitated in porous sedimentary rocks like sandstone, but in

§ Association formed in 1958 of countries comprising the EEC, it deals exclusively with the use of atomic energy for peaceful purposes.

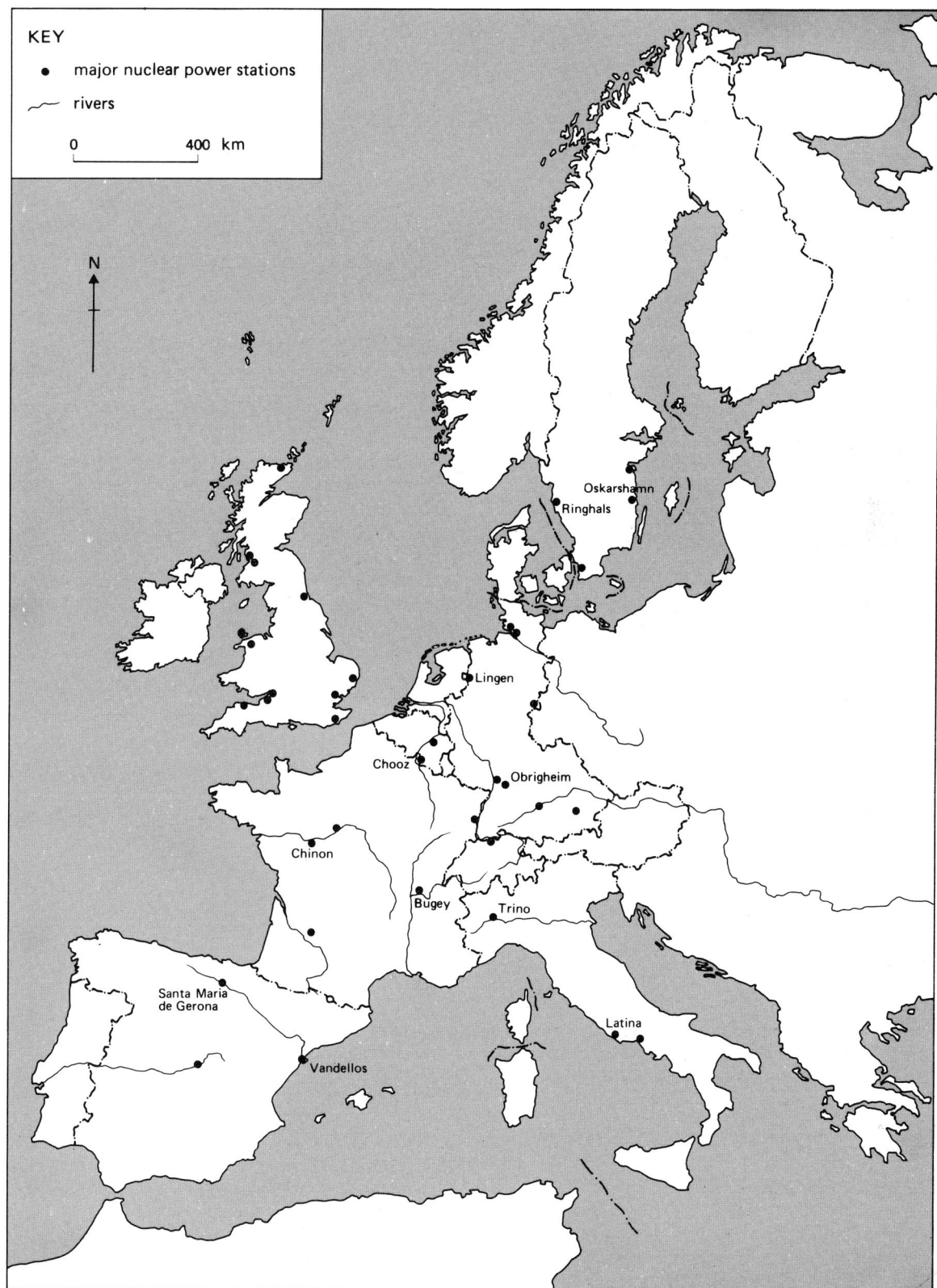

KEY

- major nuclear power stations
- rivers

0 — 400 km

N

Oskarshamn
Ringhals

Lingen

Chooz

Obrigheim

Chinon

Bugey

Trino

Santa Maria
de Gerona

Latina

Vandellos

Figure 8.22 The St Laurent des Eaux nuclear power station, situated on the left bank of the river Loire between Orleans and Blois. Electricity is produced from two 250 MW turbo-generators, and was connected to the National Grid in 1969

both forms the yield is invariably small. Thorium, too, is used as a fuel, particularly in 'breeder' reactors, where there is an end product of nuclear fuel as well as energy. France is the chief Western Europe producer of uranium, and there is a small output from Spain; with the ores yielding very little uranium the concentration plants are sited near the mines. The following table shows uranium production in Western Europe in 1972.

	Uranium production in 1972		
		1972	
Mining area	Reserves conc. uranium (in tonnes)	Ore mined (in tonnes)	Conc. uranium (in tonnes)
Crouzille (Limousin)	16,900	172,400	546
Forez (Loire)	2,900	100,700	361
Vendée (Loire)	6,900	190,700	417
Hérault (Languedoc)	12,700	—	—
Brittany	1,000	9,400	49
Massif Central	12,200	10,300	48
Spain	—	—	50

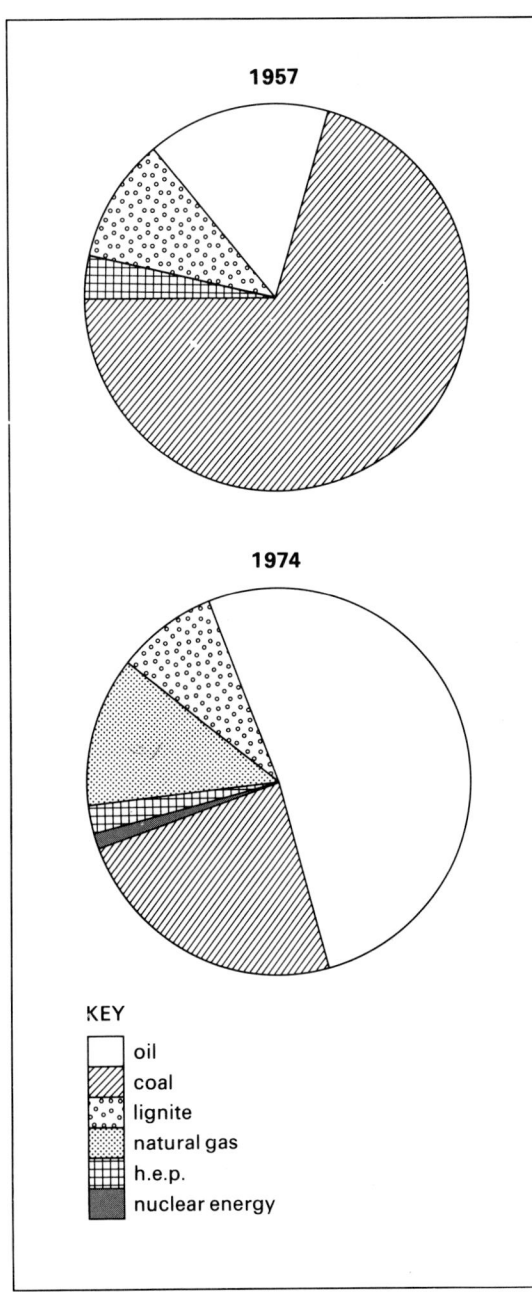

1957

1974

KEY

- oil
- coal
- lignite
- natural gas
- h.e.p.
- nuclear energy

Figure 8.23 The sources of primary energy in West Germany

The location of power stations has generally been in large production units of over 200,000 kWh on the coast or alongside rivers where water is readily available. The following examples illustrate this location factor.

Country	Site	Water source
France	Chinon	River Loire
„	Fessenheim	River Rhine
West Germany	Obrigheim	„ „
Italy	Trino	River Po
„	Latina	Coast
Sweden	Oskarshamn	Coast

To allay public suspicion of radiation dangers from nuclear power stations, developments have generally been outside areas of dense population, but the newer stations, like Barsebäck built near Malmo, indicate that these fears have little foundation.

Questions

1. With reference to the table showing sources of energy on p. 79 answer the following questions.
(*a*) For each country, study how the total energy generated is shared. Which countries derive most power from (i) coal and lignite, (ii) petroleum, (iii) natural gas, (iv) water power, (v) nuclear power?
(*b*) Give reasons to explain their importance in each of the countries.

2. (*a*) Using Fig. 8.3 name the countries fringing the North Sea in whose waters oil or natural gas has been discovered.
(*b*) From the Ekofisk field it is planned to pipe the crude oil to the UK and the natural gas to West Germany. Explain this decision.

3. Describe and account for the distribution of: (a) h.e.p. plants, (b) nuclear power plants, and (c) the crude oil pipelines in Western Europe.

4. Fig. 8.23 shows the sources of primary energy in West Germany for 1957 and 1974.
(*a*) Give reasons for (i) the increased use of mineral oil; (ii) the increased use of natural gas; (iii) the increased use of nuclear energy; (iv) the decline in the use of coal.
(*b*) Describe the problems resulting from the decline in coal production on the Ruhr coalfield. What measures have been taken to halt the decline in coal consumption?

101

9 The Rhine-Ruhr region

Coal Mining

The largest industrial concentration in West Germany is the Rhine–Ruhr region. Coal outcrops in a narrow zone along the valley of the river Ruhr and then dips northwards under a cover of sedimentary rocks where the west/east width of the coalfield reaches 120 km. The gradient is sufficiently gentle for the coal to be still accessible 900 m deep in the Lippe valley, 50 km to the north. Within the gentle northerly dip the coal measures rise in two anticlines to provide areas where coal is at a shallower depth for mining. This has concentrated the bulk of the modern mining activity in a west to east zone, following the line of the canalized Emscher valley between the Recklinghausen Ridge to the north and the Hellweg Ridge to the south. The strata in which the coal seams occur varies between 700 m and 1400 m in thickness, and is thinnest in the south, where most of the valuable coking coal seams have been removed by past erosion. The relatively undamaged coking coal seams which occur north of the Hellweg Ridge help to explain the mining concentration in this area.

The industrial development of the coalfield took place in the second half of the 19th century. Mining was initially concentrated in small pits in the Ruhr valley, but as demand grew for coking coal to supply the expanding iron and steel industry deep mines were opened on the concealed section of the coalfield. Coal mining and the steel industry have always been closely linked in the Ruhr area, and today the mines and steel plants are still jointly owned by large companies such as Thyssen, Krupp and Mannesmann. Coal mining

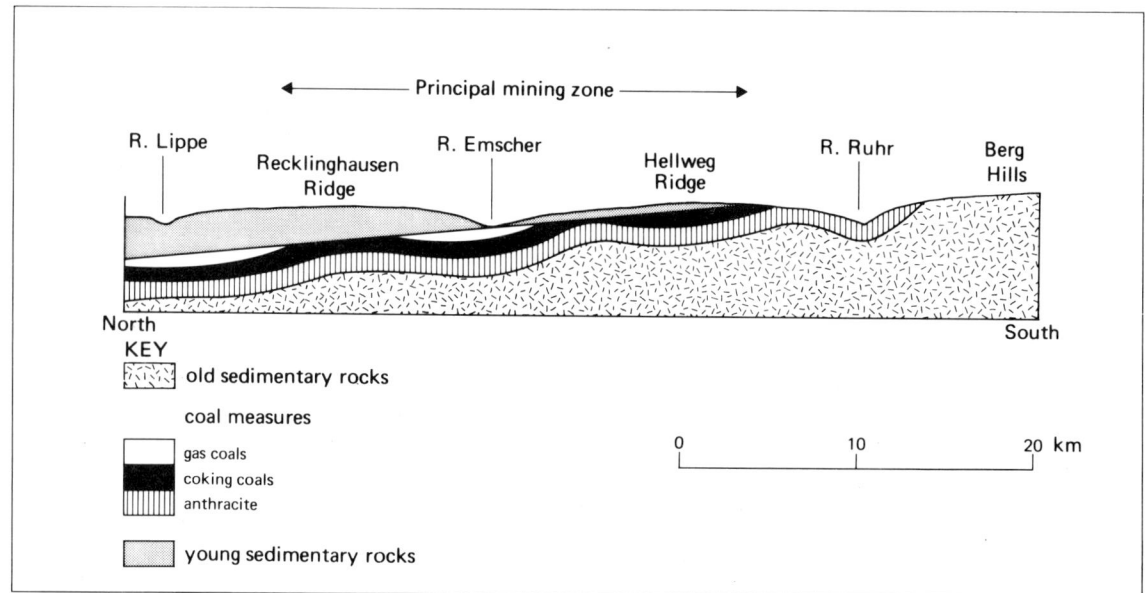

Figure 9.1 Section across the Ruhr coalfield

and steel manufacture are concentrated around the axis of the river Emscher; the Ruhr valley has little heavy industry, but provides less crowded residential conditions and a valuable source of water. To the north, the reserves under the Lippe valley have proved to be too deep for widespread exploitation, but on the west bank of the Rhine mining has been extended in recent years into an area formerly avoided because of drainage difficulties.

The reduced production on the Ruhr coalfield is illustrated in Fig. 9.2, and it can be further appreciated by the decline in the number of working pits from 183 in 1954 to 52 in 1970, and a planned 42 in 1976. To combat the competition of new fuels in the energy market, the twenty-two mining companies in the Ruhr have combined to form a new company, Ruhrköhle, which produces 95% of all coal in the region. Although the new company has improved efficiency, even with government support it has not been able to arrest the relative decline of the industry. In recent years vast amounts of coal have been stockpiled in old quarries and derelict areas, the figure standing at 9 million tonnes in 1971. Much has since been used as increased world oil prices have made coal a more economical fuel, but this may be only a temporary improvement in demand. The closure of small, uneconomic pits and a concentration upon a few mines equipped with modern machinery has helped to slow the rate of decline. The remaining deep pits, each employing over 4000 men and producing over 1 million tonnes of coal, are those in the most favourable locations to supply the electricity power stations and steel plants. The chief concentration of these remaining mines is around Rheinkamp on the west bank of the Rhine, Gelsenkirchen and Lünen.

The Iron and Steel Industry

Coking coal from the Ruhr contains a low percentage of volatile materials, and for this reason has been very suitable for steel making. In the 19th century, iron and steel plants developed alongside pits working the coking coal and were frequently owned by the same company, a legacy which remains today. Gas from coking plants has been a valuable cheap source of fuel in the furnaces, but now the West German gas grid has been converted to natural gas.

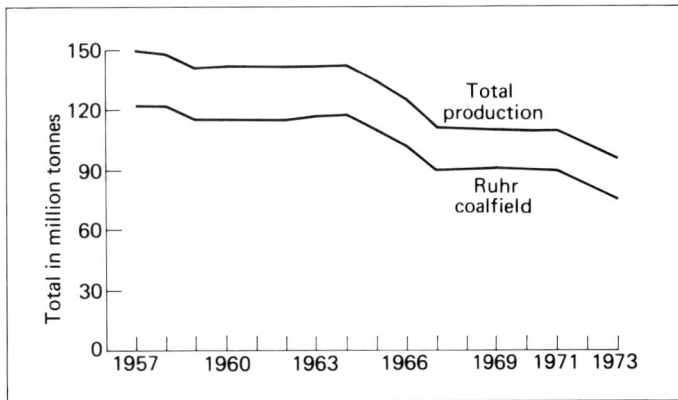

Figure 9.2 The decline in coal production in West Germany, 1957–73

As with coal mining, the steel industry was concentrated in the towns of Duisburg, Essen, Bochum and Dortmund around the Emscher valley. In the early days of metal working there was almost complete dependence upon the local resources of coal, 'black band' iron ore from the coal measures and limestone from the Sauerland plateau. However, as the industry has come to depend almost entirely

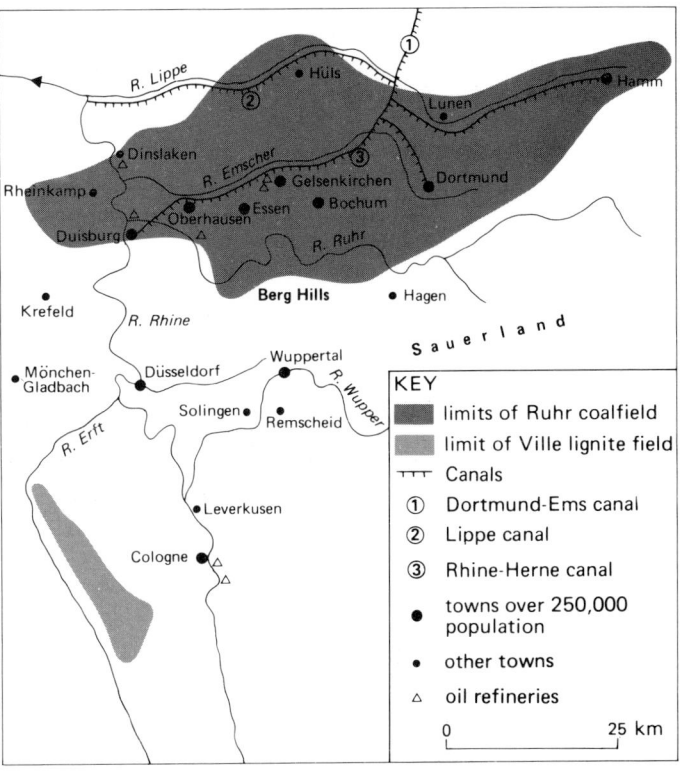

Figure 9.3 The Rhine–Ruhr industrial region

103

Figure 9.4 The Frederick the Great mine at Herne is a large, modernized pit. The Rhine–Herne canal runs alongside.

With reference to the photograph: answer the following questions.

(a) Draw a simple sketch plan of the area; (i) divide it into four contrasted types of land use, and (ii) mark the route of a line of electricity transmission cables stretching from the mine area.

(b) Write a short description of each of the land use types identified in (a).

(c) Comment upon the road, rail and water communications which serve the mine

Figure 9.5 Coal barges and a pusher unit in the Thyssen docks at Duisburg

upon imported iron ores from West Africa, Sweden, Australia and Algeria, the location has shifted to the areas where the zone of coking coal production crosses the Rhine and Dortmund-Ems waterways. The larger concentration is in the Duisburg area, where an extensive dock complex has developed to utilize the deeper Rhine routeway. The towns formerly important for steel-making now concentrate upon castings, heavy engineering goods, machine tools and special steels while attracting other industries, such as textiles and glass at Essen and motor vehicles at Bochum. The steel plants of the Ruhr produce approximately 75% of West Germany's steel output, which amounted to 49 million tonnes in 1973. The steel companies are medium-sized by comparison with those in Japan, the USA and the nationalized United Kingdom industry, the largest being the Thyssen plant at Duisburg, which produced 14 million tonnes in 1973. This relative smallness compared with competitors in the world market has meant

higher operating costs. The inland location of the industry is also a disadvantage; coast-based steel plants like those at Ijmuiden, Dunkirk and Port Talbot are able to import their iron ore directly in ore carriers of at least 50,000 tonne capacity. A factor which enables Ruhr steel to remain relatively competitive is its nearness to such large engineering centres as Essen, Bochum and Dortmund, which form a major market for iron and steel goods. However, it seems probable that mergers will occur, and a relative shift in the industry will take place to coastal locations.

Other Industries in the Region

The availability of a large source of fuel and power has produced a range of industries additional to steel making and engineering. Coal provided a useful raw material for the chemical industry, distillation processes yielding such diverse products as sulphuric acid, plastics, detergents, synthetic fibres and rubber, insecticides and dyestuffs. The chemical plants

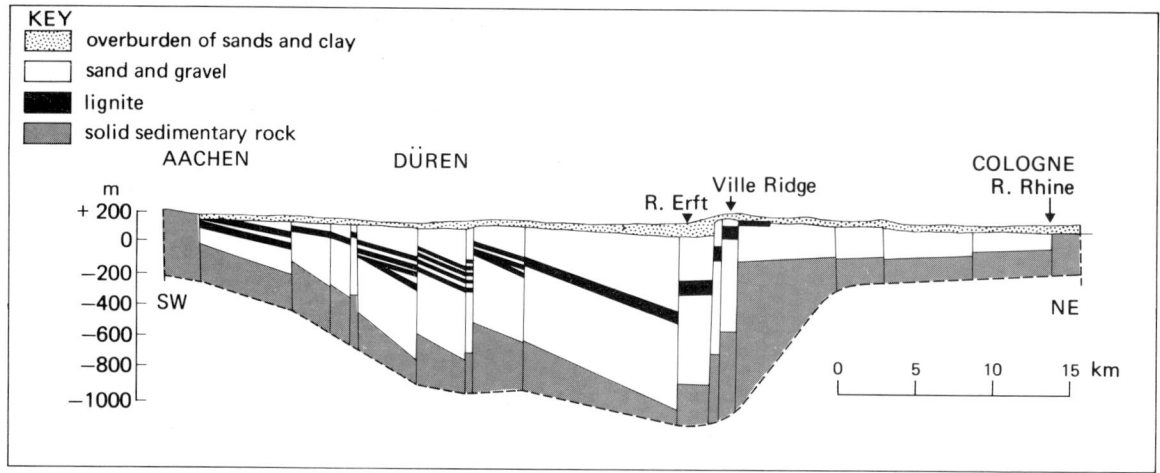

Figure 9.6 A geological section across the Rhine lignite field

are located near the coal mining centres, often on the Rhine, Rhine-Herne or Lippe waterways. As in other industries, coal has been replaced as the base raw material by natural gas and oil, and pipelines lead from the Weser-Ems and Dutch gasfields into the gas grid, which feeds such plants as those producing synthetic rubber at Hüls, dyestuffs and fibres at Leverkusen and detergents at Düsseldorf. Fuel oil is distributed by road and rail from the major refineries at Duisburg, Gelsenkirchen and Wesseling-Cologne, which lie on the crude oil pipelines from Rotterdam and Wilhelmshaven. The post-war development of oil refining and petro-chemical industries in the Ruhr has helped to absorb some of the large numbers unemployed by the contraction of the coal-mining industry.

Among other new industries which have been introduced into the coalfield area are motor vehicles (Opel) at Bochum, electrical equipment at Mülheim and textiles and clothing at Essen, Bochum and Gelsenkirchen.

Outside the mining region, industry has always had greater diversity, although the advantages of the Rhine waterway for the bulk transport of goods has produced a concentration of metallurgical, chemical, cement and timber plants, which stretch almost without interruption from Dinslaken to Bonn. South of the coalfield in the Wupper valley, the towns of Solingen and Remscheid have developed a specialist steel industry which produces cutlery, machine tools, cutting edges and precision instruments. Wuppertal is a

centre of the textile industry, but also manufactures tyres and a variety of engineering goods. Krefeld, Mönchen Gladbach, Rheydt and Viersen on the west bank of the Rhine are other textile towns which have attracted engineering and chemical industries to diversify their structure.

Cologne and Düsseldorf are the established

Figure 9.7 A giant excavator and conveyor system remove 100,000 m^3 of coal each day from the Garsdorf open pit near Cologne

The Ville Lignite Field

Lignite is a widely available but low grade fuel, and is therefore only extracted in particularly favourable locations. It often has a high moisture content, but when dried yields approximately 80% of the heat value of Ruhr coal. The fuel is usually used near the mines, where it is either burnt in thermal electricity plants (85%) or compressed and cemented into briquettes for domestic heating (15%).

West of Cologne, a thick seam of lignite extends 35 km along the Ville ridge between the river Erft and the Rhine. The shallow overburden is scraped clear and giant excavators extract the lignite from large open pits. Mining has disrupted both drainage and settlement to make much of the region swampy and derelict. Even where land has been restored, the thickness of the seam removed (up to 100 m) is such that little of the land is likely to return to normal agricultural use. The efficiency of the highly mechanized mining has enabled lignite from the Ville field to withstand the competition from oil and natural gas more successfully than coal. The output of lignite has shown a steady growth in recent years; the quantity produced for electricity generation increased at an annual rate of 10% between 1968 and 1973.

The electricity is mainly transmitted by high-tension overhead power cables from large power stations at Knapsack and other mining villages to the industrial centres of the Rhine valley. The cheapness of the electricity on the Ville field has attracted several metal working and chemical factories needing large quantities of electricity.

Figure 9.8(a–b) Land returned to use after mining.

(**a**) Grain cultivation near Frechen

(**b**) Forest and lakes near Bröhl provide recreational areas and freshwater reservoirs

major towns of the region, and between them they dominate the banking, insurance and commercial requirements of the Ruhr firms. Düsseldorf has the major airport of the region, and Cologne is a focal point of the railway and motorway systems which converge upon the Rhine valley routeway. Their industries are very broadly based, metal working and chemicals being the most important.

Questions

1. With reference to Fig. 9.6 of a geological section across the Rhine lignite field, answer the following questions.

(*a*) How is the lignite preserved in the geological structures between Aachen and Cologne?
(*b*) Estimate the thickness of the overburden on the Ville Ridge.
(*c*) Why is mining (i) concentrated chiefly along the Ville Ridge, and (ii) not carried out in the area between the river Erft and Duren?

10 The mining industries

Western Europe has an advanced industrial economy, and larger quantities of raw materials are consumed than can be met by resources within the region. This dependance upon imports has already been seen in the field of energy needs, and is equally true for most metallic ores, notably iron ore, bauxite and copper. Imports are chiefly from Australia and developing countries in Africa and the West Indies, where extensive and accessible resources are produced cheaply enough to make transportation to Europe economic. Sea transport has become increasingly efficient with the introduction of large bulk carriers for ores, grains and fuels. The growth in vessel size has had to be accompanied by extensive harbour improvements at selected European ports; notable recent developments have taken place at the ports of Bremerhaven, Maasvlaakte (Rotterdam), Dunkirk, Marseilles-Fos, and Genoa.

The increased dependence upon imports of metallic ores has not caused any marked decline in mining in Western Europe and as the world supply of some minerals has become scarce, a few long abandoned mining areas have revived. In general, however, recent European output has been virtually static, while imports of high grade ores have increased to meet the rising demand. The following statistics compare the quantities of home and imported iron ore used within the EEC.

Iron Ore

Resources in Western Europe range from the magnetite ores of Lappland, which yield up to 65% iron, to the lean carbonate ores in the sedimentary rocks of Lorraine and Salzgitter which yield less than 30% iron. The latter group do not normally enter into world trade, and mining companies are often given financial assistance by the state, particularly in subsidizing the transport of the ore. In spite of this, it seems very likely that the inland areas mining low grade ores will decline, as they are situated away from the recently developed coast-sited steel plants. While French iron ore production coming chiefly from Lorraine declined by 10% between 1964 and 1974, the Swedish output, largely from Lappland, increased by 38%. In southern Europe the most important resource is in the Bilbao region of northern Spain, where a number of haematite ore bodies are exploited. The low phosphoric nature of the ore has meant that it has been heavily worked for many years, and although Spanish output is currently at 7 million tonnes, it is likely that the steel plants of northern Spain will come to depend increasingly upon imported supplies. The table on page 109 shows the principal Western Europe ore producers and the chief mining areas.

The Lappland Iron Ore Field in Sweden

The magnetite iron ores mined near Kiruna

Iron ore consumption in thousand tonnes							
	1967	1968	1969	1970	1971	1972	1973
EEC(6)-produced iron ore	66,011	71,174	71,031	71,149	68,432	66,044	65,758
Imported iron ore	55,477	67,163	75,194	84,160	76,786	80,741	97,416

Country	Ore output (,000 tonnes)			Principal Mining areas
	1964	1970	1973	
Austria	3,563	3,997	4251	(1) Eisenerz
France	60,931	56,801	54,755	(1) Lorraine (2) Normandy
Luxembourg	6,680	5,722	3,782	(1) Lorraine
Norway	2,050	3,906	3,810	(1) Sydvaranger (2) Nr. **Mo-i-rana**
Spain	5,209	7,000	6,990	(1) Bilbao (2) Nr. Aviles.
Sweden	26,619	31,774	34,811	(1) Lappland (2) Bergslag
W. Germany	8,697	5,531	6,429	(1) Salzgitter-Peine

and Malmberget in Swedish Lappland lie north of the Arctic Circle on the same latitude as northern Alaska and northern Siberia. The problems of extracting the ore are numerous, and it was not until the beginning of the present century that the iron was mined in large quantities. In 1878 the Thomas process was discovered for smelting iron ore with a high phosphorus content, and the dream of utilizing the rich Lappland ores became a reality. A single-track railway was laid from the port of Lulea to Gallivare in 1888, and extended through Kiruna to reach the Norwegian port of Narvik in 1903. The choice of Narvik as a second outlet for the iron ore was necessary in view of the limited shipping season at Lulea which is closed by ice from 15 December to 15 May each year. The region of the iron ore deposits was uninhabited except for nomadic Lapp reindeer herders, and virtually the whole of the population of the mining towns has had to be recruited from southern Sweden and abroad.

Kiruna has a population of over 20,000 and is the principal mining centre. The workings are based upon a 250 m high outcrop of magnetite ore which extends 4 km in a north-south ridge, dipping eastwards under a cover of other rocks. Mining was originally at the top of the ridge, which has been cut into by a series of opencast quarries, but since 1962 virtually all the output has been from below ground. At the present rate of extraction it is estimated that the reserves will last for at least one hundred years, as the ore body is known to extend to a depth of over 1000 m.

The second mining centre is Malmberget; the neighbouring town of Gallivare acts as the administrative, service and shopping centre for the community. The reserves here are not centred upon a single main outcrop but are scattered. The iron yield from the ore is a little lower than the 60-65% at Kiruna, and

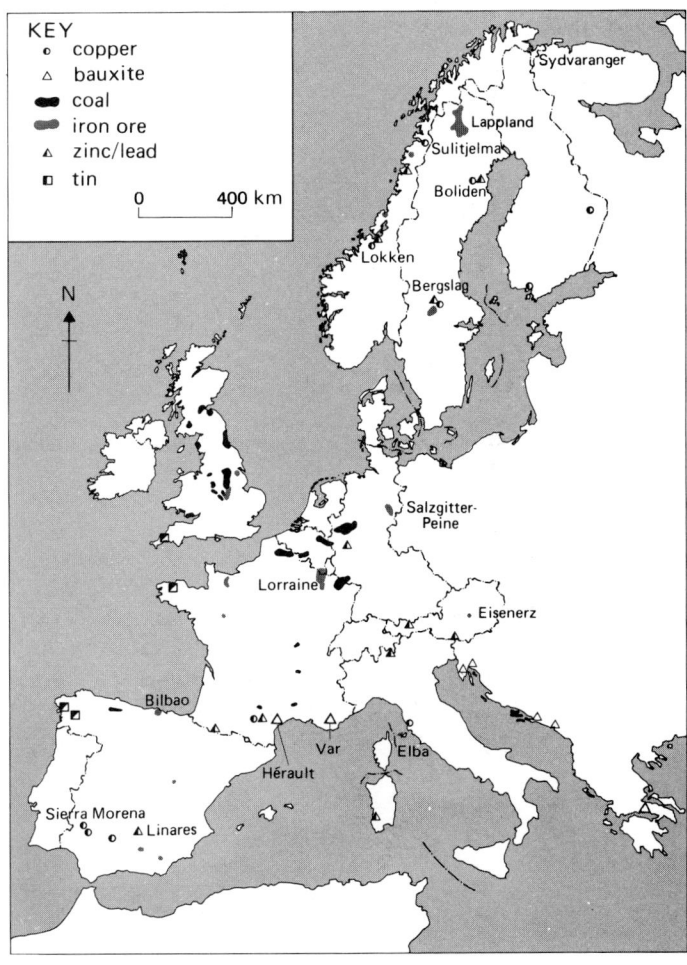

Figure 10.1 The distribution of the major metallic ores and coal deposits

109

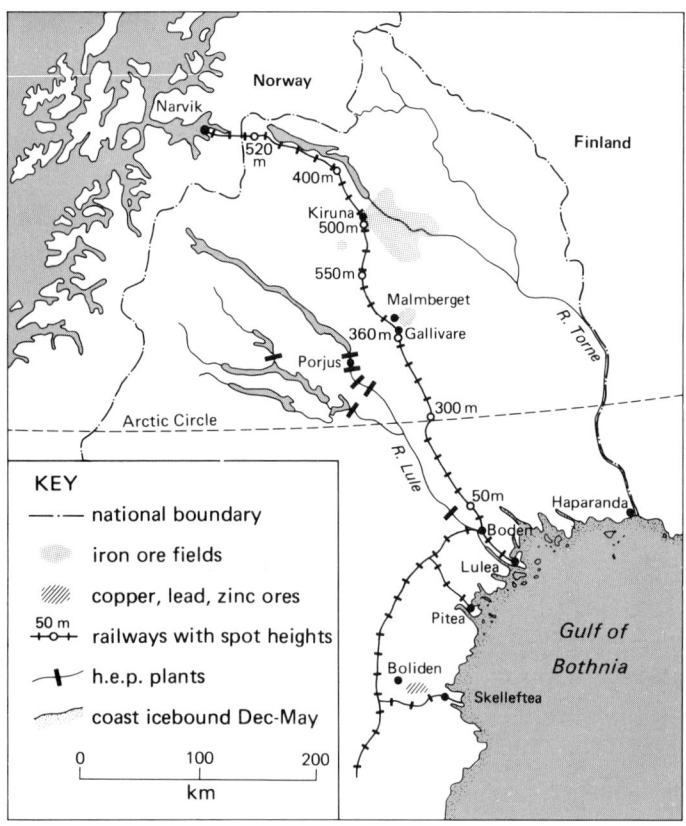

Figure 10.2 (*above*) The Lappland iron-ore field

Figure 10.3 (*below*) The township of Kiruna, with the former open-cast workings in the background

the output from the Malmberget area is crushed and concentrated at the Vitafors plant before being dispatched. The mining operation at both towns is highly mechanized and efficient, being directed by the largely state-owned LKAB company.

The present annual output of approximately 22 million tonnes from Kiruna and 8 million tonnes from Malmberget is a reflection of their relative accessibility to the major European steel-making areas. Kiruna is nearer to Narvik than Malmberget is to Lulea, while the sea journey to the principal receiving ports of Rotterdam, Antwerp and Middlesborough is 150 km shorter from Narvik. In addition, Narvik is kept ice-free in winter by the effects of the warm North Atlantic Drift and has a deeper anchorage where vessels of up to 80,000 tonnes are loaded by a continuous conveyor system. Increasingly, the ore sent to Lulea is either used in the steel plant there or exported to the steel plants in central Sweden. The principal markets are West Germany, Belgium and the United Kingdom, where Swedish ore faces competition from the high-grade, low-phosphoric ores from Australia, West Africa and Venezuela. The recent widespread introduction of the oxygen-blown process of steel-making, which requires a low phosphoric ore, has made it necessary for the LKAB company to build plant to concentrate the ore into pellets and lower the phosphorus

Figure 10.4 (*above*) An underground railway carrying ore from the mine face to the crushing plant

Figure 10.5 (*below*) The principal iron-ore quay at Narvik. One 42,000-tonne and one 80,000-tonne ore carrier can be loaded at the same time by a system of overhead conveyors

Figure 10.6 An ore train en route from Kiruna to Narvik. Each wagon carries up to 80 tonnes.

With reference to the photograph:

(a) describe the natural landscape shown in the photograph and state how you think it has influenced the route of the railway.

(b) How is the engine powered?

(c) Suggest why the line is single track.

(d) The engine is pulling 64 ore trucks; calculate the total load of ore being carried.

The latter requirements are considerable; at Gallivare the average January temperature is −11°C, and the monthly average is below 0°C for the seven months October–April. Also, the winter twilight means that the mines have to be floodlit throughout that season. In view of these difficulties, it is a great achievement that this rich iron ore resource has remained reasonably competitive in the West European market.

Bauxite

Aluminium, because of its strength and lightness, is second only to steel as a metal for general industrial use. Its uses, often in alloy form for aircraft sections and domestic hardware, have been extended to motor vehicle castings and body panels, electric cable and food packaging. The principal ore of aluminium, bauxite, is mined in a number of countries of which the most important in Europe are France, Hungary, Greece and Yugoslavia; together they produce over 20% of world output, but many West European smelters rely upon ore mined from outside the region.

The formation of bauxite is the result of rocks being weathered under humid tropical conditions to cause the removal in solution of most of the major elements in the rock, except aluminium. The material which remains after the weathering is a clay, bauxite, that has a large concentration of aluminium in it. The occurrence of the element aluminium is very common, comprising 8% of the earth's crust, but it is only occasionally found in sufficient concentrations to make mining economic. It does not matter what kind of rock has been weathered as long as the weathering conditions have been right.

As the bauxite is a surface residue it is quarried in open pits, and concentrated nearby. To produce aluminium the impurities are removed from the bauxite, reducing its volume by half, and a white powdery substance, alumina, remains. The smelting of alumina is done by an electrolytic process which consumes approximately 10,000 kWh of electricity to yield one tonne of aluminium. Consuming such vast quantities of electricity has meant that aluminium smelters have had to be located near to a large and cheap source of power. In Western Europe this has led to

content before the ore can be sold. The additional cost of this work has resulted in production expanding more rapidly in the better situated Kiruna area.

The construction of the railway has been a vital factor in the development of the iron-ore field, and today trains, each carrying over 2000 tonnes of ore, link Kiruna to Narvik. Equally important has been the provision of electricity from a series of hydro-electric plants on the Lule river. The electricity is used to power the railway, the steel furnaces at Lulea and the light and heat requirements of the mines and the urban communities around.

the location of smelters near to hydro-electricity plants, often in relatively remote parts of Norway and the Alpine countries. In recent years the development of the large thermal electricity power station, fired by the transportable fuels, gas, oil, coal and uranium, has caused the aluminium smelting industry to be less tied to hydro-electricity and the mountain regions of Europe. Smelters built near Lünen in the Ruhr region, at Fusina near Venice, and those planned for Dunkirk and Wilhelmshaven show how the location has moved to the major industrial markets.

Bauxite Mining in South-Eastern France

France produces approximately 5% of the world's bauxite, output coming chiefly from the departments of Var and Hérault in the south-east of the country. Bauxite was first mined in this area in 1821 at Les Baux, and the initial discovery of a method for refining aluminium was made by Héroult at Froges near Grenoble. These strong traditions have made France a pioneer in the utilization of aluminium, and in 1938, 680,000 tonnes of bauxite were mined, comprising over a quarter of the world's total. Although France's

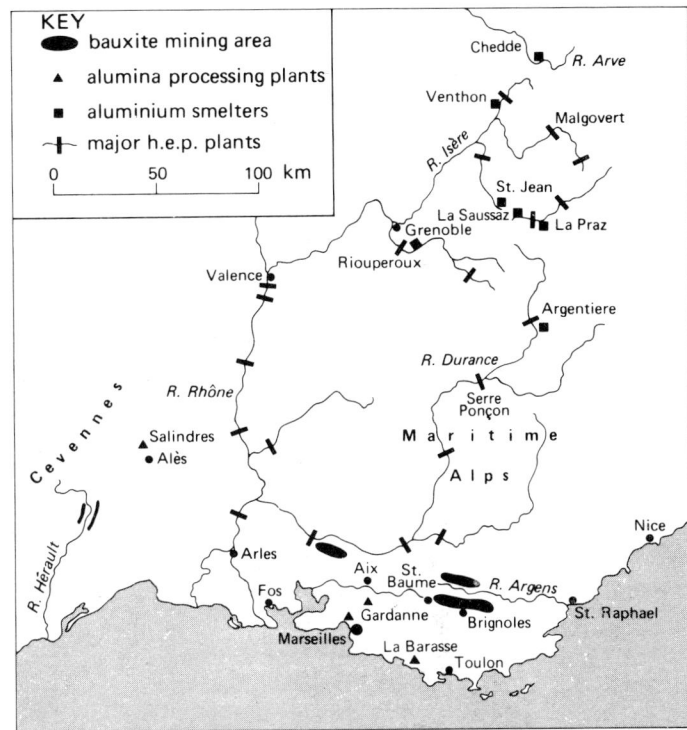

Figure 10.7 (*above*) The bauxite deposits of south-east France, and aluminium-processing plants

Figure 10.8 Opencast bauxite quarries near Brignoles, Provence

Figure 10.9 The aluminium smelter at Argentière in the Maritime Alps

relative importance has declined with the exploitation of resources in Jamaica, Surinam, Guyana and Australia, production increased to 3·3 million tonnes in 1973.

The bauxite occurs in pockets in the limestone hill country that fringes the Mediterranean coast of France. The chief mining area is in the upper valley of the river Argens and its tributaries, where shallow quarries have been cut into the wooded ridges that separate the valleys. Brignoles, Sainte-Baume, Tourves and Le Luc are important centres. The ore is taken by road to Gardanne and La Barasse for reduction into alumina, and then sent to aluminium smelters powered by local hydro-electricity in the valleys of the Maritime Alps, notably at Riouperoux (Romanche valley), St Jean (Maurienne valley) and Chedde (Arve valley), or exported from the ports of Toulon and St Raphael. Most of the smelters in the Maritime Alps and Pyrenees are long established and have a small production capacity of less than 30,000 tonnes per annum. The plants at L'Argentière (est. 1910) and Auzat (est. 1908) are both being modernized and their output increased.

The other important area of bauxite mining is on the sides of the tributary valleys of the river Hérault flowing southwards from the Cevennes. The main centre is Bédarieux, and the alumina reduction plant is at Salindres near Alés. The alumina is then sent to the smelters of the Maritime Alps and the Pyrenees.

In the Var and Hérault departments lie the bulk of French bauxite reserves, which were estimated at 60 million tonnes in 1974, with a further 190 million tonnes of lower quality ore. Reserves are also known to exist in the Ariège valley area of the Pyrenees, but it seems likely that French aluminium smelters will begin to use increasing quantities of foreign ore with home production rising only slowly. The works at Nogueres near Pau in the western Pyrenees has the largest output of the French aluminium smelters, and while utilizing cheap hydro-electricity generated in the area, it depends upon imported alumina. The proposed building of a smelter on the north French coast at Dunkirk, and the backing French companies are giving to the extraction of bauxite at Fria in Guinea, Greece and Australia, suggest that this may be the future pattern.

Other Non-Ferrous Metals

In the extraction of the major non-ferrous metals, i.e., copper, lead, zinc, tin, chrome and nickel, West European output falls far short of its requirement, and there is great dependence upon imported ores. The major foreign sources of these ores are as follows:

Copper:	Zambia, Zaire, Chile, Canada
Lead and Zinc:	Australia, Canada, Peru, Morocco
Tin:	Malaya, Indonesia, Bolivia
Chrome:	South Africa, Turkey, Rhodesia
Nickel:	Canada

The occurrence of these ores is associated with ancient igneous rocks, and when injected along joints and bedding planes in neighbouring sedimentary rocks, they can be found some distance from their igneous source. This limits their main distribution in Europe to the Baltic Shield and the upland areas affected by igneous intrusions. Although there are numerous outcrops in these areas, only rarely have they proved sufficiently extensive to justify the high costs of mining. The metal content of the non-ferrous ores is invariably low; in the case of copper the European deposits average 2–5% metal. This means that most workings must be near the surface and that the smelting of the ores is done near the mine; it is only under such conditions that the small, scattered European mining areas can remain competitive with foreign suppliers developing more extensive mineral fields.

In Sweden the sulphide ores of Boliden yield copper, lead and zinc, and at Röros, Lokken and Sulitjelma in Norway similar ores are refined for their copper content. In north-

ern Italy important yields of lead and zinc are obtained from mines in the Adda valley, and in West Germany from mines in the Harz mountains and Westerwald. The distribution of the major workings of non-ferrous minerals is shown in Fig. 10.1, and it can be seen that the greatest exploitation of a variety of minerals occurs within the plateau areas of central Spain.

Sierra Morena Mining Region of Southern Spain

The Paleazoic rocks of the Meseta form a marked west/east structure of high ridges or 'sierras' and valleys occupied by long westerly-flowing rivers. The Sierra Morena lies between the Guadiana and Guadalquivir valleys and rises to over 1000 m with a steep fault scarp marking its southern edge. This edge is fretted with valleys drained by rivers flowing into the Guadalquivir, and it is in these valleys that most of the mineral exploitation occurs.

The region contains a wide variety of minerals which have been extracted since the 15th century but have not given rise to any marked industrial development. This can be explained by the minerals being scattered, the power resources being inadequate and the limited

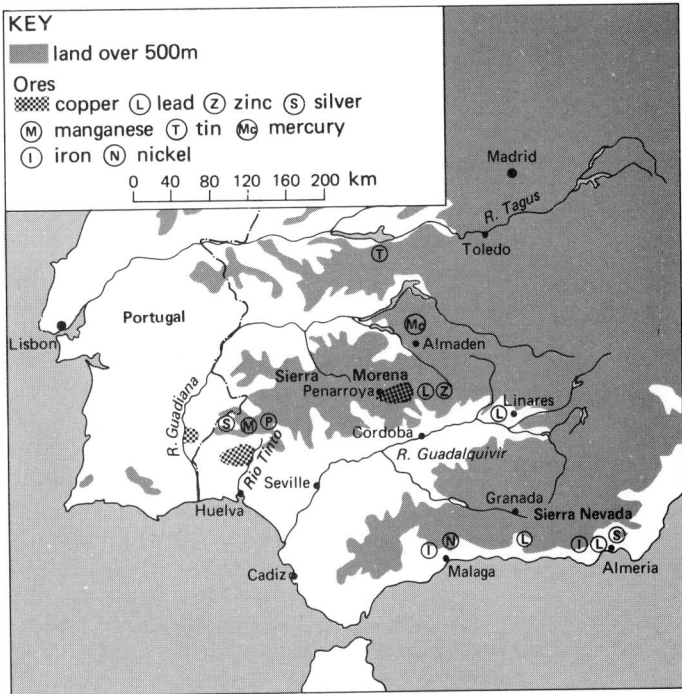

Figure 10.10 The principal mining areas of southern Spain

115

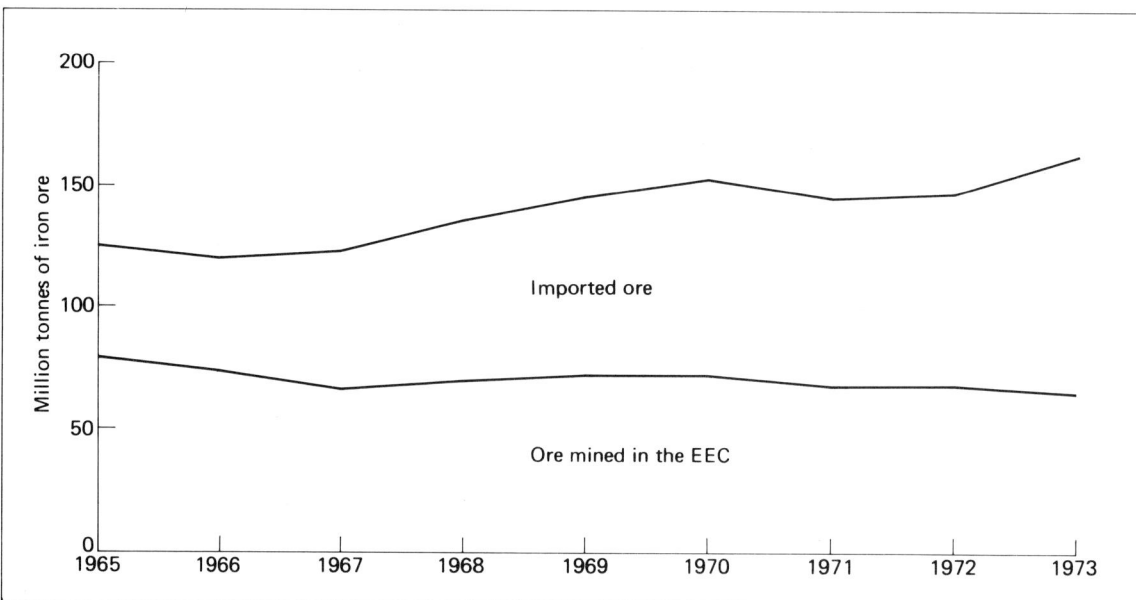

Figure 10.11 The supply of iron ore in the EEC countries of West Germany, France, Italy, Netherlands, Belgium, Luxembourg

Spanish communications network making the utilization of the resources difficult. Also, much of the development was in the hands of foreign companies, notably the British at Rio Tinto and the French at Huelva and Penarroya, who did not encourage industrial development in the region. Although the amounts are less than in the past, significant quantities of copper, lead, iron pyrites and mercury are exported to other West European countries.

The western and central sections of the Sierra Morena yield lead/zinc ores and iron pyrites, which are mined and smelted near Penarroya, using thermal electricity generated from nearby coal resources. In the Rio Tinto valley copper is extracted from large shallow pits and sent by rail to Huelva, where it is smelted and then exported. The port is situated on a deepwater ria and handles most of the mineral exports of the region. Other minerals mined in the area include manganese near the Portuguese border and iron ore. The eastern section of the Sierra Morena is equally well endowed with a number of workable mineral deposits, but it suffers from having poorer access to the coast. Linares, an important lead mining and smelting centre, has gradually developed a wider range of industrial activities in response to the government's efforts to disperse industrial growth away from

Madrid and Barcelona. To the west of Linares, uranium mined in the Sierra Morena is treated at Andujar and copper is mined and smelted near Cordoba. On the north side of the Sierra Morena, approximately 20% of the world's supply of mercury is extracted and smelted at Almaden, the bulk of the output being exported.

Questions

1. Suggest reasons to explain why the exploitation of mineral resources of Swedish Lappland and the Sierra Morena in Spain have not led to large scale industrial development.

2. With reference to Fig. 10.1 comment upon the distribution of the European deposits of iron ore, bauxite and copper in relation to:
(*a*) power resources for smelting;
(*b*) major industrial areas where the ore will be needed;
(*c*) communications.

3. With reference to Fig. 10.11 and the text:
(*a*) what was the total amount of iron ore used in the EEC in 1970, and what percentage was imported?
(*b*) Describe the trends shown on the graph.
(*c*) Name the country producing most iron ore in the EEC in 1970.
(*d*) Name *three* countries exporting large quantities of iron ore to the EEC.

116

11   The metal-smelting industries

Owing to the inability to produce its own food and energy requirements, Western Europe has developed a wide range of industrial products for export in order to earn the revenue necessary to import these goods. The most important export is machinery and engineering goods, which make up approximately 40% of the total exports. Although heavily committed to industry, most European countries have insufficient home-based supplies of fuel and raw materials to support these industries. Many raw materials are imported and this has increasingly caused industries to choose locations near to the coast, where they can take advantage of bulk imports by sea. This particularly applies to the metallurgical, chemical and bulk food processing industries, while those producing such consumer products as textiles, foodstuffs and electrical goods favour a location accessible to the main centres of population.

Metallurgical industries

1 Iron and Steel Industry

The raw materials necessary for the manufacture of pig-iron in a blast furnace are iron ore, coking coal and limestone. Pig-iron is an impure, brittle metal which is of little value to industry until it is refined further to make steel. Steel can be made by a number of conversion processes, of which the most important are the open hearth, the electric arc, the Thomas process for basic ores and the oxygen-blown process. The latter process, in which oxygen is injected into the furnace from above, has proved a valuable technological advance in producing high-quality steel quickly and cheaply. New plant has had to be built for this process, usually at coastal sites where the advantages of receiving ore and coke in bulk can be realized. The steel industry occupies two principal types of location—*deepwater coastal sites* or *near sources of coal and iron* ore. The latter location is illustrated by steel plants on the Ruhr, Franco-Belgian and St Etienne coalfields and the northern Spain, Bergslag and Norrland iron-ore fields. Coastal locations of the steel industry are numerous, but among the most important sites are those at Mo-i-Rana and Oxelösund in Scandinavia, and Ijmuiden, Bremen, Dunkirk, Fos, Genoa, Naples and Taranto in southern and Western Europe. Several others are planned or under construction at Maasvlakte (nr Rotterdam), Zelzate (nr Ghent) and Sagunto (nr Valencia). The cost of constructing a modern steelworks is beyond the resources of small companies, and new developments have generally resulted from companies combining together and receiving financial aid from the state.

These coastal plants are deliberately located to make use of raw materials from outside their local area, and supplies are received from a variety of countries. Good quality coking coal is restricted to a few areas in the world and the West Virginia coalfield in the USA, together with the Ruhr region, supplies most of Western Europe's needs. Iron ore is currently available in greater quantities than steel plants require, which means that there are many suppliers competing for the European market. Ore is imported from Labrador, Sierra Leone, Guinea, Mauritania, Venezuela, Western Australia and several other areas where the demand for metallurgical products is small and the ore is available for export.

Steel production in Western Europe has steadily increased at a rate of approximately 7% per annum since 1963. The main producers have remained the same, but some of the smaller countries, notably Belgium, Spain and the Netherlands, have more than doubled their output by developing new plants at

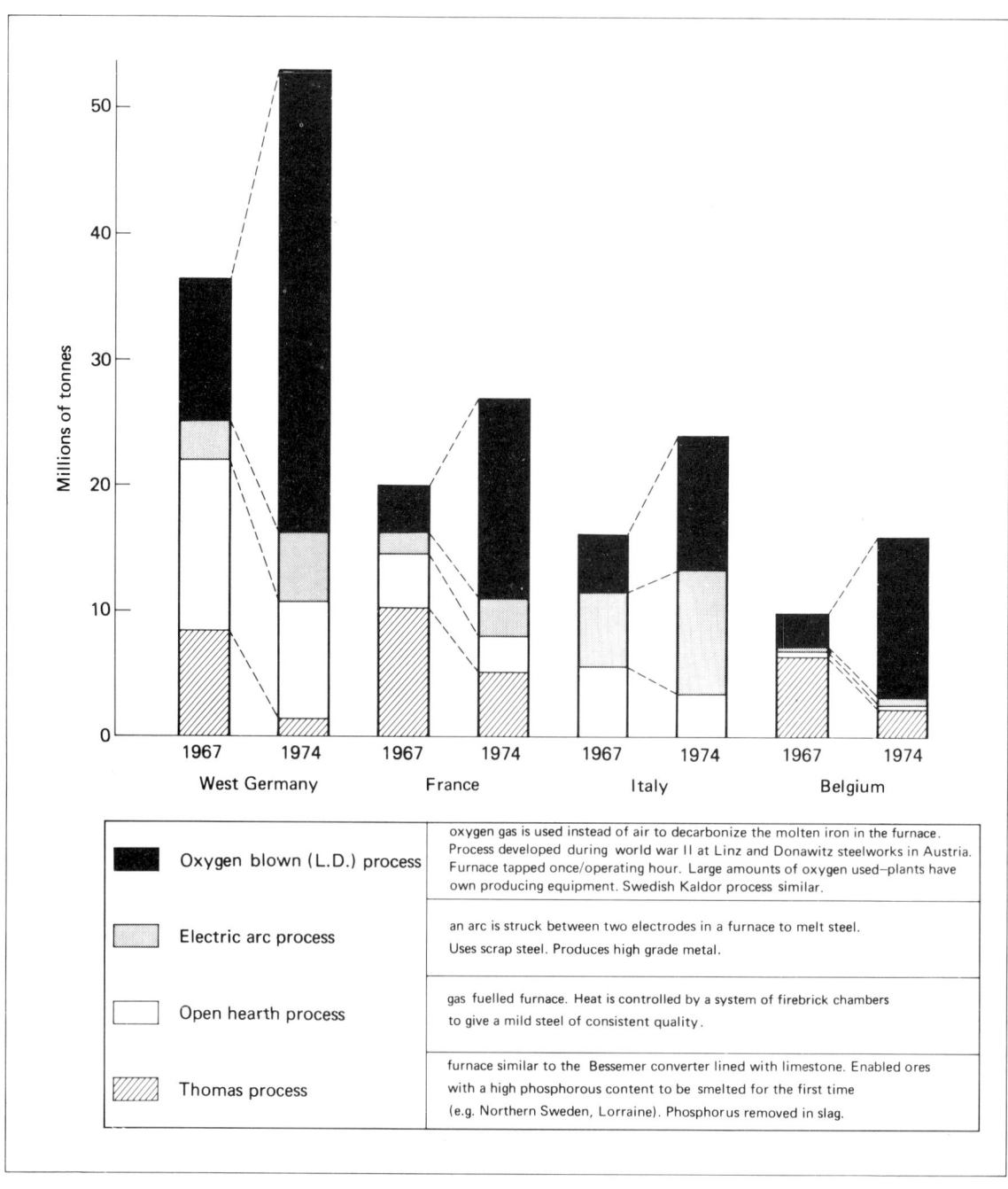

Figure 11.1 A comparison of the processes used for steel production in four West European countries

Figure 11.2 (*opposite*) The distribution of major steel-producing areas

coastal sites. The pie-graphs in Fig. 11.3 show how each country's share in West European steel production has changed since 1963. It illustrates how the major producers, whose industry was built on home-based coal and iron ore deposits, have lost ground to countries who have modernized their steel industry around coastal locations.

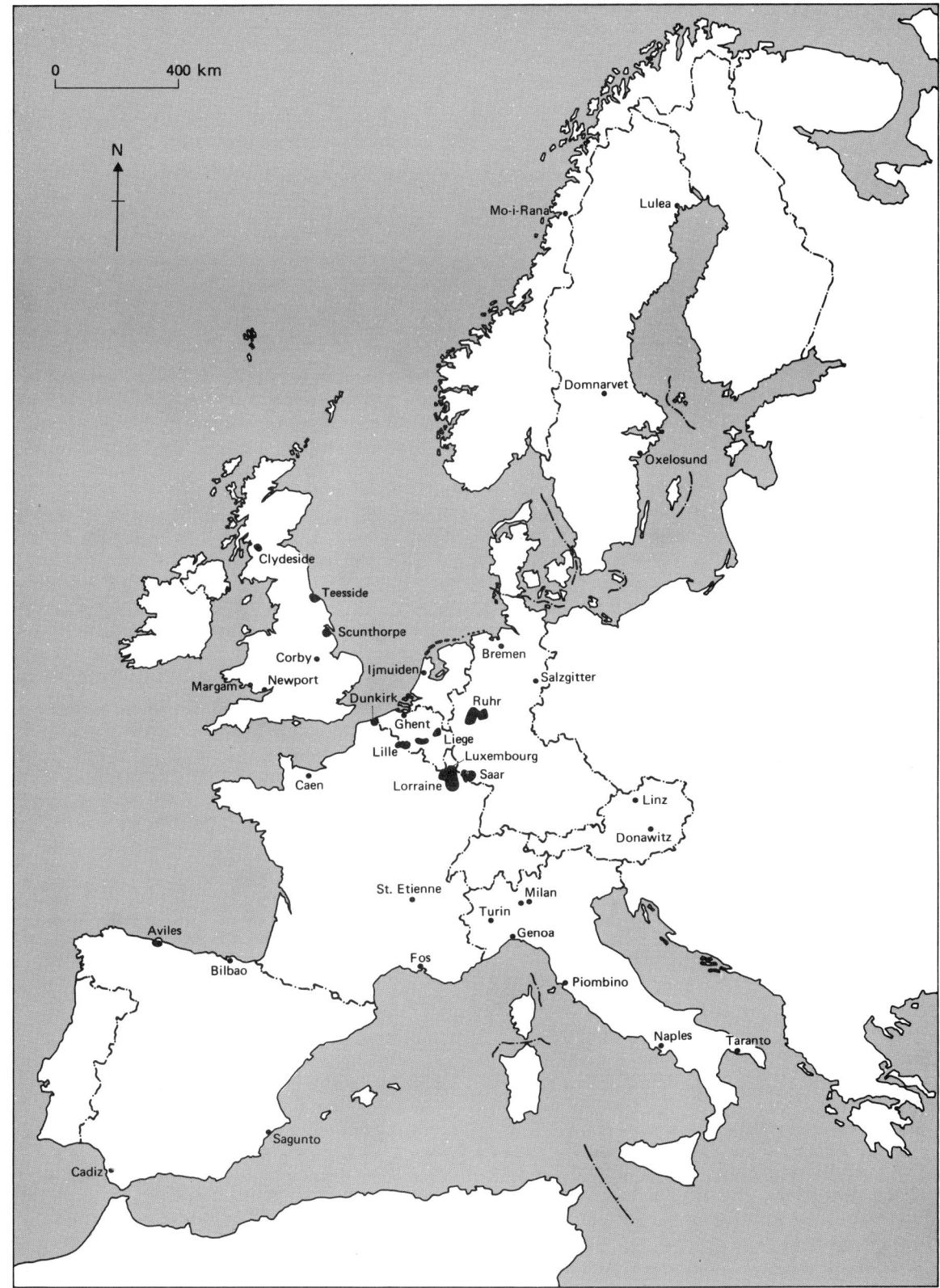

0   400 km

N

Mo-i-Rana   Lulea

Domnarvet

Oxelosund

Clydeside

Teesside

Scunthorpe

Corby   Ijmuiden   Bremen   Salzgitter
Newport
Margam   Dunkirk   Ruhr
            Ghent   Liege
        Lille   Luxembourg
        Lorraine   Saar   Linz

Caen   Donawitz

St. Etienne   Milan
            Turin   Genoa
Aviles   Fos
Bilbao   Piombino

                Naples   Taranto

Sagunto

Cadiz

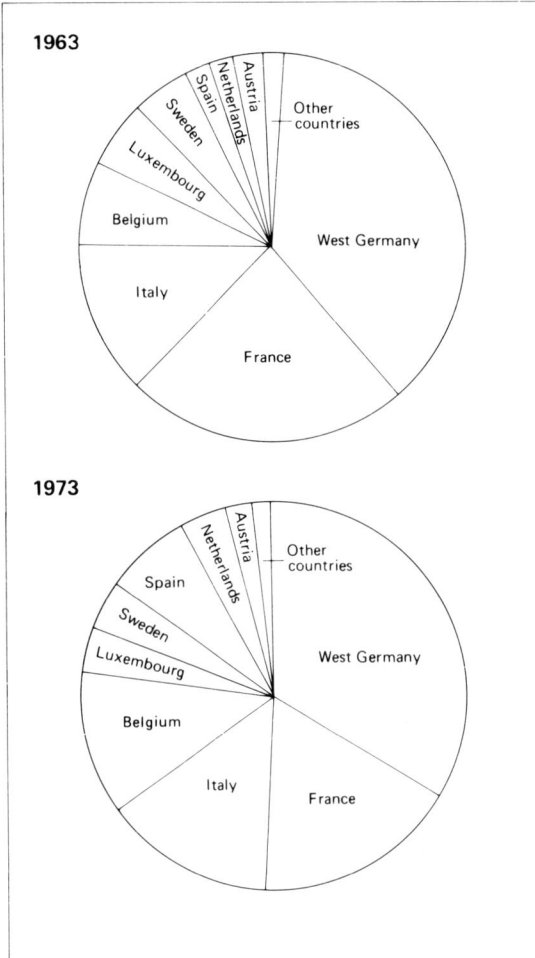

Figure 11.3 Steel production in 1963 and 1973

A Study of the Integrated Steelworks at Dunkirk

The French steel industry has seen its share of world production fall from 4·3% in 1965 to 3.6% in 1973, while the share taken by Italy, Belgium and the Netherlands has increased. The new steel plants developing at Dunkirk and Fos, which are economically located at deepwater coastal sites, are expected to reverse this trend. The policy is designed to gradually transfer primary steel making from such established inland sites as Lille and Denain on the Nord coalfield and Longwy, Thionville and Nancy on the Lorraine iron orefield to coastal locations which can take advantage of bulk shipments of cheap foreign coal and ore. The French policy is very similar to that of Britain, where the principal new developments have been built at Teesside, Humberside and in South Wales.

The integrated steelworks at Dunkirk was begun early in the 1960's by the USINOR company on a flat, coastal plain site of 500 ha, one-fifth of which was reclaimed from the sea. Initially the works situated west of the town depended upon the artificial tidal harbour which was started in 1939 and completed after the war. The docks have been added to on several occasions, and the two mineral berths which extend alongside the steelworks can now receive 120,000-tonne ore carriers: further extensions to the harbour will enable vessels of up to 300,000-tonnes capacity to dock. Rapid handling facilities are a feature of the docks and have opened up the possibility of Dunkirk becoming an ore-importing port for other steel-making areas in Western Europe. In recent years the ore imported into Dunkirk has been used in the following proportions:

Dunkirk works	Steelworks in the Nord and Lorraine areas	Steelworks outside France
48%	43%	9%

The port is served by an electrified rail link to the steelworks of Lorraine and the Nord, and a canal for 3000-tonne barges to Lille and Valenciennes connects with the Belgian and West German systems. These facilities and the motorway links to Lille and Paris have attracted shipping companies to Dunkirk, and a large container terminal has been built.

Pig-iron is produced in the blast furnaces and transferred to three 160-tonne oxygen-blown converters, which have an annual steel-producing capacity of approximately four million tonnes. By the construction of a further three converters of 220-tonne capacity, steel production was raised to a planned eight million tonnes in 1976. Although just 80 km from the mines of the Nord coalfield, the furnaces have come to depend almost entirely upon imported coking coal—chiefly from the West Virginia coalfield in the USA. Limestone, quarried in the nearby Boulonnais district, is carried to the works by road and rail. Iron ore, partly in pellet form, is obtained from a variety of sources, reflecting the over-production that has occurred in the world

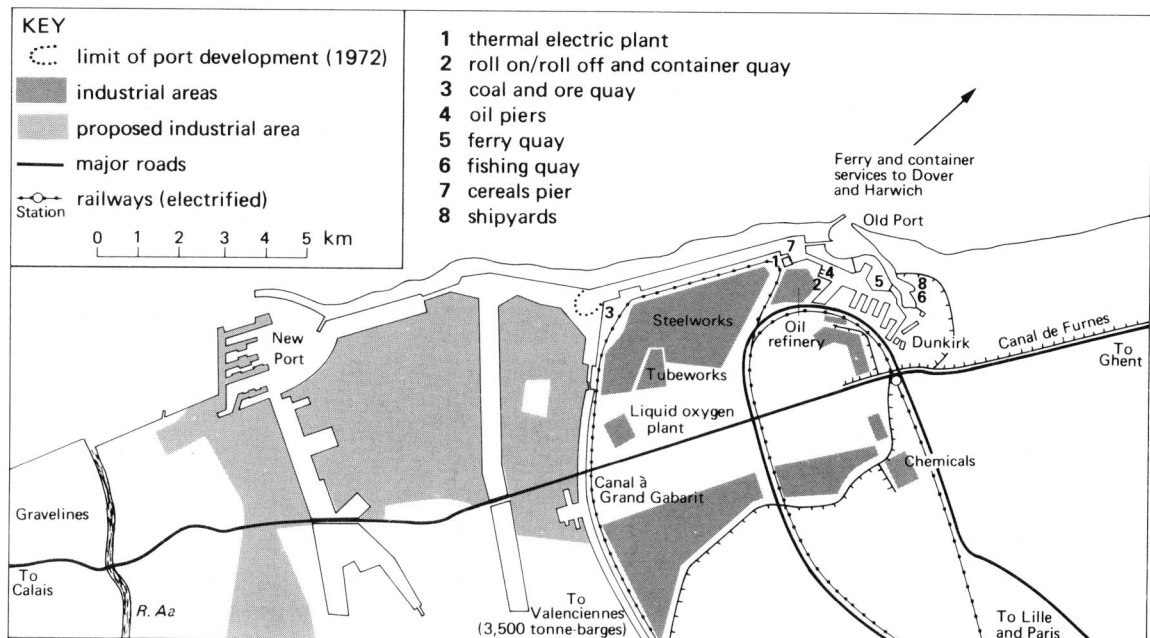

KEY

- :::: limit of port development (1972)
- ▓ industrial areas
- ░ proposed industrial area
- — major roads
- ⊶ railways (electrified)
- Station

0 1 2 3 4 5 km

1 thermal electric plant
2 roll on/roll off and container quay
3 coal and ore quay
4 oil piers
5 ferry quay
6 fishing quay
7 cereals pier
8 shipyards

Ferry and container services to Dover and Harwich

Old Port

New Port

Steelworks

Oil refinery

Tubeworks

Liquid oxygen plant

Dunkirk

Canal de Furnes

To Ghent

Chemicals

Canal à Grand Gabarit

Gravelines

To Calais

R. Aa

To Valenciennes (3,500 tonne-barges)

To Lille and Paris

Figure 11.4(a) (*above*) The site of Dunkirk

Figure 11.4(b) (*below*) The position of Dunkirk

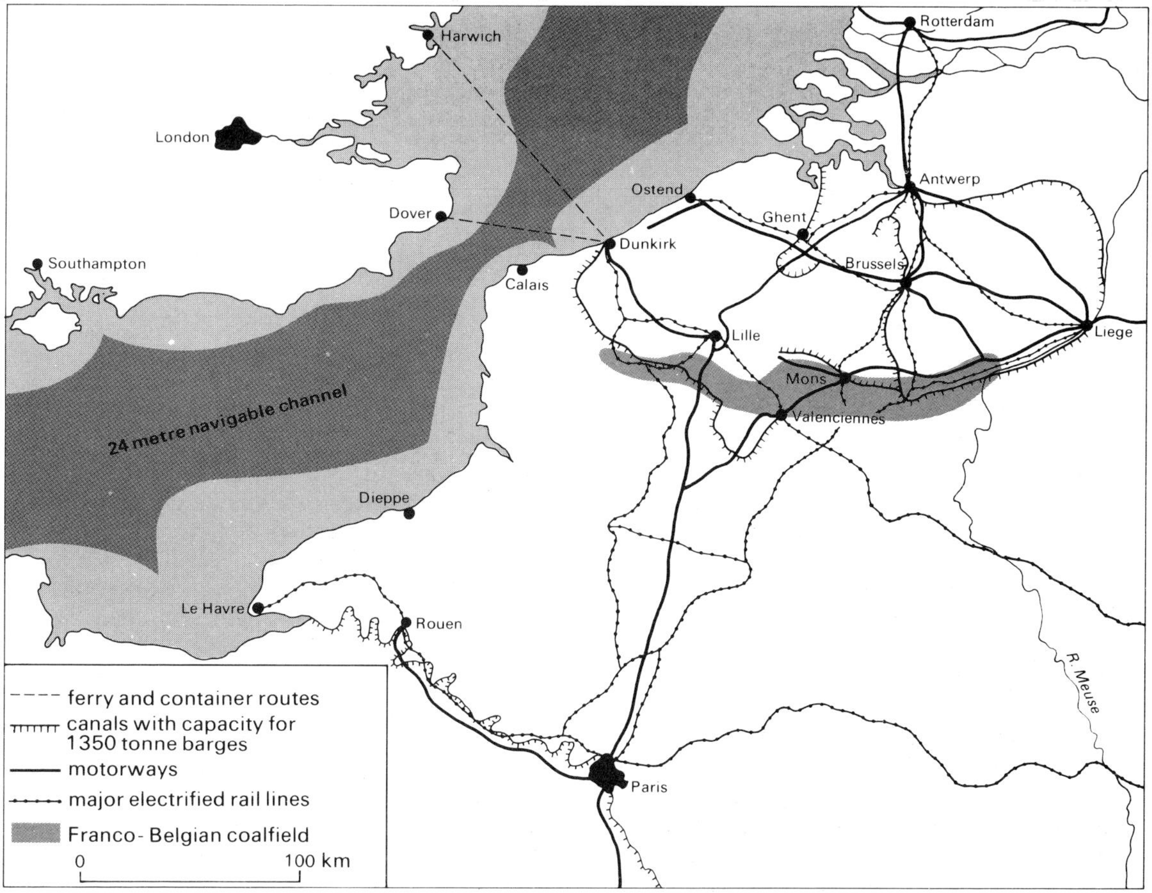

Harwich

Rotterdam

London

Ostend

Antwerp

Dover

Ghent

Southampton

Dunkirk

Brussels

Calais

Liege

24 metre navigable channel

Lille

Mons

Valenciennes

Dieppe

Le Havre

Rouen

R. Meuse

Paris

- – – – ferry and container routes
- ⊤⊤⊤ canals with capacity for 1350 tonne barges
- — motorways
- •••• major electrified rail lines
- ▓ Franco-Belgian coalfield

0   100 km

Figure 11.5 Dunkirk: the USINOR steelworks

recently. In a typical year (1970) non-phosphoric ores all containing above 60% iron content were received from the following sources:

Country	Mines	Quantity of ore (tonnes)
Mauritania	F'Derik, Tazadit	1,550,000
Liberia	Mano River, Bomi Hills, Nimba	1,250,000
Brazil	Itabira	925,000
Peru	Marcona	295,000
Australia	Hamersley Range	292,000
Spain	Granada	173,000
Sweden	Kiruna	151,000
Norway	Fosdalen	115,000
Algeria	Ovenza	112,000
Angola	Cassinga	50,000

The main product of the USINOR works is flat, rolled steel in the form of heavy plate, coiled strip and sheet. The molten steel leaving the oxygen-blown furnace is formed into ingot slabs of between 13–32 tonnes each by a process of continuous casting. The slabs are then reheated, rolled and sheared in the rolling mill. Electric power for the mill is supplied from a thermal power station alongside, which is fuelled by gas produced in the blast furnace process. The high-temperature steel furnaces are fuelled with oil from the Dunkirk refinery, while oxygen is piped from a liquified oxygen plant to the nearby furnaces and to the works at Denain, 120 km away.

The steel is used locally in the shipyards, for the manufacture of oil and gas pipes and for oil storage tanks. The rolling mill, opened in 1973 at Mardyck 2 km south of Dunkirk, will produce steel sheet for the motor vehicle industry, household goods and furniture. In addition, the deepwater port will undoubtedly attract other refining industries to the area: an aluminium smelter is planned, to add to the Antar and BP oil refineries already situated there. However, the major oil distribution

Figure 11.6(a) Conveyor carrying pellitized ore to the furnaces

Figure 11.6(b) Iron-ore dock

port for the region is Le Havre, and with its established pipeline network it seems unlikely that there will be any large increase in oil refining at Dunkirk. Shipbuilding, particularly bulk carriers and oil tankers, together with textiles and engineering, are established industries, but the major new growth of the town is likely to be as a transit port for bulk cargo and container traffic. At the beginning of 1974 the USINOR works had over 8000 employees, and the new town of Deux Synthes has been built to accommodate the increased population.

2 Aluminium Smelting

Like steel production, the aluminium smelting industry of Western Europe depends heavily upon imported ore; only in France are there substantial deposits of bauxite. The choice of site for aluminium smelters has been guided by two main factors:

(1) access to sea-borne bulk imports of alumina, and

(2) a location within easy reach of large quantities of electricity.

The second factor tended to favour locations in mountain areas where there existed a large potential resource of hydro-electricity with few alternative uses for it. The Alps, Pyrenees and Scandinavian mountains each have important centres for smelting, but the additional asset of the deep-water, ice-free Norwegian coast has made that area the main location for the industry in Western Europe. However, conditions have recently begun to change and as the Norwegian plants are relatively isolated the country's domination may be threatened. The major smelters built recently have a capacity exceeding 100,000 tonnes of aluminium per annum, and to achieve this production an electricity power supply of 200,000 Kw is needed. As the best hydro-electricity sites in Europe have already been exploited there are very few areas remaining where water power can be generated on this scale.

With large quantities of electricity now widely available from recently built thermal power stations, the advantages from locating smelters nearer to the chief markets for aluminium have been realized. This has led to a marked growth of the industry in West Germany, Italy and the UK. The new smelters at Lünen in the Ruhr, Fusina near Venice, and at Holyhead (Anglesey) illustrate this trend.

123

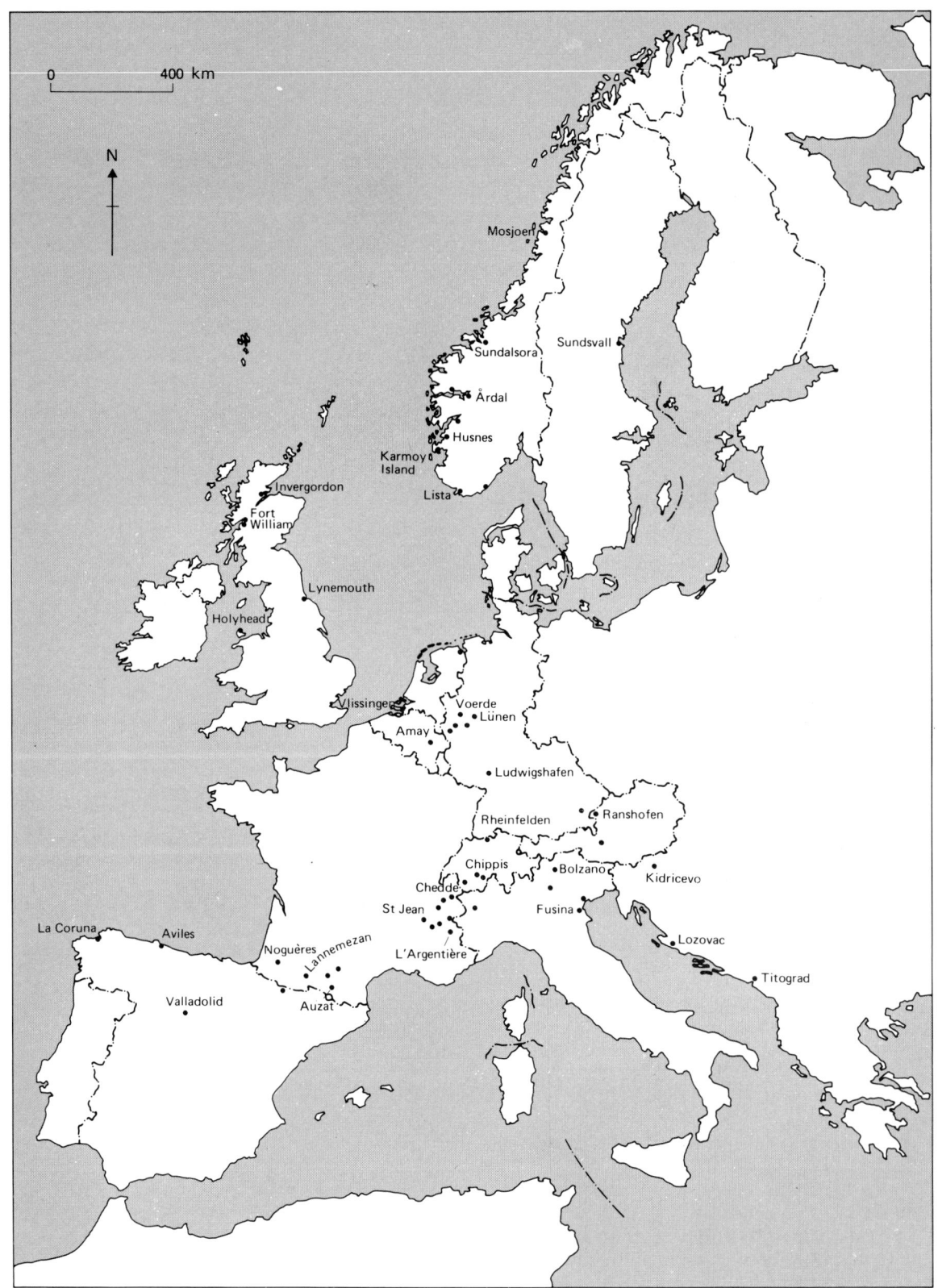

Figure 11.7 (*opposite*) The distribution of major aluminium smelters in Western Europe

Production of aluminium in Western Europe has increased at an average rate of 10% per annum in the ten years up to 1974. The producing countries are shown in Fig. 11.8, where the important role of Norway can be clearly seen. The metal, with its valuable properties of lightness and strength, is increasingly used in alloy form, particularly for aircraft and motor vehicle construction, and for a variety of domestic utensils.

Aluminium Smelting in Norway

The importance of the industry in the Norwegian economy can be judged when one considers that aluminium is the country's major single export, earning over 10% of the value of all exports. Approximately 15% of Norway's electric energy goes to the aluminium plants, which are mainly located at deep-water fjord sites along the west coast. Unlike some European countries, Norway imports its raw material as pure aluminium oxide or alumina; the reduction of bauxite ore having taken place in the producing country. Alumina is imported from the Caribbean countries, Jamaica, Surinam and Guyana, and increasingly from Australia. The establishment of alumina-producing plants near the bauxite deposits has been financed by the large international aluminium companies, who, unlike the oil companies, were encouraged in their investment by the relatively stable political situation in these countries.

The largest aluminium smelter in Norway is at Årdal, near the head of the Sogne Fjord. The plant, completed early in the 1950s, is owned jointly by the state and the international company, Alcan. Since it first came 'on stream' production has been periodically increased and the present annual output is approximately 200,000 tonnes. However, the government made this expansion conditional upon a reduction in the discharge of fume pollutants. The quantity of dust, tar and fluorine discharged hourly into the atmosphere has been reduced from 84 kg in 1964 to 50 kg in 1971, and a further reduction to 40 kg must be achieved by 1981. In Norway this national awareness of the dangers of atmospheric pollution has led to similar controls

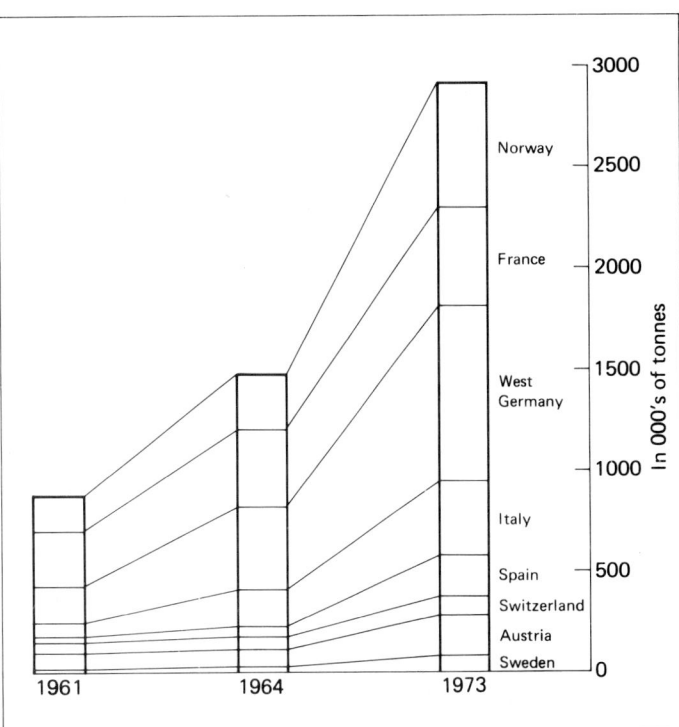

Figure 11.8 A comparison of the major aluminium producing countries, 1961, 1964, 1973

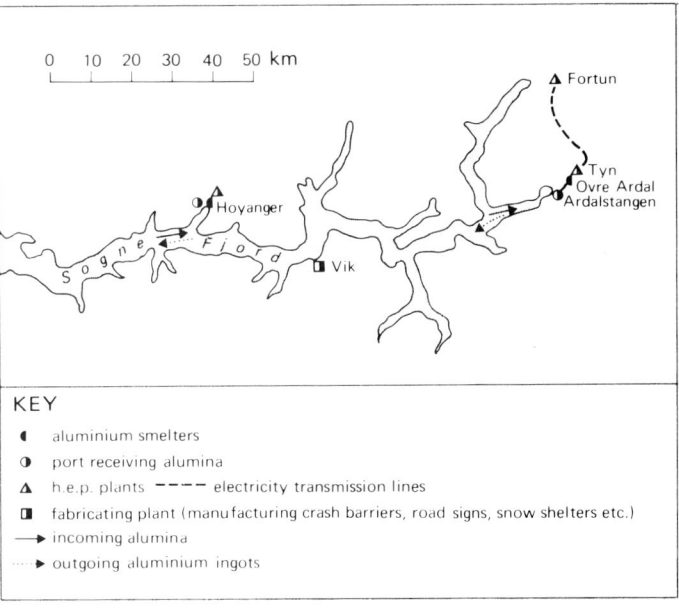

Figure 11.9 Aluminium smelting in the Sogne region of Norway

Figure 11.10 (*above*) The aluminium works at Årdalstangen; the smelter at Ovre Årdal is further along the valley

Figure 11.11 (*right*) Aluminium ingots awaiting dispatch at Årdalstangen

being imposed upon the newly-opened smelters at Karmöy Island near Stavanger (1967) and Lista (1971).

The bulk of Norwegian production is exported to other West European countries in the form of aluminium ingots; less than 10% of the total production is retained in Norway. Aluminium retained is mostly used in the Oslo area, and manufactured into a variety of engineering and domestic products for the home market. The small size of this industry is due to the following three factors.

1   With a population of 4 million, the Norwegian home market is small, and discourages manufacturers from establishing consumer industries on a large scale.

2   The cost of transporting consumer products to the centres of population in Europe.

3   The high tariffs applied to these products entering the EEC area.

It is clear that the Norwegian industry has developed to supply the West European industrial market. However, as new smelters are built and increasing amounts of aluminium are re-cycled from scrap, this traditional outlet for Norwegian metals will become increasingly competitive. New markets further afield are now being developed; in 1973 23% of the total production was exported to countries outside the EEC (9), including 25,000 tonnes to China.

Non-Ferrous Metal Industries

The supply of non-ferrous metals to the engineering and electrical industries of Western Europe is met chiefly by imports from abroad. The European ores are insufficient and large quantities of copper, lead, zinc, nickel and tin are imported. The metals are either imported in refined or partly-refined form, and are usually smelted and processed into alloys near the port of entry. The principal centres of the non-ferrous metal industry are Antwerp, Hamburg and the Ruhr region, while smaller developments exist at most major ports. Other centres of importance are located in the non-ferrous mining districts at Boliden (Sweden), Córdoba (Spain) and Brixlegg (Austria). In addition to being located at ports within easy reach of the factories requiring the metal and near mines, small refining units have been established in the mountain areas of Europe to smelt the metal electrolytically at sites where hydro-electricity can be provided cheaply. The plants producing ferro-alloys at Kristiansand, Heroya and Odda in Norway, in the Bergslag area of central Sweden, and in the Trento-Adige region of northern Italy illustrate this location.

The supply of ores for smelting are obtained from a wide variety of sources, but there is concern that the world's reserves of some metals are approaching exhaustion. In an attempt to maintain a reliable supply of ore many European companies have negotiated contracts with mining companies which guarantee supplies for periods of 10, 15 or 20 years. This approach has become particularly necessary to ensure supplies of lead and zinc, as some producing countries have developed their own refining plants and prefer to sell metal rather than ore.

As resources have become scarce, the importance given to the recovery and re-cycling of scrap copper, lead, zinc and other valuable metals has increased. Belgium has one of the largest non-ferrous metal smelting industries in Europe, and approximately one third of the output is from re-cycled materials. The industry is centred upon Antwerp and the refined metals and alloys are distributed among a variety of electrical and engineering industries in Belgium and the other EEC countries.

A further problem which the industry is having to contend with is the disposal of toxic waste from the metal smelters. Attempts are being made to prohibit the uncontrolled dumping of waste in rivers and offshore waters, and some progress is being made here as water, fishery and conservationist organizations begin to work together. In addition to finding alternative means for disposing of solids, the quantity of pollutants discharged into the atmosphere can be reduced if refineries are designed to include this factor.

Questions

1. With reference to Figs. 11.1 and 11.3 describe and explain the recent changes which have occurred in the West European steel industry.

2. (a) Describe the location of the aluminium smelting industry in Western Europe.
(b) Name *two* important producers of aluminium. What factors have influenced the siting of smelters in these countries?
(c) Name *three* countries exporting bauxite to Western Europe.

3. (a) Antwerp and Hamburg are important centres for non-ferrous metal smelting; suggest reasons for this development.
(b) On page 115 several countries are listed as main suppliers of non-ferrous metal ores. For each, name *one* European country with which it has particularly close cultural and trade links.

4. (a) With reference to Fig. 11.4(a) and Fig. 11.5, draw an outline plan of the dock area and on it label the site of each of the following features (using the initial letters indicated):

blast furnaces (F), ore stockpiles (O), oil storage tanks (T), a thermal power station (P), a mobile dock crane (C), a conveyor system (S).
(*b*) Give reasons to account for Dunkirk's importance as a steel-producing centre.

5. (*a*) On an outline map of the world, mark and name the countries and mining areas supplying the Dunkirk steelworks with iron ore.
(*b*) Draw a bar graph showing the proportions supplied by each country (see page 122).

12　The engineering industries

After the Industrial Revolution, most manufacturing industry developed near to the major coalfields, which supplied both a source of power and, in the case of chemicals, a raw material. The provision of alternative sources of energy and the construction of an efficient network of road, rail and water communications has enabled the manufacturing industries to disperse and develop in locations away from the coalfields. The locational pattern in Western Europe today illustrates both of these influences. The coalfield industries, often when coal itself has ceased to be significant, remain important because of the large investment in factory plant and the nearness to an area of dense population, which provides both a labour force and a market for the goods produced. The dispersal of industry from the coalfields has focussed upon areas which have alternative sources of power available, such as the Rhône valley, northern Italy and central Switzerland, and to the major centres of population growth well-served by communications—notably the capital cities and principal ports. Intermediate locations between the coalfields and the major centres of population has brought industry to many small towns and villages lying near important communication routes.

Engineering is the industry which deals with the final stages in metal manufacture, and access to steel and other raw materials is important in its location. Individual industries are usually concerned with either the mass production of particular components or the assembly of these components into various types of machines. Location near to associated industries and services has frequently caused growth in areas which would appear to have few specific advantages for industry. Developments in the small towns of Bavaria illustrate this process.

A branch of engineering fundamental to all others is the machine-tool industry, which provides the reliable, accurate machines designed to mass-produce the many engineering components. The industry uses only relatively small amounts of top quality steel but requires a high level of technical skill. It has tended to remain located in the old established steel and engineering areas like the Ruhr, where machinery and equipment are manufactured for every industry. The manufacture of heavy engineering goods, such as bridges, cranes and mining equipment, is also found principally in the established metal-working centres of the Ruhr, Sambre-Meuse, Luxembourg and Lorraine areas. This location reflects the need of the industry to be within easy reach of a plentiful supply of steel, which is both difficult and expensive to transport overland. Other branches of the engineering industry, particularly those concerned with high-value consumer goods, are less confined to a location near to the steel plants. The motor vehicle, electrical engineering and precision engineering industries are widely dispersed but stay within reach of markets; at the same time being conveniently placed to receive a reliable supply of components and raw materials.

One of the most rapidly growing sectors of the engineering industry is that concerned with the manufacture of electrical equipment, ranging from large items such as generators, electric motors and switchgear, to domestic appliances, radios, televisions, telecommunication equipment and computers. The manufacture of heavy electrical equipment has tended to develop from engineering and is located in metal working areas such as the Ruhr, where Mulheim is a particular centre. Factories producing light electrical appliances are at Eindhoven (Netherlands), Stuttgart, Nürnberg, Milan, Stockholm and Paris.

The importance of the engineering industry, in all its forms, to the economy of Western Europe cannot be over-estimated. It is the variety of the engineering products that has enabled the economy to develop to its present level, and allowed the population to enjoy a high standard of living. Engineering products form the cornerstone of West European export trade, no other single industry approaching it for value of goods exported.

The Shipbuilding Industry

In Western Europe the shipbuilding industry is in relative decline; the following statistics of merchant shipping tonnage launched by the major shipbuilding countries show only a modest rate of increase.

Merchant shipping tonnage launched (in ,000 tonnes)		
	1964	1973
Denmark	242	920
France	510	1134
Italy	368	754
Japan	4085	15673
Netherlands	226	896
Norway	409	1071
Spain	217	1568
Sweden	1021	2517
West Germany	890	1980
Total for world	10,264	31,520

Although the overall tonnage launched in the period 1964–73 has doubled, this has been at a time when world output has trebled; and Western Europe's share of world shipbuilding has slumped from 48% in 1964 to 36% in 1973. There has also been a decline in the number of ships built, and the increased tonnage launched reflects the emphasis upon the large bulk carrier for ore, grain, oil and gas. Bulk carriers of up to 100,000 tonnes can enter most of the major West European ports, but crude oil tankers of up to 470,000-tonnes capacity have been built for offshore unloading.

The other area of specialist development has been the vessel designed for carrying standard-sized containers for transfer to road, rail and waterway systems. By using standard $13 \times 2 \cdot 5 \times 2 \cdot 5$ m containers, a dock berth can handle up to twenty times more freight and reduce costs by 50%. The saving in time enables one vessel to do the work of several conventional cargo ships. The introduction of the large bulk carrier and the container ship at a time of rising construction costs has meant an overall reduction in the number of ships required from the shipyards of the world. In competing for this shrinking market, governments have attempted to protect their industry by giving financial assistance to companies refitting their yards to build the larger vessels now required. Additionally, the decline in crude oil traffic resulting from the 1973/4 price increases, has brought about cancellations and reduced orders for supertankers from the shipyards.

The industry is now so widely subsidized that its survival in some areas, such as Clydeside in the UK and Hamburg and Kiel in West Germany, can only be attributed to this policy. The giving of subsidies has distorted the recent development of the industry in Western Europe, but it is noticeable that there has been growth in the less heavily industrialized countries, particularly Sweden, Spain, Italy and Denmark. The marked expansion in

Figure 12.1 Prefabricated bow section being added to vessel in Naples shipyard

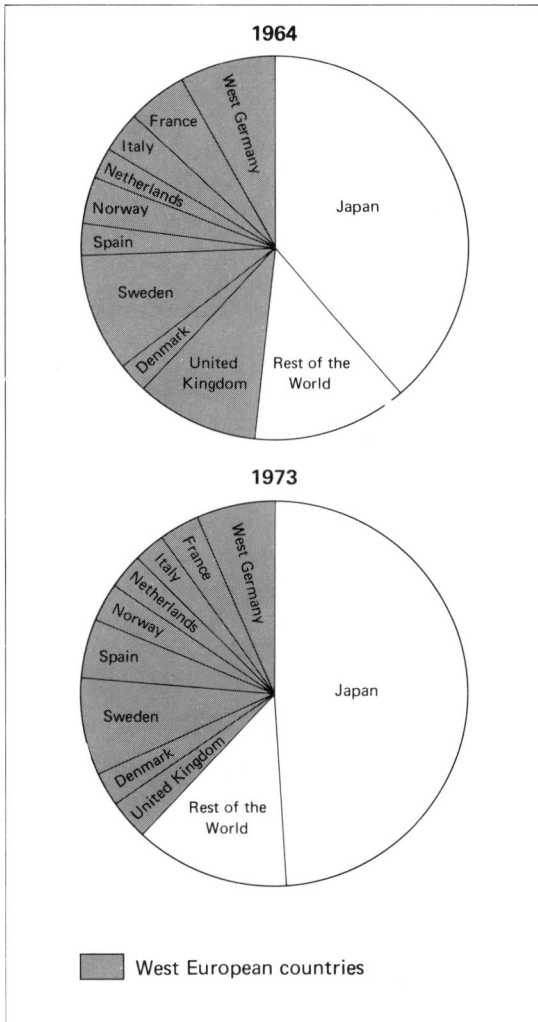

Figure 12.2 The relative importance of the world's major shipbuilding nations in 1964 and 1973

helped to keep the industry alive. Among techniques developed in Japan and the USA are (1) the construction of the stern section first to enable the fitting-out of this section to take place while the remainder of the ship is being built, (2) the construction of bow, stern and superstructure sections at adjacent yards, being brought together for assembly and (3) covered yards where construction is not delayed by bad weather.

The principal factors in the location of the shipyards of Western Europe are as follows:

1 a sheltered deep-water site suitable for launching and trials;

2 a gently-sloping shore for the slipways and shipyard plant; the construction of large tankers has usually required extensive dredging operations;

3 a nearby or cheaply accessible supply of steel and engineering and electrical components, brought to the yard for assembly;

4 a plentiful supply of labour, including a pool of skilled design and engineering staff;

5 a potential local demand for ships—hence, shipyards are often located near major cargo ports, where many shipping companies are to be found.

Shipbuilding is an industry which requires a large labour force, and as labour is scarce and therefore costly in Western Europe, the expanding centres of the industry have tended to be in areas where there is a labour surplus. The dominance of Japan and the expansion in southern Europe in the period 1950–70 was chiefly the result of lower labour costs, but this advantage has gradually disappeared as wages have risen, and now the most attractive areas for the future are Spain, Greece and Yugoslavia, and possibly Singapore and Hong Kong. The industry seems only likely to survive in the industrialized countries of Western Europe with further State aid to compensate for high production costs. Such aid should not be directed just towards maintaining existing plant but to new plant designed for greater efficiency and output to meet current shipping demands.

The Italian Ship-Building Industry

Although not the largest shipbuilding nation in Western Europe, the tonnage launched from Italian yards rose from 368,000 tonnes to 754,000 tonnes in the period 1964–73. In 1956 shipbuilding joined several public

southern Europe at Bilbao, Cadiz and El Ferrol in Spain, and at Genoa, Naples and Monfalcone in Italy shows the advantage of lower labour costs in these areas. However, in spite of the growth of the industry in the south there are several important yards in northern Europe, notably Hamburg, Kiel, Rotterdam, St Nazaire, Goteborg and Odense. The demand for drilling rigs and production platforms for the North Sea gas and oil fields has provided an important new market, while the combined efforts of companies amalgamating into larger units and concentrating upon improved design and construction methods has

Figure 12.3 The major centres of shipbuilding and steel manufacture in Italy

Figure 12.4 A supertanker under construction at Monfalcone

industries, such as gas, oil and electricity, to come under State control as part of the Institute for Industrial Reconstruction (IRI). The degree of State control and financial aid varies between shipbuilding companies, but most of the larger ones are virtually State enterprises, comparable with the nationalized coal, steel and power industries in Britain. The influence of the State can be seen in the steel and shipbuilding developments at Taranto and Naples, which are growth centres for the economic improvement of southern Italy.

State involvement in developing industry in the economically depressed south has been necessary as national wage agreements have removed the potential advantage of the area's cheaper labour. Therefore the development of

industry must be considered as part of a deliberate government policy to raise living standards in the region. Developments like the massive integrated steel plant at Taranto, now the largest in Italy, have been called 'cathedrals in a desert', for the highly-paid steel workers live in an area of rural poverty.

A factor important in the success of the Japanese industry has been the close link established between steel producer and shipbuilder, and large corporations like Mitsubishi own both steel works and shipyards. In Italy a similar advantage is apparent, as both industries are under state control, and the Naples, Livorno/Piombino and Genoa sites are located close to steel supplies (see Fig. 12.3). Together with the Venice/Monfalcone area, these shipbuilding centres will provide the basis for the industry in the future.

The Motor Vehicle Industry

In the past fifty years the manufacture of motor vehicles has grown from a small workshop industry producing powered carriages and cycles to become one of the most important branches of engineering in Western Europe. The demand for vehicles in Europe and abroad has continued to grow, and production and assembly is widely distributed (see Fig. 12.5). The rapid growth of the industry has favoured the large firms with the finances available to expand their factories and so production in Europe is dominated by a few companies. The major European manufacturers are Volkswagen, Daimler-Benz, Renault and Fiat, together with the American-controlled Ford, General Motors (Opel) and Chrysler (Simca) groups.

The growth of the industry in Western Europe is chiefly due to the influence exerted by the following factors.

1 The development of a successful motor vehicle by *pioneers in the industry*, such as Karl Benz at Stuttgart and Louis Renault at Paris, provided the basis upon which the modern industry at these cities has been built.

2 The advanced *metal-working* and *engineering industries* in Europe were able to supply the mass-produced components for the rapid assembly of vehicles. It is a feature of the location of the industry that its centres have remained near or accessible to supplies of steel body pressings and engineering components.

3 The motor vehicle plant, with its extensive assembly tracks and workshops, requires *large, flat sites*. Each stage in the growth of a company has been marked by new developments beyond the original parent factory. The larger firms now build vehicles at a number of separate factories. For example, Daimler-Benz now only produces engines at Stuttgart; cars are manufactured at Böblingen, 20 kilometres west of Stuttgart; buses at Mannheim and commercial vehicles at Karlsrûhe.

4 The industry, although using a lot of machinery, is one which employs a *large labour force*. The construction of a vehicle is a complex process, only part of which has been fully automated. The need for a large labour force has directed the industry to well populated areas, as illustrated by the recently built plants at Bochum (Ruhr region) and Genk (Belgium) where a labour force, displaced by closures in mining and heavy industry, was available.

5 The availability of an efficient road, rail or waterway system for the *rapid transit of new vehicles* to the main centres of distribution and to ports for export. The rivers Rhine and Seine are both used for the transport of vehicles on long, flat-decked barges; specially designed rail wagons can carry over 300 vehicles per train, and the European motorway network allows the extensive use of large vehicle transporters.

The Volkswagen (VW) Motor Vehicle Plant at Wolfsburg

The construction of the VW plant was begun in 1938 at Wolfsburg in an agricultural area with no tradition in engineering. It was a project planned and financed by the state to produce a 'people's car' (Volkswagen), at a location that was relatively central in Germany and alongside the Berlin–Hanover rail line and the Mittelland Canal. Situated on the edge of the North European Plain near the poor farming country of the sandy geest, the new town offered the industrial jobs and opportunities the region lacked. The population of Wolfsburg is approximately 100,000, and in 1972 the VW factory was employing 59,000 people. The rapid post-war growth of the car industry, and Wolfsburg's position only 20 km from the East German border, has attracted many refugees from eastern Europe into the town. The social and welfare services, including the provision of accommodation, organized by the company in the attractive open site of Wolfsburg, have also brought in workers from many parts of the EEC, particularly Italy, and further afield. The recession, which began in 1974, in the car industry has brought about a reduction in the workforce at VW. Until industries which are unrelated to car production are introduced, the fortunes of Wolfsburg and VW will remain inseparable.

The factory is sited on the level surface, between the river Aller and the Mittelland canal. It extends for 1·5 km alongside the canal and occupies 2 ha of land on the north side, while the town of Wolfsburg is built on rising land to the south. The separation of town and factory has enabled the latter to expand as one unit without the difficulties that have arisen at motor vehicle plants in confined urban sites, like those at Stuttgart and Paris. Many employees travel to work by car, and vast areas of land to the north of the factory and along the south bank of the canal are laid out as car parks. The canal is crossed by a dual carriageway bridge

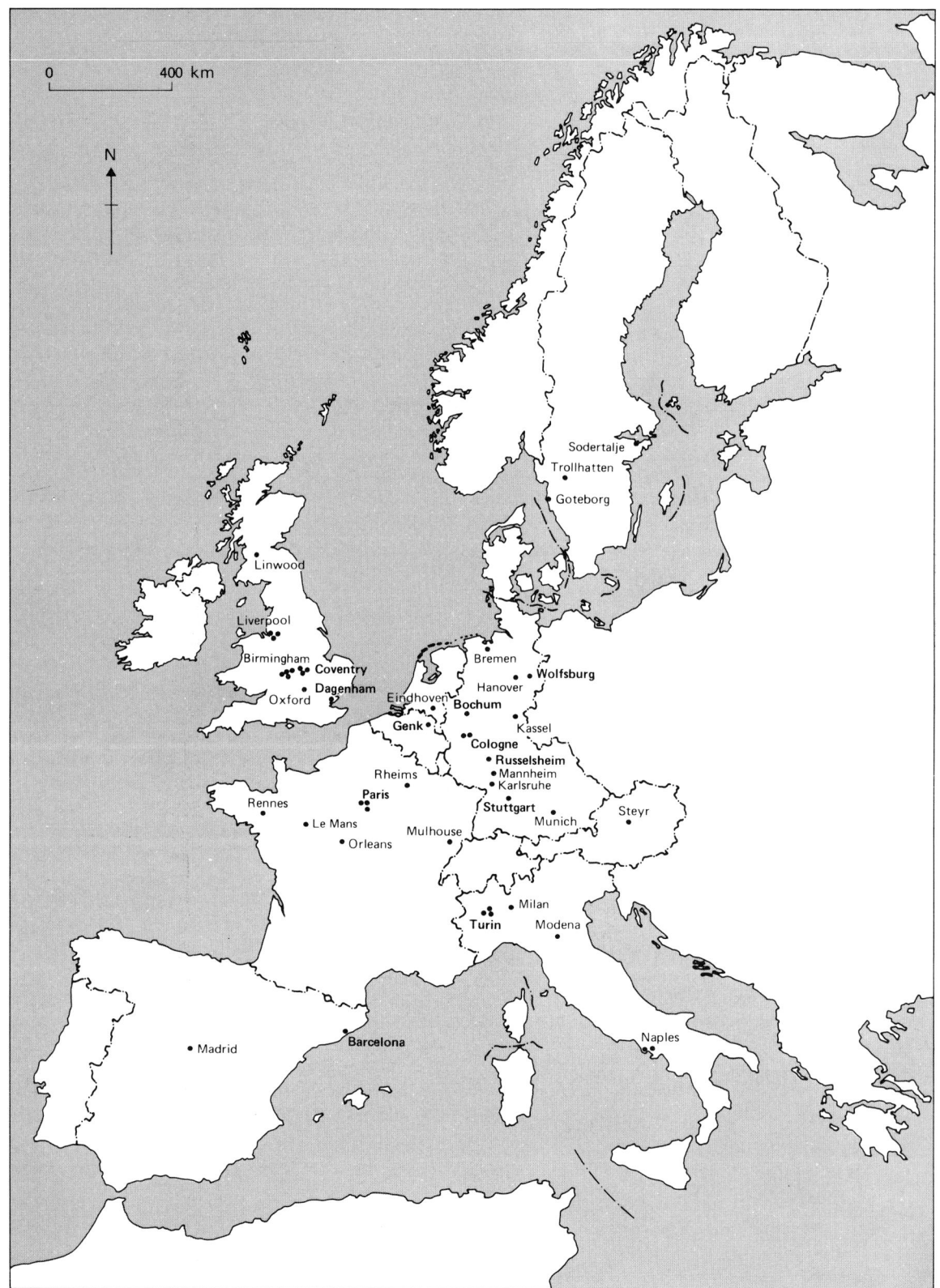

400 km

N

Linwood

Liverpool

Birmingham

Coventry

Dagenham

Oxford

Eindhoven

Bochum

Genk

Bremen

Wolfsburg

Hanover

Kassel

Cologne

Russelsheim

Mannheim

Karlsruhe

Rheims

Paris

Le Mans

Orleans

Mulhouse

Stuttgart

Munich

Steyr

Rennes

Milan

Turin

Modena

Madrid

Barcelona

Naples

Sodertalje

Trollhatten

Goteborg

and two pedestrian tunnels to give access to the factory from the south.

At Wolfsburg there has always existed a close planning relationship between the town authorities and the VW management. This has been possible as the Federal and State government planned and financed the growth of the town; at present they are the principal shareholders (40%) in the VW company.

The development and success of the Wolfsburg enterprise has been almost entirely built around the production of one car, the Beetle. The first cars of this design were built in 1937 from a design by Ferdinand Porsche, but because of the wartime disruption and destruction, only 25,000 had been built by 1948. From then on, production, particularly for export, was greatly increased, and by February 1972 over 15 million Beetles had been built, replacing the Model T Ford as the most popular car. To meet the demand for this and other vehicles the Wolfsburg factory had to be extended several times, and new assembly lines were opened at Hanover in 1956, Emden in 1964 and Salzgitter in 1970. In addition, large, specialist component factories have been built at Kassel and Braunschweig. The VW organization has also expanded to include the Audi plant at Ingolstadt, NSU at Neckarsulm and Porsche at Stuttgart.

The management of the VW organization is centred at Wolfsburg, the main producing unit with important communication links. To achieve an efficient movement of raw materials and components between the various VW factories and their suppliers, and for the distribution of the finished vehicles, great reliance is placed upon the Federal railway network. Road transport is only used for the movement of small quantities of goods, while the Mittelland Canal

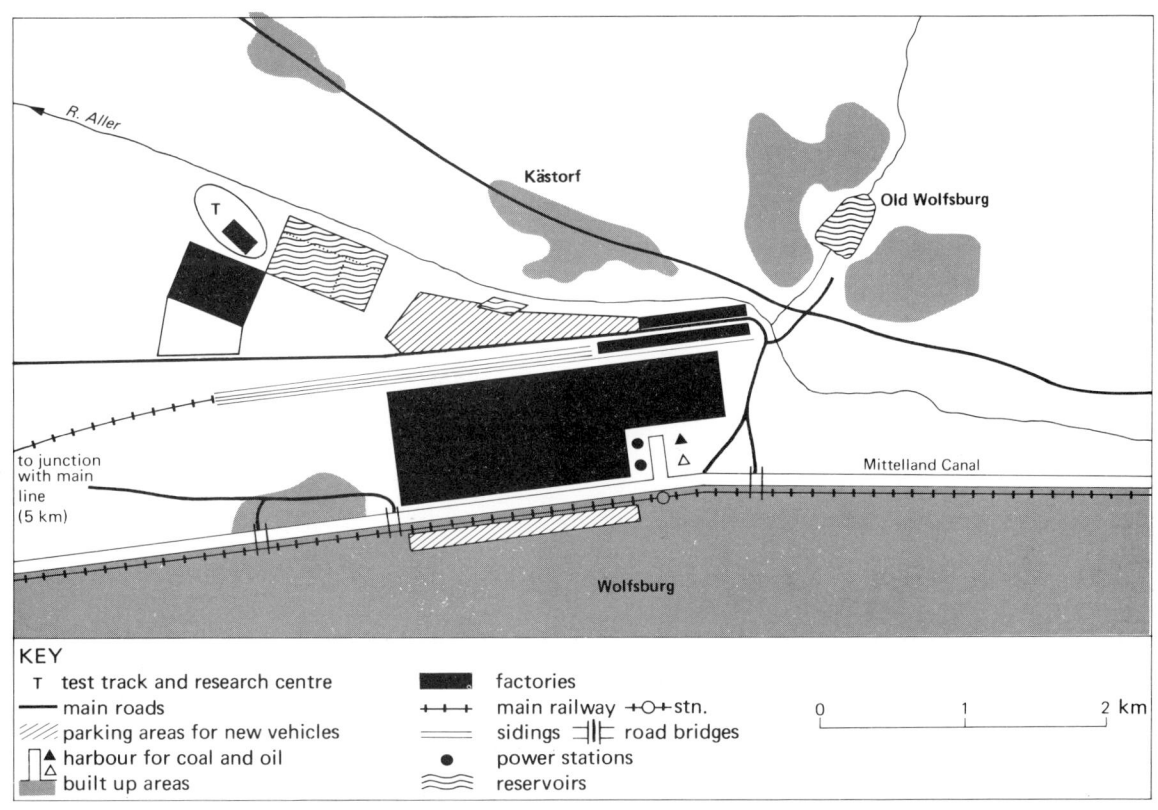

KEY

T test track and research centre	▬ factories
— main roads	+-+-+ main railway +○+ stn.
▨ parking areas for new vehicles	══ sidings ⊐‖⊏ road bridges
harbour for coal and oil	● power stations
▮ built up areas	∿ reservoirs

0   1   2 km

Figure 12.6 A plan of the site of the Volkswagen factory at Wolfsburg

135

Figure 12.7 The Volkswagen motor-vehicle factory at Wolfsburg

is chiefly used to carry coal and fuel oil to the twin thermal-power stations which serve Wolfsburg's needs. The railways carry coils of steel sheet from the Ruhr, engines from Hanover, transmission units from Kassel, and axles from Braunschweig into the Wolfsburg sidings, and carry out up to 300 new vehicles per train in specially designed double-deck freight wagons.

In recent years over 1 million cars have been exported each year by Volkswagen, the major overseas movements being from the following ports:

Destination	Ports used
North America	Emden, Bremen, Hamburg
United Kingdom and Ireland	Emden, Antwerp, Ghent
Scandinavia	Lubeck

The modern cargo vessels can each transport up to 3000 cars. On the North American service, the ships are usually converted into bulk carriers for coal, ore or grain by the removal of their car decks for the return journey. Where there is a land link, car export into European countries is almost entirely by rail.

The Aircraft Industry

The aircraft industry is widely distributed in Western Europe, but only in France is it on a large scale, employing over 100,000 people. As in the motor vehicle industry, the small manufacturer has found competition intense, and the individual producing unit is continually being enlarged as a result of amalgamations and co-operative ventures. The industry has considerable state support with research projects and contracts for military aircraft, which often provide the basis for civil aircraft developments.

The close relationship with the motor vehicle industry arises because both industries are dependant on the same sources for engines and machine components. Turin, Paris, Bremen and Munich are among the towns important for both aircraft and motor vehicle production. The more widespread distribution of the aircraft industry is an indication of the absence of any dominating locational factor. Aircraft sell for such high prices that the costs involved in transport of raw materials, components and the finished products appear insignificant in overall production costs; the availability of a suitable site and sufficient labour are more important considerations. The following factors help to explain the development of the aircraft industry in Western Europe.

1 The industry in West Germany, France and Italy was stimulated by the Second World War, but the extensive destruction of airfields and factories gave the industry a poor base to build upon in the post-war years. Controls on aircraft production in West Germany and Italy further delayed the industry's recovery, but in France the industry has regained much of its earlier prestige.

2 The demand for aircraft since 1950 has been very great, particularly to service the trans-Atlantic routes where there are close cultural and commercial links with Europe. The aircraft industry of the USA has benefitted most from this increased demand, but the growing European industry has provided many aircraft for short- and medium-distance routes.

3 The pre-war aircraft factories were small, but the demand for larger, more technically complex aircraft has forced many to merge into large companies, like the French Aerospatiale, which operate a number of plants producing components for assembly at specific sites. International co-operation to spread the development costs of new aircraft has currently been established between British and continental firms in the following projects: the Concorde Supersonic Airliner (BAC and Aerospatiale), the Jaguar military strike aircraft (BAC and Breguet) and the A300B Airbus (Hawker-Siddeley, Aerospatiale, Fokker and Deutsche Airbus). In addition, several

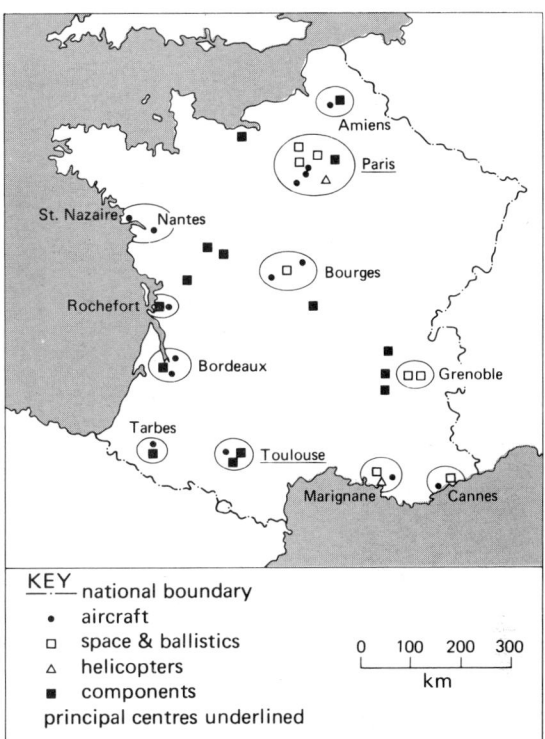

Figure 12.8 The distribution of the aircraft and space (Aerospace) industry in France

military aircraft of American design are built under license for European airforces in West Germany, Belgium and the Netherlands.

4 As proximity to sources of raw materials and components is not an over-riding consideration, other factors often determine particular locations. In West Germany and France wartime military aircraft factories were dispersed to relatively remote districts where there was less danger of air raids; like the Augsburg factory, some have remained at these locations. Aircraft assembly plants located in Bavaria and southern France benefit from the drier, less cloudy conditions, enabling aircraft to be tested throughout the year. In both of these areas industrial development has been recent, and large open sites, like that at Marignane near Marseilles, have been available for aircraft construction. The need for a skilled labour force in an industry which does not lend itself to mass production means that the larger factories keep to areas where a work force can be recruited, although key workers are often drawn from further afield.

137

Figure 12.9 The St Martin aircraft factory near Toulouse where the French Concorde is assembled

5 Research and development costs of new aircraft are high, and most companies receive some government aid in financing new projects. In return, governments exert considerable influence in deciding the location of new aircraft plants.

Questions

1. Under the headings of: site and position, source of components, communications, markets, and labour supply, describe the development of the motor vehicle industry at either Turin or Paris. Illustrate your answer with a sketch map.

2. (*a*) Study Fig. 12.2 and describe the changes that have occurred in the world distribution of the shipbuilding industry.
(*b*) Choose (i) *one* country which has increased its share of new ships built in the world and (ii) *one* which has seen its share decline. Suggest reasons to explain the change that has occurred in each country.

3. With reference to Figs 12.6 and 12.7:
(*a*) describe the site of the Volkswagen motor vehicle plant;
(*b*) what evidence is there to suggest that most of the development has been (i) recent, and (ii) planned?

13 The manufacturing industries

Although metal working and engineering provide the principal forms of employment in most West European countries, there exists a variety of other manufacturing industries.

The chemical industry is closely related to the provision of a reliable supply of raw materials, and it is mainly located at the major ports and centres of heavy industry. Textiles are more widely distributed, having developed in many cases from a cottage industry, and the industry has remained important in rural locations in Switzerland, Bavaria and Alsace, while also being strongly represented in the densely populated areas. The food processing industry is principally located either in the main centres of population, where demand is strong and the communications systems are efficient, or at the major ports where the facilities for import, processing and distribution are available. The manufacture of cement and building materials is an important industry throughout the heavily built-up areas of Europe, where the renewal and construction of houses, factories and roads is continually taking place. Limestone for cement making, brick clays, sands and gravels are widely available in the sedimentary lowlands of central and southern Europe, where the major urban areas are situated.

The Chemical Industry

The chemical industry is concerned with separating raw materials into their various elements and regrouping them to form new products. The raw materials are called 'organic' if they have originated from animals and plants, and 'inorganic' if from mineral ores, air and water. Organic raw materials are chiefly coal, oil, wood and natural gas; the products these yield include petrol and diesel fuels, plastics, synthetic fibres and fertilizers. Inorganic raw materials, particularly limestone, pyrites and the salts of sodium, potash and nitrate from former dried-up lakes and seas, yield nitric and sulphuric acids and such alkalis as soda ash and caustic soda, for use in glass and soap making respectively.

The locations of the chemical industry are relatively diverse and concentrations are found (1) near a source of raw material (2) near areas where there is a large demand for chemicals (3) in areas where there is a cheap source of power and (4) at coastal sites where raw materials and finished products can be assembled and distributed in bulk.

1 *Near a source of raw material.* Organic chemicals were first produced in large quantities from the distillation of coal, and the industry is still well represented on the Ruhr and Franco-Belgian coalfields. This is in spite of an almost complete change-over to oil and natural gas as the main raw materials. The high cost of scrapping and resiting chemical plants, together with the importance of the local industrial and domestic demand, has caused the industry to remain at its original location, although the raw materials have changed. Other concentrations at sites where the raw material is produced are at Ravenna (natural gas), Delfzijl (salt) and Mulhouse (potash).

2 *In areas with a large demand.* The development of a network of crude oil pipelines has enabled refineries and petro-chemical plants to be established in areas where there is a large demand. The chemical plants, stretching from Duisburg to Bonn and from Frankfurt to Karlsrühe in the Rhine valley, at Feyzin in the Rhône valley, Klarentahl in the Saar and Milan in the North Italian Plain, show the wider location of the industry.

3 *At sites where there is a plentiful supply of power.* The coalfields originally provided the power for the chemical industry, and became important locations. Soda ash made from blending limestone and common salt, and caustic soda and chlorine produced from the separation of brine, relied on the power generated from coal. The cheap hydro-electric power sites in the Alps, the Pyrenees and south-west Norway attracted chemical industries using electrolytic separation. The manufacture of nitrates, by fixing nitrogen from air, is important at Rjukan in Norway and Chippis in Switzerland. Electric power, now widely available from grid networks, has reduced the importance of this type of site, except where the site is in a good position for receiving raw materials and distributing its finished goods.

4 *At sites served by bulk water transport facilities.* Until the advent of the oil and natural gas pipeline networks, a coastal or inland waterway site offered the most attractive location to the chemical industry. It explains the coastal location of the industries at Hamburg, Rotterdam and Le Havre for petro-chemicals based upon imported crude oil, and inland developments served by the deep Rhine waterway at Leverkusen, Ludwigshafen and Basle. In addition, such a site provides abundant water, which is equally important whether used as a raw material, a coolant or a convenient place for depositing soluble waste. These sites remain important today, although the inland ones are much less dependant upon water transport for their supplies of fuel and raw materials.

The West German Chemical Industry

West Germany is the leading West European producer of synthetic fertilizers, sulphuric

Figure 13.1 The Bayer chemical plant and synthetic-fibre factory at Dormagen, built alongside the Rhine waterway

acid, plastics, synthetic fibres, caustic soda, soda ash, chlorine and pharmaceutical products. The West German industry earns almost twice that of its nearest rival, France. In all European countries the industry is dominated by a few large companies which have grown as a result of amalgamations. Among the major companies are Bayer and Hoechst in West Germany, which are of equivalent size to ICI in the United Kingdom and Montedison in Italy.

The variety of factors which influence the location of the chemical industry can all be found in West Germany, and the present day pattern is of four main producing areas, two of which are closely connected with the densely populated Rhine Valley.

1 *The Ruhr–Rhine region.* The organic chemical industry developed to supply the large and expanding demand for chemicals in the region, and because of the availability of coal, both as a raw material and fuel. Today coal has been replaced by oil and natural gas, fed into the region by pipe-line. The principal refineries are on the river at Duisburg, Dinslaken and Wesseling and inland at Gelsenkirchen. Plastics, insecticides and synthetic fibres produced at Dormagen and synthetic rubber at Hüls are chiefly made from either natural gas or the residual products after the petroleum fuels have been distilled from the crude oil at the refineries. Many important acids, notably sulphuric acid, are obtained as bi-products of metal and oil refining at Duisburg, Essen and Gelsenkirchen. Brine from the salt domes of the Weser-Ems area is piped south to the Ruhr region, for use in the production of alkalis for glass, soap, detergent and dyestuffs manufacture. The Bayer factories at Leverkusen and Wuppertal were originally established to provide the dyestuffs for the textile industry of the region.

Although the Ruhr-Rhine region has come to rely increasingly on pipeline transport for crude oil and finished products, the Rhine waterway is still used for carrying some bulk raw materials, such as pyrites for sulphuric acid manufacture, and for distributing finished chemical products.

2 *The middle Rhine region.* The chemical industry of this region has not developed from local raw materials, but from the ability of the rivers Rhine and Main to provide bulk transport facilities to the docks at Frankfurt and

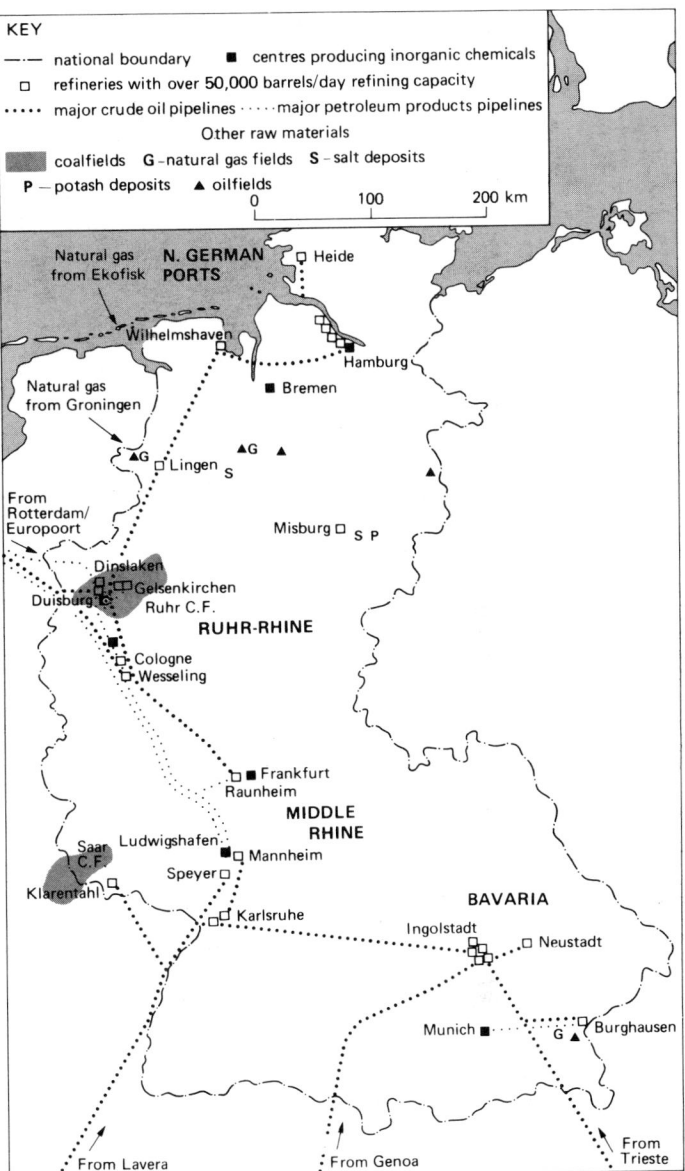

Figure 13.2 The centres of the West German chemical industry

Ludwigshafen/Mannheim, the growing local demand and the centrality of the location within Western Europe. Water transport has been partly replaced by the crude oil pipeline from Rotterdam to a site west of Frankfurt and from Lavera on the Mediterranean coast to Karlsruhe and Speyer. These refining centres produce a range of petrochemical products, many of which are distributed along the two products pipelines that

141

Figure 13.3 Barge traffic on the river Rhine, near Kaub

follow the Rhine valley. The most established chemical centre is Ludwigshafen, which has long been dominated by this one industry. Chemical works stretch for 6 km along the Rhine, producing fertilizers, dyestuffs, plastics and acids.

3 *The Bavarian region.* The industry owes its remarkable recent growth at Ingolstadt to the construction of the Trans-Alpine-Pipeline from Trieste. The choice of Ingolstadt was determined by the availability of a large, level site for the chemical plant, the growing demand from Bavarian industry for chemicals and the relatively central position of the area in Western Europe. In addition to the industry at Ingolstadt, the cheap hydro-electricity of the Alpine Foreland has been used for many years with limestone and Ruhr coal to produce carbide, nitrogenous fertilizers and insecticides at a number of small towns west of Munich; Burghausen being the largest. A branch from the TAP has been constructed to provide the raw material for the industry on a more economical basis, using oil as the raw material.

4 *The North Sea ports.* The estuaries of the rivers Elbe and Weser and Jade Bay offer good sites for the assembly of raw materials in bulk, and all have chemical developments. Before the oil pipeline network was built these sites, together with those along the river Rhine, provided the most economical siting for the industry. Refineries have been built at Hamburg, Bremen, Emden and Wilhelmshaven, the terminal for the North-West European Pipeline. At Hamburg the smelting of nonferrous metals, particularly copper, from imported ores is an important 'port' industry, and chemicals are produced from the biproducts of this process. Other raw materials, such as pyrites, timber and mineral salts, are imported into the region, and give the chemical industry a broad basis.

The general trend within the West European chemical industry is for the further development of petro-chemicals. The oil and natural gas discoveries in the North Sea are likely to stimulate further growth along the coastline at sites where the minerals can be brought ashore economically. In southern Europe the North African oil and gas resources are being increasingly utilized with the similar stimulus to the chemical industry of selected Spanish, French and Italian ports.

The Textile Industry

In Western Europe the industry is largely dependant upon imported natural fibres—wool, cotton, jute and silk—but produces its own synthetic fibres. Textile fibres are light in weight and have a high value, and can be economically transported over long distances to the factory. Raw wool is imported from Australia, Argentina and South Africa; raw cotton from the USA, Egypt, India and Peru; jute from India and Bangladesh and raw silk from the Far East.

The manufacture of yarn from these imports has tended to remain in a location near to a source of power. Producing centres in the lower Rhineland, Belgium and northern France are all near to coalfields, while those in northern Italy and south-west France rely upon hydro-electricity generated from mountain rivers. The most rapidly growing section of the industry is that of synthetic fibres, and its development has often been in areas not previously associated with textiles. As power is now widely available from the national electricity grids, the factors of labour supply, proximity to associated industries and services and access to markets have become more significant in the siting of textile factories. The large cities of Paris, Rome, Brussels, Vienna and Dusseldörf all have important luxury finishing industries, while the growth of the mass-produced cheaper products in Portugal, Spain and Italy reflects their labour surplus (particularly female) and lower production costs.

Figure 13.4 Textile mills and synthetic-fibre plants in the crowded narrow valley of the river Wupper at Wuppertal. With reference to the photograph:
(a) draw a simple contoured sketch map.
(b) Mark and label on the map: (i) the routes of four different forms of transport; (ii) the industrial areas; (iii) the residential areas, and (iv) the areas of open ground that are not built upon.
(c) Describe and account for the pattern of land use shown on the map you have drawn

The manufacture of the different types of textile shows a varying pattern in Western Europe. Production is no longer intended to meet essential clothing and household needs but to satisfy the customer's desire for change. In these circumstances the demand for textiles is less consistent than in the past, and it is the cheaper fabrics that have sold well. Cotton has been faced with severe competition from light synthetic fabrics and from massive imports of cotton goods from countries with lower production costs, notably Hong Kong, India and Portugal. The decline in the production of cotton goods has affected all the traditional producers in Western Europe. Woollen goods, although affected by the challenge from synthetic fibres, have retained their importance. The absence of large scale foreign imports into Western Europe from the Far East reflects the lack of local demand for woollen goods in this area of hot climates. In Western Europe the woollen, knitwear and clothing industries of Portugal, Spain and Italy have expanded at a more rapid rate than those in the north, where there is little surplus labour to keep production costs down. The production of the relatively expensive fabrics, linen and silk, have both shown a slow decline in most countries, while the output of coarse fabric from jute, sisal and hemp has maintained its position.

The factors which account for the distribution of the industry today can be summarized as follows.

1 *Location near a major source of power.* This factor helps to explain the industry at Wuppertal and Krefeld near the Ruhr coalfield, Roubaix and Verviers near the Franco-Belgian coalfield, and the textile towns of Switzerland, Austria and northern Italy, using hydro-electricity from the Alps.

2 *Location near a source of raw material.* The Flemish linen industry is still supplied with local flax; the Spanish textile towns of Leon and Burgos rely upon merino wool from the Meseta; while the production of synthetic fibres shows its heaviest concentration near some centres of the petro-chemical industry.

3 *Location near ports for the import of raw materials.* The cotton industry at Goteborg, Borås and Norrkoping in Sweden, at Rouen in France and Barcelona in Spain illustrate this factor.

4 *Location near important areas of demand.* Although this factor is of less significance than in industries not concerned with a light, high value product, the most densely populated areas all have important textile industries, notably the Rhine–Ruhr region, Flanders and northern Italy.

5 *Location near a supply of soft, unpolluted water.* Although this factor alone would be unlikely to determine the siting of a textile works, it is an important local consideration. Soft-water streams, like the Wupper off the Rhine Uplands and the Moselle off the Vosges, have been important local factors in the choice of mill sites at Wuppertal and Epinal respectively.

6 *Location near a plentiful source of labour.* Textile mills located in coalfield areas have the advantage of a power supply, a large local demand for textiles, the availabilty often of dyestuffs and bleaches and a plentiful supply of labour. The newer mills located in the Barcelona area and northern Italy have chosen sites where labour, particularly female machinists for knitwear, has been plentiful.

The Belgian Textile Industry

The industry in Flanders was first established in the thirteenth and fourteenth centuries, and an international trade in cloth developed using imported English wool. Ghent was the centre of the industry, and at this time was second only to Paris among European cities.

The major growth of the Belgian industry came with the Industrial Revolution and the introduction of linen and cotton manufacture to Flanders. Ghent became the most important cotton town, the ship canal to Terneuzen built in 1827 providing a route for the raw cotton imported from the USA to enter the region. Linen manufacture was centred upon Kortrijk and other small towns in the Lys and Scheldt valleys, where the raw flax was grown, and the soft river water could be used for 'retting'— the process of separating the fibres from the flax stalk. Woollen manufacture, once exclusive to Flanders, has developed in a new location near to the Liege coalfield, at Verviers. This pattern of cotton and linen in Flanders and wool at Verviers had developed by the mid-nineteenth century and still dominates the distribution of the industry today.

The Ghent area, with its concentration upon cotton textiles, providing half of the total Belgian output, has been particularly affected by the decline of the industry. Since 1957 the labour force in textiles has been greatly reduced and many small firms have closed. The remaining industry has been re-organized and modern machinery introduced. There is now relatively less dependence upon cotton, although it is still of major importance, and increasing numbers of textile mills using synthetic fibres have been established. Synthetic fibres* of the cellulose group (rayon) and non-cellulose group (nylon, terylene, orlon) are produced to be used separately or mixed with cotton.

The textile finishing industries are important in Ghent—clothing, carpets and furnishing fabrics being made. In addition the industry of the area has been given greater variety by the deepening of the ship canal to take vessels of up to 60,000 tonnes. This has led to the introduction of many new industries, including an oil refinery, a steelworks and a car assembly plant, and Ghent is now second only to Antwerp among Belgian ports.

The Verviers area is equally dominant in the manufacture of woollen goods, although it has fewer natural advantages than the flat, coastal site of Ghent. The town is built on the hill slopes of a narrow tributary valley of the river Ourthe, which joins the Meuse near Liege. The original reasons for the development of woollen textiles at Verviers were:

1 the local source of raw wool from the Ardennes;

2 power provided by water mills driven by the fast flowing river;

3 the water was soft and suitable for washing and dyeing cloth;

4 the restrictions imposed by the powerful cloth guilds in Flanders in the fifteenth century caused many weavers to move to new towns, and some settled at Verviers;

5 the railway linking Liege to Aachen (1844) gave the area the reliable connection it needed for its imported wool and an outlet for the finished woollen goods. The industry is also located in several small towns near Verviers, and a wide range of goods is produced.

* Cellulose fibres are produced from vegetable or animal materials (chiefly wood pulp). Non-cellulose fibres, polymers, are the bi-product of the chemical industry, being derived from coal, oil and natural gas.
The three types of non-cellulose fibre are:
(a) polyamide-nylon (b) acrilic-orlon (c) polyester-terylene.

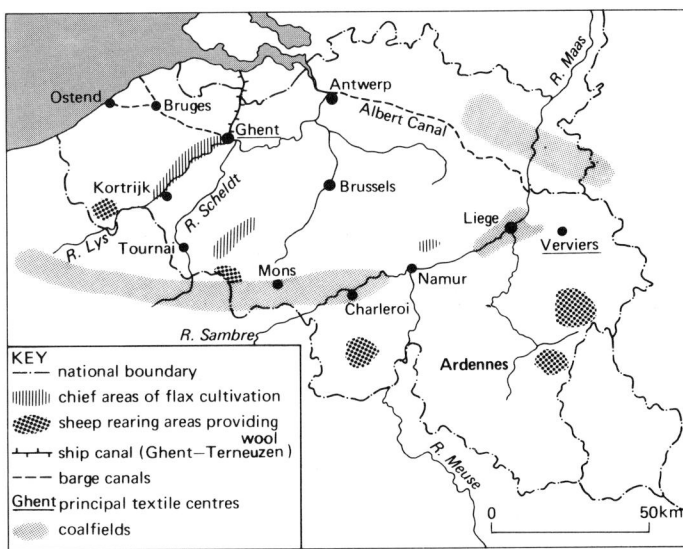

Figure 13.5 Factors which have influenced the location of the Belgian textile industry

The textile industry centred upon the towns of Ghent and Verviers is of considerable importance to the Belgian economy, and in 1973 textiles made up 7% of the total value of exports. Altogether, over half of the total Belgian production is exported, the principal markets being the other EEC countries (75%), and the USA. Exports are increasingly in the form of high quality finished goods rather than semi-finished cloth and yarn; in 1973 finished goods comprised approximately 75% of exports, compared with 43% in 1950.

Questions

1. What factors have favoured the development of (a) the chemical industry at Rotterdam and (b) the textile industry at Wuppertal?

2. Figs. 13.1 and 13.4 show synthetic fibre plants in contrasted locations. Using these photographs:
(a) describe the physical landscape and built-up area of Wuppertal and Dormagen.
(b) Which area do you consider the most economical producer of synthetic fibre? Explain your choice.

145

Production of textile yarns (,000 tonnes)						
	Cotton		Wool		Synthetic Polymers	
	1964	1973	1964	1973	1964	1973
Belgium	95	65	62	84	6	6
France	300	280	147	155	52	112
Italy	204	200	164	199	52	151
Netherlands	75	40	24	11	18	72
Portugal	74	84	14	16	1	0.9
West Germany	299	215	92	87	78	398

3. With reference to the table (left) answer the following questions.

(*a*) Which countries have shown a growth in the production of (i) cotton (ii) wool (iii) synthetic polymer yarns since 1964?

(*b*) Which countries have shown a decline in the production of (i) cotton, (ii) wool yarns since 1964?

(*c*) For which type of yarn has there been (i) the largest overall growth and (ii) the least overall growth in the period 1964–73?

(*d*) Choose *one* country as an example for each of the following, and explain the change in its output. (i) An increase in wool yarn production; (ii) a decline in cotton yarn production; (iii) an increase in synthetic polymer yarn production.

146

14 Communications

Water, rail, road and air transport all have important roles to play in Western Europe, and the demand is such that they are frequently in competition with each other, rather than combining in a single system. In Scandinavia there has had to be considerable integration between water, rail and road systems to provide a reliable service in this thinly populated region. In some cases government subsidies have influenced development, particularly in protecting railways against competition from road transport. For example, the state has subsidized rail freight rates to Hamburg in an attempt to direct traffic from south Germany to this port in compensation for the loss of east European traffic since 1948. The densest communication system follows the gentle surface of the North European Plain, with off-shoots extending inland along the major valleys. The Alpine ridges of southern Europe comprise the most difficult physical barrier, but are crossed by major communication lines at an increasing number of points as tunnels, bridges and viaducts are built through the mountain passes.

Figure 14.1 The Europa bridge near Innsbruck: a section of the motorway linking Italy and West Germany across the Alps

Figure 14.2 (*above*) Dunkirk: the container berth and roll-on/roll-off ferry

Figure 14.3 (*below*) The ferry berth at Rodby Havn. The motorway ends left of the berth and the railway terminal is in the centre (Denmark)

Sea Transport

The industries of Western Europe depend upon sea transport to provide a supply of raw materials from abroad and to export finished products. The peninsula structure, with numerous bays and arms of the sea, means that no part of Western Europe is further than 500 km from a seaport. Water transport is ideal for the bulk movement of non-perishable goods such as crude oil, mineral ores and timber, where the relatively slow speed of the journey is compensated for by low freight charges and regular delivery. For the movement of perishable foodstuffs, specialist refrigerated vessels are used for delivery to the ports for onward distribution by road and rail. The most significant recent development in sea transport, additional to the increase in the size of vessels, has been the introduction of specialist cargo ships for carrying standard-sized containers and of vessels with roll-on/roll-off facilities. The advantage of these techniques is a much quicker turn-round for the vessels in the docks, and a considerable saving in handling costs. Most of the major European ports now have modern container terminals with facilities for the rapid transfer of containers to railway flat-wagons or to road trailers. The roll-on/roll-off method of transport using loaded road trailers has the disadvantage of leaving the expensive trailer equipment idle during the sea journeys—mainly short sea crossings between the British Isles, Scandinavia and the North Sea ports.

The importance of sea transport to Western Europe can be judged from the size of the merchant shipping fleets of the various countries. Of a total gross world-shipping tonnage of 311 million tonnes in 1973, approximately 50% was registered in West European countries.

The West European ports with over 30 million tonnes of cargo passing through in 1973 were as follows: Rotterdam, Marseilles, Antwerp, Le Havre, Dunkirk, Hamburg, Genoa, Trieste and Augusta (Sicily). All of these ports are major importers of bulk raw materials, particularly crude oil. The harbour facilities built for the large tankers and bulk carriers have provided attractive conditions for vessels carrying other kinds of cargo, and these ports are also of major importance for the import of foodstuffs and industrial raw materials, and the export of manufactured

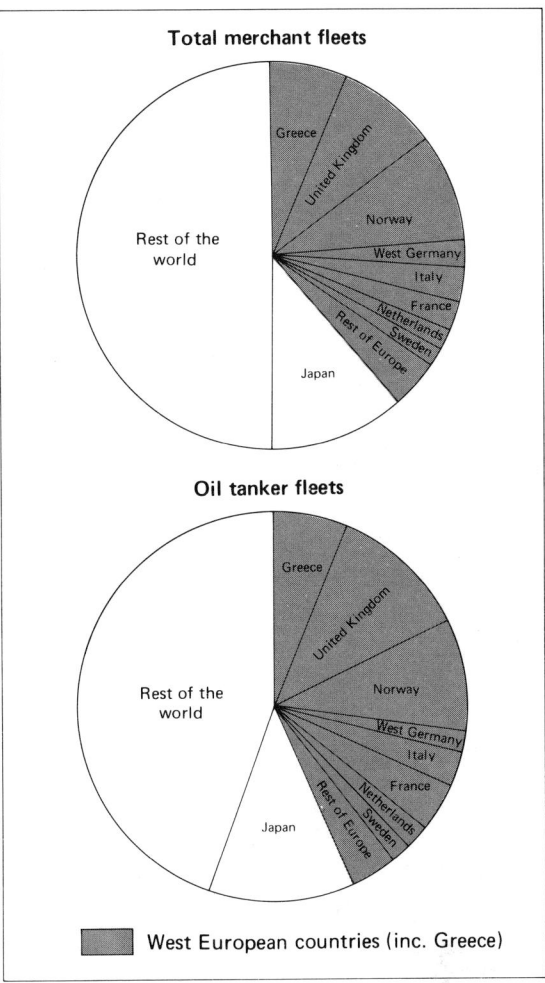

Figure 14.4 Composition of the world's merchant shipping fleet

goods. The location of the major seaports is around the North Sea/Channel coast, where shipping routes converge to serve the densely-populated areas of the North European Plain. An area of secondary importance includes the ports of the western Mediterranean—a developing industrial region.

Although the vast majority of Western Europe's seaborne traffic involves cargo movement, passenger services are important in some areas. The deeply-indented, steep coastline of Norway and the island nature of Denmark have both led to the development of regular, scheduled ferry services, connecting with road and rail timetables to provide an integrated Scandinavian transport system. In

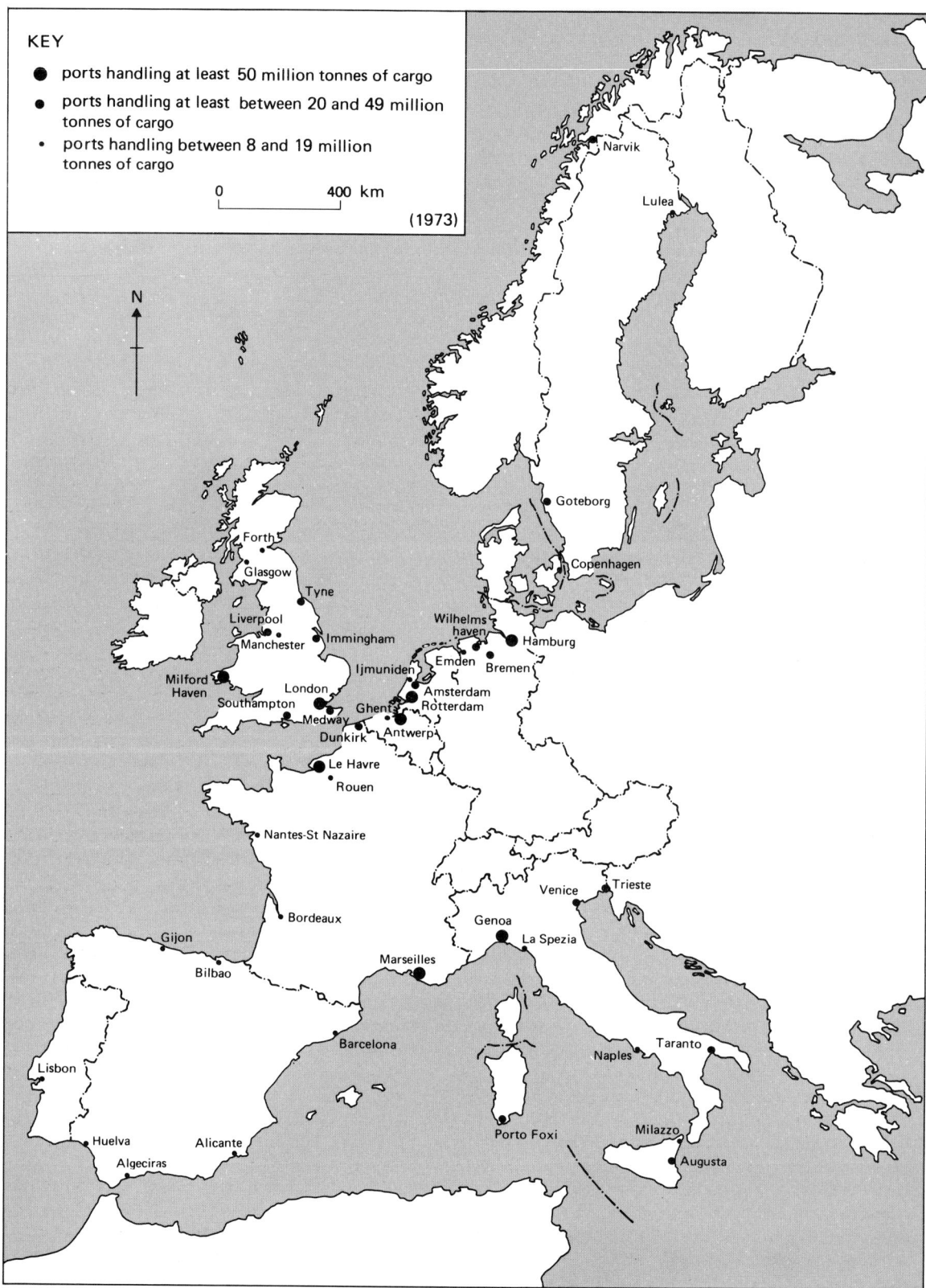

KEY

● ports handling at least 50 million tonnes of cargo

● ports handling at least between 20 and 49 million
   tonnes of cargo

· ports handling between 8 and 19 million
   tonnes of cargo

0   400 km

(1973)

N

Narvik

Lulea

Goteborg

Copenhagen

Forth

Glasgow

Tyne

Liverpool

Manchester

Immingham

Wilhelms
haven

Hamburg

Emden

Bremen

Milford
Haven

London

Ijmuniden

Southampton

Amsterdam
Rotterdam

Medway

Ghent

Dunkirk

Antwerp

Le Havre

Rouen

Nantes-St Nazaire

Venice

Trieste

Bordeaux

Genoa

La Spezia

Gijon

Marseilles

Bilbao

Barcelona

Naples

Taranto

Lisbon

Huelva

Alicante

Algeciras

Porto Foxi

Milazzo

Augusta

150

Figure 14.5 (*opposite*) Distribution of the major seaports

other parts of Europe the transport of passengers shows considerable seasonal variation, the movements across the North Sea and English Channel reaching a peak during the summer holiday season. The ports with the largest movement of passengers, over 2 million people passing through each year, are Naples, Ostend and Calais.

Inland Waterways

The rivers Seine, Rhine, Elbe and Danube provide important navigation routes, extending the bulk transport of raw materials long distances inland. Ports capable of handling seagoing vessels, such as Rouen, Paris, Duisburg and Basle, have developed far inland in continental Europe. The four major waterways are linked by canal systems, which are at present being improved to a miniumum standard in order to allow the passage of barges with a 1350 tonne capacity. A fifth major river, the Rhône, which in the past has never provided a reliable through-route, is being regularized by a series of navigation schemes designed to link with the Rhine and establish a route from the North Sea to the Mediterranean. As in Britain, Western Europe has many narrow, out-dated canals of limited commercial use, but of recreational value for sailing and holidays. Where these canals have a commercial future they are being deepened and widened to handle the standard 1350 tonne vessel; the Main-Danube canal is at present being rebuilt. The improvements have brought about a change in the inland waterway fleets—the number of vessels has fallen while their average size has increased from 385 tonnes in 1965 to 435 tonnes in 1974.

The traffic carried on inland waterways is wide ranging, but as with sea transport, the bulk movement of raw materials is the most economic and makes up most of the traffic. The transport of crude oil on the inland waterways has declined with the construction of pipeline networks, but the distribution of petro-chemical products from refineries frequently sited near waterways has remained important. The quantity of petroleum products carried on inland waterway tankers in West Germany has increased slightly in recent

years and approximately 40 million tonnes is carried each year. Coke, iron ore, limestone, pyrites and timber are examples of raw materials carried by water, while a range of manufactured goods and foodstuffs are often transported on specially designed barges, including ones for carrying containers. The inland waterways have always offered attractive sites for industry, where flat land, a water supply and raw materials were all readily available. Examples of important industrial areas on inland waterways are around Rouen on the Seine, Duisburg-Bonn on the Rhine, Lyons on the Rhône, and Linz on the Danube.

The great rivers of Europe all pass through a number of countries, linking those without a coastline, like Switzerland, Austria and Czechoslovakia, with the sea. No tariff barriers exist on European rivers and traffic passes freely between countries, the only artifical barrier to movement being between the free enterprise system of Western Europe and the state control of Eastern Europe. This particularly affects movement on the Elbe and Danube, where western shipping companies find it difficult to compete for traffic when virtually all cargo is reserved for the state controlled companies. The countries where the great rivers reach the sea have developed inland-waterway fleets to handle the goods carried on the rivers. The Dutch, Belgians and West German fleets carry a greater tonnage of goods destined for other countries than for internal customers. The Dutch fleet is the largest in Western Europe, being engaged in movements along the small canals within the Netherlands and along the Rhine waterway. Many of the vessels are under 250 tonnes capacity, contrasting with the larger vessels of the West German fleet, which is principally working deeper and wider waterways. The transfer of goods from ocean-going vessels or warehouses to inland-waterway vessels is called *lightering*, and Rotterdam, Antwerp and Le Havre are the principal ports engaged in this work.

The Rhine Waterway System
Navigation on the river Rhine extends 950 km upstream to Basle, where the river is 230 m above sea level. Although the river has always offered a valuable means of transport it was not until the mid-nineteenth century that

151

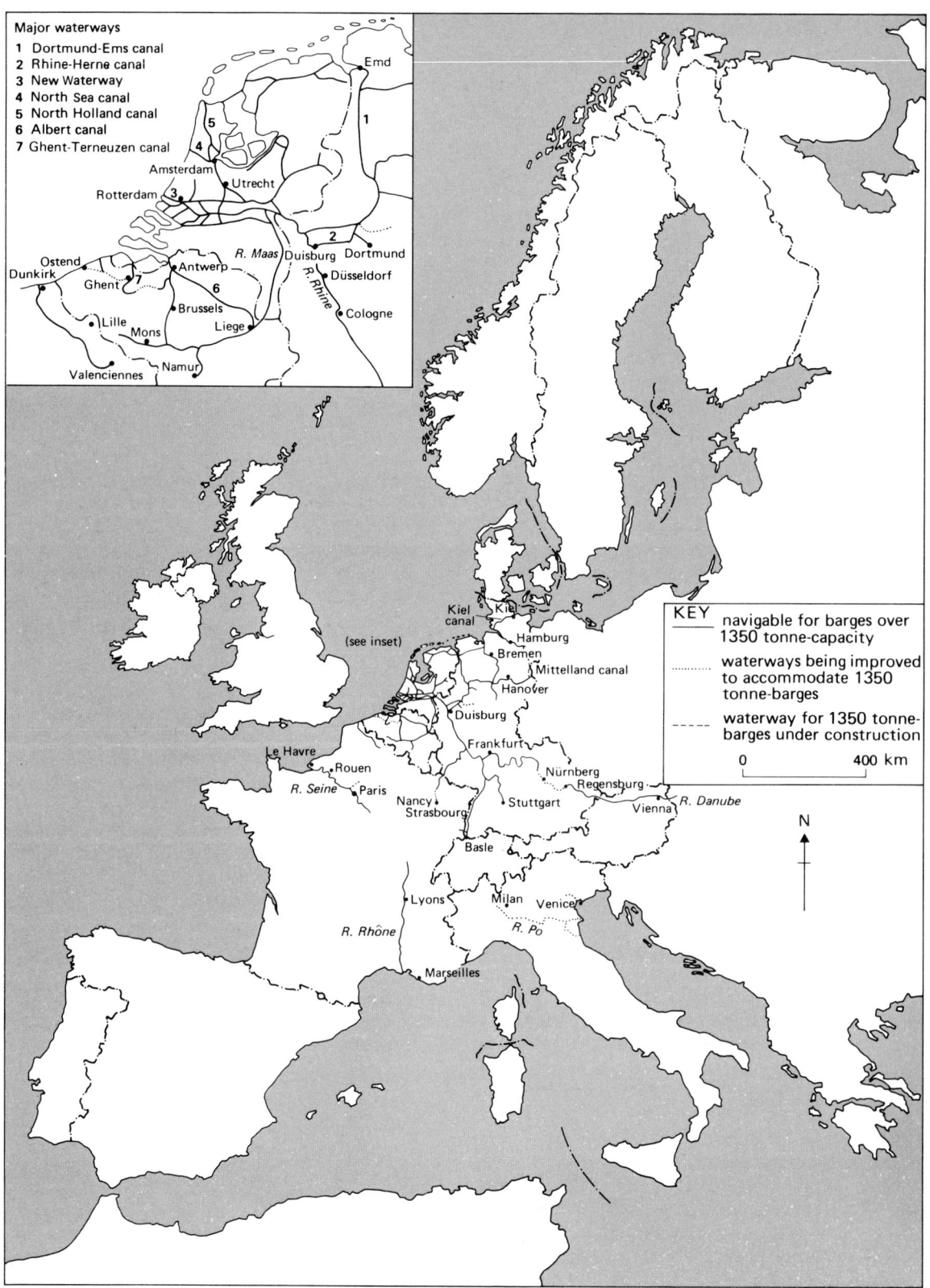

Major waterways
1 Dortmund-Ems canal
2 Rhine-Herne canal
3 New Waterway
4 North Sea canal
5 North Holland canal
6 Albert canal
7 Ghent-Terneuzen canal

Emd

5

4

1

Amsterdam

Utrecht

Rotterdam 3

Ostend

Dunkirk

Ghent 7

Antwerp

R. Maas

Duisburg Dortmund

2

Düsseldorf

R. Rhine

6

Cologne

Brussels

Lille

Mons

Liege

Valenciennes

Namur

Emd

Kiel canal Kiel

Hamburg

Bremen

Mittelland canal

Hanover

(see inset)

Duisburg

Frankfurt

Le Havre

Rouen

R. Seine Paris

Nancy

Strasbourg

Nürnberg

Regensburg

Stuttgart

Vienna R. Danube

Basle

Lyons

Milan

Venice

R. Rhône

R. Po

Marseilles

KEY
navigable for barges over 1350 tonne-capacity
.... waterways being improved to accommodate 1350 tonne-barges
– – – waterway for 1350 tonne-barges under construction
0   400 km

N

152

Figure 14.6 (*left*) Major waterways

Figure 14.7 (*right*) A comparison of the size of vessels of the inland waterway fleets of Belgium, France, West Germany and the Netherlands

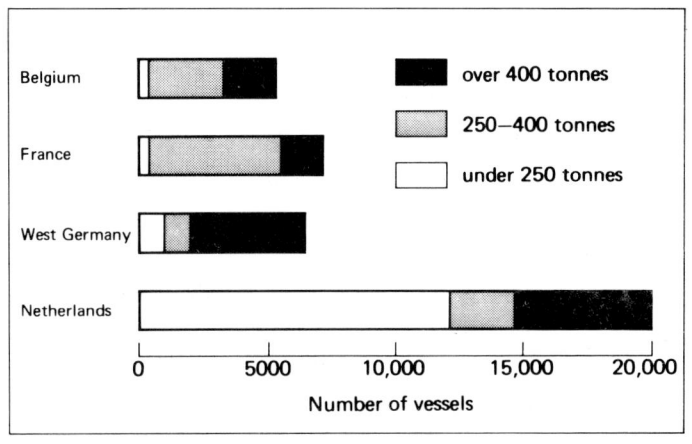

improvements were made to the channel to make the river navigable along its full length to Basle. The shallow rocky sections of the gorge where the river crosses resistant bands of quartzite were deepened by dynamiting, and the meandering, divided channels in the rift valley were straightened and embanked. The Grand Canal d'Alsace, begun in 1927 to bypass the difficult Strasbourg–Basle stretch, has enabled 2000-tonne barges to use this section of the river, while the dams regulating the navigation provide sites for hydro-electricity generation. The seasonal problem of ice flows, which normally affect the navigation for 12–16 days each year, fog and periodic low water in autumn and winter, are relatively minor difficulties on a river that is a wonderful natural asset to Western Europe The present importance of the waterway can be best judged by the volume of traffic moving past the town of Emmerich on the German/Dutch border. In 1973 this was 133 million tonnes, while the principal river ports of Duisburg, Strasbourg and Mannheim handled 44 million, 12 million and 10 million tonnes of traffic respectively.

The importance of the river in the past can be judged by the numerous castles commanding movement along the river, particularly in the gorge area. The occupants of each castle, often representing a small independent state, were able to exact tolls from vessels passing along the river. Transport was costly and liable to many delays, and until the small independent states disappeared with the emergence of a united Germany in 1870, the river was not used to its full potential. The river flows through Switzerland, Germany, France and the Netherlands and today free passage exists along its entire length. The establishment of unrestricted movement on the Rhine encouraged the improvement of navigation on the major tributary rivers, the Moselle, Main and Neckar. These now connect with the other great rivers of Europe to provide through-navigation between the North Sea, Mediterranean Sea and Black Sea. The improvement of the shallow, meandering Moselle was completed in 1964 and included

Figure 14.8 (*below*) The Rhine waterway system

153

Figure 14.9 The harbour of Duisburg, the largest inland port in Europe

the construction of 14 dams, some with h.e.p. installations, to provide a route for 1350-tonne barges between the steel and engineering towns of Lorraine and the Rhine.

Until recent years, much of the traffic on the river Rhine has revolved around supplying the Ruhr coalfield region with raw materials, particularly iron ore, and distributing coke, iron and steel goods, chemicals and manufactured products to other parts of the Rhine basin. The river provided a cheap means of transport for bulk commodities, and the movement of coal from the Ruhr was fundamental to the establishment of chemical industries at Frankfurt, Ludwigshafen, Mannheim and Basle. The carriage of timber, grain, cement, building stone and mineral ores has led to the location of industries processing these materials at river-side sites. The decline in coal shipment followed by the loss of the bulk movement of crude oil to pipelines has been partly compensated for by the increased

carriage of petro-chemical products. Only in a few areas are these required in such quantities to make specialist-product pipeline construction economic.

The Rhine valley divides into four main sections; the upper valley above Basle, the rift valley between Balse and Mainz, the gorge section from Mainz to Bonn, and the Rhine plain and delta.

The Upper Rhine Valley

In Switzerland the river is too steep and shallow for navigation, except where it passes through Lake Constance, which is used for commercial traffic and tourist craft. The steep-sided, flat-floored upper valley is a region of dairy farms and forest, tourist resorts like Davos, and small industrial towns using hydro-electric power. The major power developments are above Basle at Schaffhausen, where the river falls over 100 m from Lake Constance. The electric power has attracted

154

Figure 14.10 Basle harbour

chemical and metal working industries to the area, including aluminium smelting at Rheinfelden. These industries are supplied with their raw materials through the port of Basle, which can be reached by barges with a 2000-tonne capacity. The upstream journey for laden barges takes 4–5 days from Rotterdam to Basle, the journey downstream, often of empty or partly laden vessels, takes at least one day less. It is planned to extend the navigation upstream to Schaffhausen. Basle is the third largest town in Switzerland, and an important bridge point upon which road and rail communications focus. These routeways distribute many of the goods carried into the river port. The imports of Basle include grain, oil, coke, metals and textile fibres which help to support the engineering, textile and chemical industries of the town.

The Rhine Rift Valley

This section extends for 300 km from Basle to Mainz, the valley averaging 40 km in width between the fault escarpments of the Vosges and Black Forest. The floor of the valley is choked with sediments and provides a gentle surface across which the river channel divides and meanders. The area is predominantly agricultural with vines and orchard crops on the lower hill slopes, grain and market garden crops on the drier parts of the flood plain and pasture land near to the river. The river improvements begun in the nineteenth century included the embanking of a main channel to prevent flooding, followed by the construction of a new deep channel, the Grand Canal d'Alsace, running parallel with the river for 100 km north of Basle. Port developments at Karlsruhe, Strasbourg, Ludwigshafen, Mannheim, Stuttgart, Mainz and Frankfurt attracted new industries dependent upon raw materials brought into the area. These include chemical, engineering and paper industries, while others like brewing, tobacco and flour milling are based upon local resources. The two largest urban areas, Frankfurt, a great banking and industrial city, and Stuttgart, the home of Daimler-Benz and the administrative centre of the region, both owe much of their importance to the communications of the Rhine valley.

The Rhine Gorge

The river is entrenched in a steep, narrow valley with few areas of flat land for settlement. Here, although there is a large volume of traffic passing through, the riverside area has been unable to profit industrially from the advantages of bulk transport. Only in the Neuwied Basin, north of Coblenz, are the valley sides low and gentle to allow the development of metal working, engineering, paper and cement works. Elsewhere, the gorge area has been terraced to grow vines for wine making in the small villages stretched out along the sides of the river, while the many castles which enhance the scenic attractiveness of the area help to provide the basis for a thriving tourist industry. Apart from Coblenz, the small river ports are chiefly concerned with tourist traffic and the local movement of agricultural produce.

Figure 14.11 Castle overlooking the river Rhine near Coblenz. Vines are grown on the steep terraces

The Rhine Plain and Delta

The level nature of the land surface, the industrial resources of the Ruhr coalfield and cheap water transport have made this area one of the most densely-populated industrial regions in the world. In spite of competition from other forms of transport the river is intensively used, with the large dock complex at Duisburg forming the hub of the water-transport system. The need to carry cargo at the lowest cost, i.e., with the least number of crew, has led to the development of large vessels with a capacity of up to 2500 tonnes being guided by 'pusher' units. The advantage of pushing rather than pulling a barge train of up to four barges is that the wash from the propeller blades does not foul and slow the following barges. The chemical and metal-working industries which dominate the riverside from Cologne to Rotterdam have caused a great deal of pollution to the river, which the authorities are now attempting to control. Pollution on the river is a cumulative process and has its worst effects in the Netherlands. In 1971, owing to particularly heavy pollution of the river, drinking water was rationed in Rotterdam. The high concentration of soluble salts in Rhine water is also harmful to crops grown on the flood plain; a recent analysis revealed that 41% of the salts in the river had originated from the indiscriminate dumping of waste from the French potash mines in Alsace.

Rail Transport

Western Europe, with approximately 140,000 km of track, has the densest rail network in the world. It was largely developed in the nineteenth century as a result of the growth of large urban and industrial areas. The railways were built from a national view point, the main lines radiating from the capital cities to the frontiers; this pattern is clearly discernible in France, Germany and Spain. Only a few international lines like the Ostend-Vienna were built with this specific intention in mind, although the standard 1·5 m gauge used in Western Europe has posed no barrier to international movement. The fullest rail development is across the flat North European Plain, and extends along main valley routes like the Rhine and Rhône. The international character of the Rhine valley is shown by the growth of the important transit ports near its mouth; Rotterdam, Amsterdam and Antwerp all rely in part upon rail transport. Antwerp, having no direct waterway link with the Rhineland, has relied upon the rapid movement of raw materials and manufactured goods by rail; in 1974 Belgian railways handled over 5 million tonnes of transit traffic.

The role of the railway system in Western Europe can be summerized as follows.

1 To provide an alternative to water transport for the bulk movement of goods. The principal lines connecting ports and major industrial areas have been improved and electrified for the use of trains carrying 2000 tonnes of freight.

2 To provide fast inter-city links for passengers. For journeys of up to 500 km and taking approximately 5 hours, rail travel remains competitive with air transport. Important inter-city lines of this type are Paris–Strasbourg, Paris–Lyons.

3 To provide fast suburban services for commuters travelling daily into cities. Most major cities have important suburban networks serving an area of up to 75 km from the centre.

4 To provide a specific amenity in areas where other land transport services are lacking. The railways from Kiruna to Narvik and from Bergen to Oslo are examples which cross the barren Scandinavian Mountains, and reach heights of 525 m and 1300 m respectively.

Rail communications have lost a great deal of traffic to road transport over the past twenty-five years, the more extensive road systems providing a flexibility the railways cannot match. Roads are used and financed by private and public traffic, whereas the railways can only be used for scheduled public services. To reduce this disadvantage, all the major European rail systems are state owned, and receive considerable government subsidy. After a period of decline, the West European systems have begun to fulfil the role of serving the whole of the European community rather than just national requirements.

Figure 14.12 Central station in Milan. Milan is the focus of the north Italian rail system, with lines running north across the Alps into Switzerland

Figure 14.13 (*left*) The motorways of Western Europe

Road Transport

The use of roads for passenger and freight movement has increased dramatically during the past twenty-five years. The greater flexibility of roads over other forms of transport, together with increased wealth which has enabled many families to own a car, has caused a large increase in road building and improvement. In 1973 there were 10·9 million commercial vehicles and 7·6 million cars (representing 1 car per 4·2 people) on the roads of Western Europe.

The road improvement programme has, like the railways, generally been undertaken from a national rather than a European viewpoint. The system of designated international 'E' roads crossing Europe only occasionally coincides with sections of motorway, which have usually been built as part of a national network. The most developed motorway network, begun in the 1930's, is in West Germany where the system follows two parallel routes along the Rhine valley and from Munich to Hamburg, with various connecting motorways. The decision to focus part of the system upon Hamburg was taken with the intention of directing some south German traffic towards the port as compensation for the loss of its East European hinterland. The Italian system is based upon the 'autostrada del sole' running the full length of the country with branches to Milan, Turin, Genoa and Venice in the north. The following statistics showing the length of motorway in kilometres, illustrate the increase in construction during the 1960's.

	France	Italy	Netherlands	West Germany
1963	348	1269	506	2992
1970	1542	3981	979	4461

Figure 14.14(a) (*below*) The approach to the Mont Blanc road tunnel at Coumayeur (Italy). The tunnel is over 1200 m above sea level and 11.6 km long

Figure 14.14(b) Bridges across the Little Belt link Jutland and Fyn. The 1700-m bridge in the foreground was opened in 1970

Unlike the railways, roads have exerted a very strong influence on the siting of industries and residential areas. The mobility of a labour force using road transport has attracted many industrial firms to sites on main arterial roads or near to motorways. These industries are particularly those engaged in the manufacture of light, high-value engineering and electrical goods, where raw materials are needed in relatively small quantities, and road transport provides the ideal means of transport. The location of light-industry factories away from the main cities, but near important roads, has been a feature of recent industrial growth in southern Germany.

Road transport has become increasingly important in serving ports. The development of the roll-on/roll-off ferry and the container ship has made it essential for ports to have efficient road, as well as rail and waterway, links.

The motorways serving Bremen, Hamburg, Genoa, Naples, Antwerp and other European ports have been instrumental in developing this close integration between land and sea transport.

The growth in demand for road transport has led to the improvement of many difficult routes. In the Alps the Mont Blanc tunnel provides a link between the north Italian cities of Milan and Turin, and Geneva and Lyons. In Scandinavia a replacement six-lane road bridge has been built between the Danish island of Fyn and Jutland, while between the Swedish mainland and the island of Oland, the longest bridge in Europe, 6070 m in length, is nearing completion. Clearly, more roads will be built, some damaging local environments, but overall the road seems most likely to connect and integrate the European transport system, breaking down the nationalistic attitudes that have prevailed in the past.

Figure 14.14(c) The Storstrum bridge, connecting Zealand and Falster, is 3211 m long and was built in 1937

Air Transport

Air transport has the great asset of speed, but can only carry small freight loads. It is therefore primarily used for passenger travel and is in competition with rail and road transport systems for journeys of above two-hours duration. The high purchase price and operating costs of aircraft make short distance travel relatively costly and in these circumstances air transport is only used when a fast journey is essential. Although freight movements are increasing, they are reserved for small, light, high-value goods, such as jewelry and precision instruments. The largest aircraft can carry up to 100 tonnes of freight, often in standard sized containers. An interesting example of air freight transport is the carriage of valuable plants and cut flowers grown under glass at Aalsmeer, near Amsterdam. The blooms are dispatched by air all over the world from the nearby international airport at Schiphol.

Figure 14.15 (*right*) The major airports

Western Europe is a relatively small area for air transport to have strong advantages over other forms of passenger transport. Most countries have one major state-owned national airline which operates international and European services. Smaller charter airlines exist, particularly for tourist traffic, but do not normally offer many regular scheduled services. The numerous national airlines again illustrate the lack of integration in European transport; the aircraft of the major airlines frequently fly with an average annual load capacity of only 55%. With the rationalization brought about by increased fuel prices, air transport is beginning to increase its competitiveness with other forms of transport. The most important routes for international traffic are those to North America, while in Europe the growth of holiday charter flights to southern resorts has been very spectacular. With

Figure 14.16 Le Bourget airport, now closed, is in a congested, built-up area

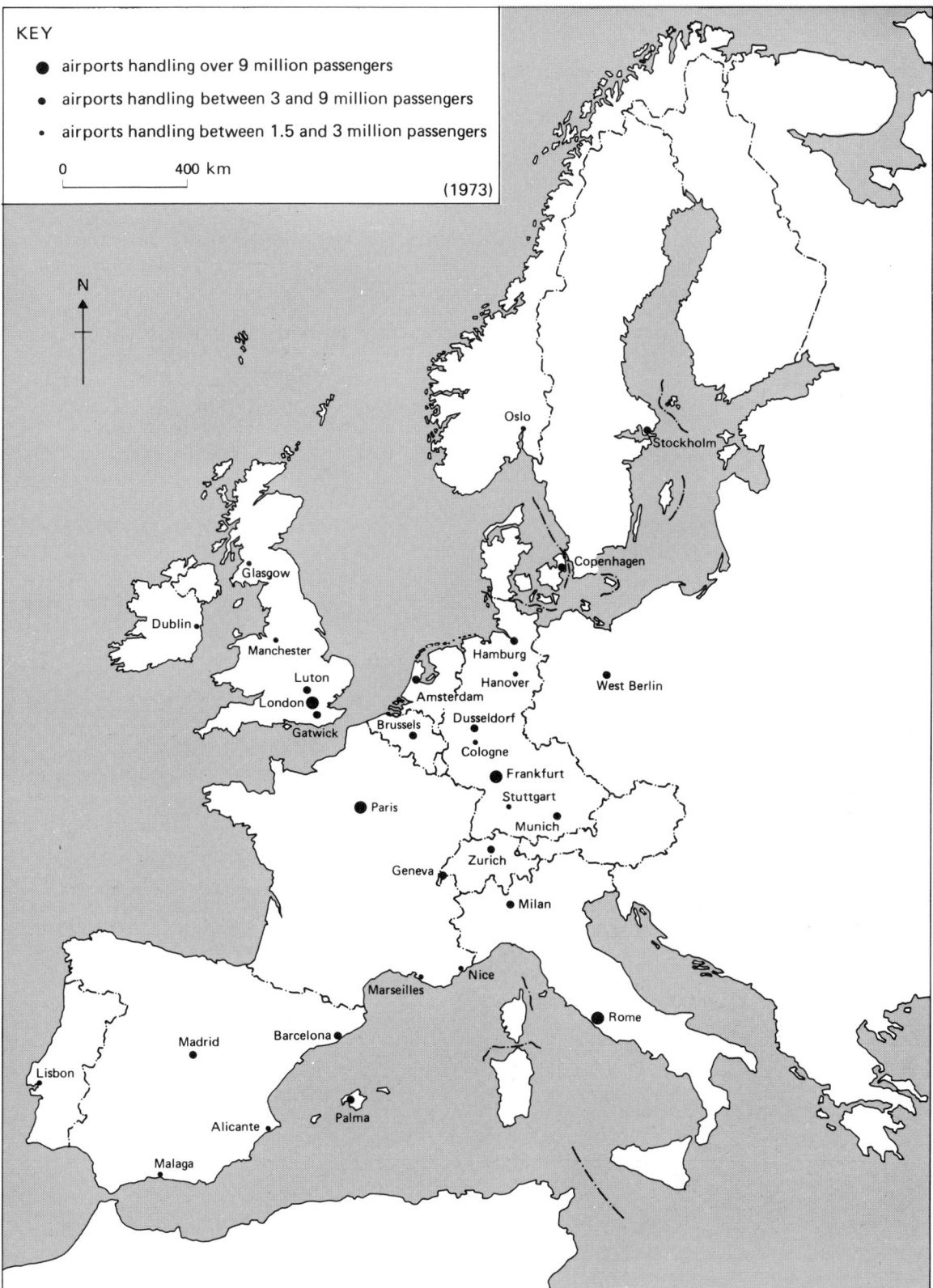

KEY

- ● airports handling over 9 million passengers
- • airports handling between 3 and 9 million passengers
- · airports handling between 1.5 and 3 million passengers

0   400 km

(1973)

N

Oslo

Stockholm

Copenhagen

Glasgow

Dublin

Manchester

Hamburg

Hanover

West Berlin

Luton

London

Amsterdam

Dusseldorf

Brussels

Gatwick

Cologne

Frankfurt

Paris

Stuttgart

Munich

Geneva

Zurich

Milan

Nice

Marseilles

Rome

Madrid

Barcelona

Lisbon

Alicante

Palma

Malaga

Figure 14.17 The Charles de Gaulle airport showing the control tower and reception terminal

aircraft filled to capacity, a transport charge of approximately £5 (1974) per passenger/hour enables tour operators to offer holidays at a sufficiently low cost to attract very large numbers of people.

The growth of air transport was stimulated by the development of the aircraft industry during the Second World War, and the availability in the immediate post-war years of surplus military aircraft. Since then, the demand for new airports has consumed large areas of land, usually some distance from the main built-up area, and major land transport links between city centre and airport are included in all current expansion schemes. The Charles de Gaulle airport at Paris is sited 22 km north of the city, and covers 3000 ha. It is designed to handle up to 50 million passengers per year and was opened in 1974. An express rail service and motorway provide the link with central Paris. The development of short take-off (STOL) and vertical take-off (VTOL) aircraft may bring airports nearer the city centres, but only when pollution and noise hazards are reduced. The high operating costs of helicopter travel have prevented this form of transport from providing the type of economical link required.

The very great demand for passenger and freight transport in Western Europe has produced a system developed along nationalistic lines with considerable competition between the various forms of transport. Only the waterways, with major rivers passing through several countries, have been developed from an international rather than national viewpoint. Airlines duplicate each others services, railway electrification programmes have frequently been developed solely on a national basis, and several motorways, notably Italian, end at frontiers. The transport ministers of the EEC are giving priority to the integration of the communications systems and recognize the following as areas where improvements are particularly overdue.

164

1 Motorways designed mainly to meet national requirements should be linked to establish a European network.

2 Regular scheduled air services should be established between major European cities. At present there are few direct services except those between capital cities.

3 Co-operation between the state railway authorities to extend the standardization of rolling stock and passenger and freight charges. A plan has been considered by the EEC Council of Ministers for the merger of the railway authorities of the member countries into one company.

4 Increased investment in the development of high-speed vehicles, such as the French gas turbine train and the British Advanced Passenger Train.

The EEC, enlarged in 1973 to include the United Kingdom, Denmark and Eire, will require further development of an integrated transport system and links will be needed between the British and continental motorways through improved ferry connections across the English Channel and North Sea.

Questions

1. With reference to Fig. 14.4, answer the following questions.

(*a*) Suggest reasons for the importance of the West European countries in the composition of the world merchant shipping fleet.
(*b*) Norway (4 million) and Greece (9 million) have two of the smallest populations in Europe, but two of the largest merchant shipping fleets. Explain the reasons for this.
(*c*) What are the factors which have led to the development of a large oil tanker fleet in France but not in West Germany?

2. Study Fig. 14.15 and answer the following questions.

(*a*) Name *five* capital cities which contain their country's major airport;
(*b*) Give reasons to explain this connection by making detailed reference to the particular countries named in (*a*).

3. The Low Countries and West Germany have the best developed system of inland waterways in Western Europe. Give a reasoned account to explain this development.

4. The Scandinavian mountains, Pyrenees and Alps are the principal physical barriers to land communication in Europe. For each of the mountain systems write an account of the major routes which cross them and assess their importance.

5. With reference to the bridges shown in Figs 14.14(b) and 14.14(c):
(*a*) describe the differences and similarities you notice in the construction of the two bridges;
(*b*) name the communications each bridge carries;
(*c*) list the physical factors you consider were important in deciding the exact site of each bridge;
(*d*) refer to an atlas map of Denmark and list the major towns connected by the communications carried by each bridge.

15 Population distribution and settlement

Western Europe is among the most densely populated areas of the world, and several countries have population concentrations comparable to those along the eastern seaboard of the USA and the plains of India, China and Japan. Only in the mountainous high-latitude areas of Norway and Sweden can the population distribution be considered sparse. The following table illustrates the size and density of the population of certain countries in 1973.

Population statistics for selected countries (1973)

Country	Total population (millions)	Population density (per km²)
Belgium	9·7	320
China	814·2	85
France	52·1	95
India	574·2	175
Italy	54·8	182
Japan	108·3	291
Netherlands	13·4	329
Norway	3·96	12
Spain	34·8	69
Sweden	8·1	18
Switzerland	6·4	156
United Kingdom	55·9	229
USA	210·4	22
West Germany	61·9	249

The distribution of population reflects the relative importance of three factors:

1   access to important agricultural and industrial resources;

2   the availability of relatively level, well-watered land;

3   a mild, humid climate without extremes of temperature or precipitation.

Where these factors occur together, as they do in many parts of Western Europe, dense concentrations of people have gathered.

Conditions Which Have Influenced the Choice of Settlement Sites

The initial reason for the establishment of settlements was man's primary need for shelter and his inclination to live in communities with fellow men. The decision of where the settlement should be built was usually arrived at through the consideration of a number of factors. It is only rarely that one single factor can be attributed as the reason for the choice of a particular site, and clearly certain sites proved more favourable than others. The principal conditions which helped to determine a successful site are as follows.

1   *A reliable water supply.* Accessibility to stream water, springs or wells has always been an essential requirement for any size of settlement. In addition to being a source of drinking water, streams frequently provided a site for a water mill, which gave some settlements an added advantage with the development of this form of power in medieval times.

2   *Dry sites.* Sites close to rivers in exposed lowland areas were generally avoided in the past, the dual threat of floods and attack by enemies making them unpopular. Early settlements in river plains made use of any elevated feature, even if only a few metres above the river. The mounds in the Rhine delta, and the Seine and Elbe river terraces are examples of dry point sites settled from an early date. More popular waterside sites were those in the middle and upper valleys where the steeper sides provided greater security.

3   *Sites which were easy to defend.* Many of the older European towns illustrate the importance of this factor—Paris, Rome and Stockholm being good examples. Dominating hill- and valley-side situations, river and offshore islands, and the land within a meander, still distinguish the medieval centres of many towns from their modern suburbs.

4 *Access to agricultural land.* A reliable food supply was important to early settlements, which were usually situated near to level well-watered land that supported a farming population. The plains were often forested, being progressively cleared for agriculture and to provide level land for building.

5 *A river crossing point.* Where other factors combined to produce a settlement near a shallow or narrow section of a river, crossing points by ford and later by bridge were developed. Such settlements became focal points for communications and trade, and frequently grew to be the chief towns of a region. The names of several important European towns include evidence of the value of river crossings: Frankfurt, Saarbrücken, Bruges, Innsbruck, Pont à Mousson, Ponferrada.

6 *A port.* Before the development of mechanized transport, rivers provided the principal means for the carriage of merchandise. The small sea-going vessels in use were able to penetrate deep into Europe and important trade and transhipment ports

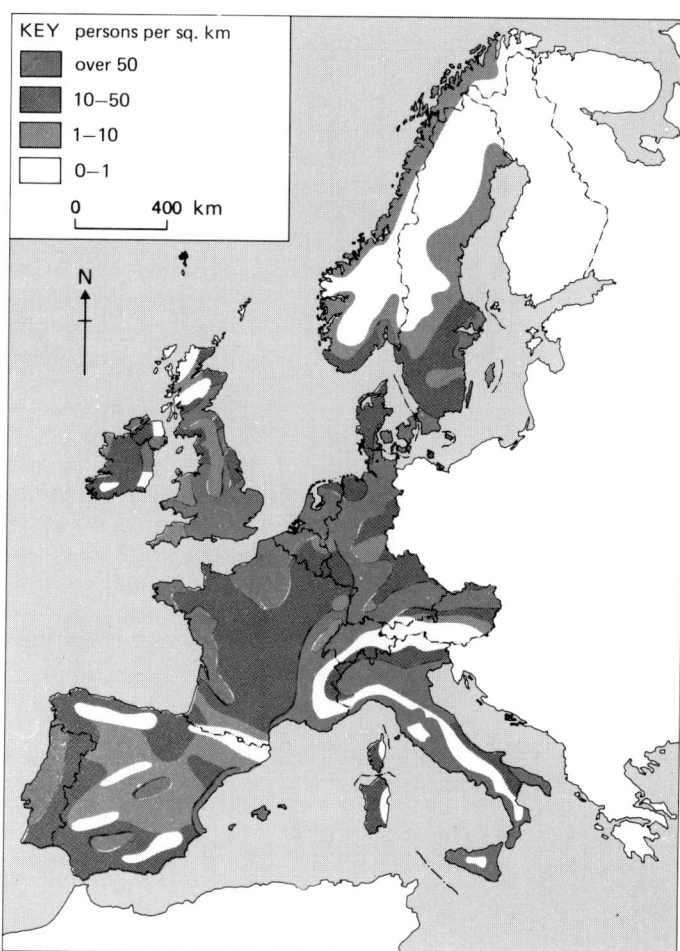

Figure 15.1 The distribution of population

Figure 15.2 The medieval walled town of Carcassonne in south-west France

developed at the upstream limits of navigation. The Romans established many of their principal towns at such locations, e.g., Cologne, Paris and Cadiz. Although the importance of these towns as ports has reduced with the increase in size of vessel, they remain major centres of commerce and industry.

7 *A location near an important mineral resource or power site.* The Industrial Revolution of the 19th century brought with it a major period of town development. The large labour force needed to support mining and industry was drawn from the rural areas, and led to the establishment of new towns and an expansion in the size of existing towns and villages. The areas to be first affected by rapid urbanization were the Ruhr and Franco-Belgian coalfields and Lorraine iron-ore field, followed by the towns and ports along the principal lines of communication. Where mineral deposits occur in remote highland regions, urbanization has been of a less permanent nature than on the North European Plain. Except where large reserves exist, as at Kiruna in Sweden, mining communities have often drifted away and the town has fallen into decay with the exhaustion of the mineral resource. At Röros in Norway the town has developed a second function with the decline of its copper mines, and has become a small tourist and service centre for farming and forestry.

8 *A southern aspect and sheltered position.* Alone, neither of these factors is likely to cause a settlement to develop, but where other favourable conditions exist, shelter and aspect often determine the particular position of a settlement. In south-west Norway the northern shores of the Sogne and Hardanger fjords are far more fully settled than the north-facing southern shores. Coastal settlements have always utilized islands and promontaries to protect their port activities; a feature illustrated by the Breton fishing ports of Lorient, Concarneau and Douarnenez.

A Classification of Settlements

Settlements may be considered by their size, shape and function, or combinations of these factors.

Size
The size of a settlement reflects:

1 the demand for the facilities and services a settlement can offer;

2 how favourable the conditions are for its growth.

In rural areas unrestricted of marsh and mountain, a clear pattern can be seen. Each settlement unit has a distinct function, the smaller being within the influence of the larger to give a region an overall form. Settlement units can be classified according to size.

Figure 15.3 Concarneau, Brittany. The fishing harbour is sited within a sheltered inlet

Figure 15.4 The Ruhr conurbation

Isolated building: usually occupying a favourable local site within the context of a farm or area of extractive industry.

Hamlet: a cluster of buildings housing a population of usually less than 50 people, with few amenities.

Village: a farming community which can number over 1000 people. A village usually contains a church and provides the every-day shopping facilities required by the community. In areas within 50 km of expanding industrial towns, new housing and industry is altering the form and function of the rural village.

Town: the farming town or market centre traditionally dominated the life of an agricultural region, offering the extra choice and facilities the village could not provide. With its established communication facilities the market town became a growth centre for light and service industries. Industrial towns have developed chiefly in the past 100 years, many from rural villages fortuitously sited near valuable mineral resources. Their rapid growth, often along the outcrop of the mineral being exploited, has given many industrial towns a fragmented, sprawling character, unlike the more nucleated form of the market town.

Neighbouring towns, which are related to each other by their economic activities but remain physically unconnected, form an agglomeration: the towns of the Rhine–Main region in West Germany illustrate this form.

City: the city has no precise place in a classification of settlements by size. It can be defined as a settlement of larger or similar size to a town, but with a wider geographical sphere of influence and a traditional role in administration and trade. State and provincial capitals are usually referred to as cities, together with many smaller settlements which were once of greater regional importance than they are today (i.e., those being centres of church administration and containing a cathedral).

Conurbation: the physical growth of urban areas during and since the Industrial Revolution has joined many neighbouring towns into one continuous built-up area, or conurbation. Industrial areas like the Ruhr coalfield illustrate this characteristic best, but many smaller regions, such as the Amsterdam and Rotterdam areas of the Netherlands and Marseilles–Fos in France, show a similar tendency. The uncontrolled growth of towns, producing

169

conurbations and resulting in overcrowded living conditions, is considered undesirable. Most large urban areas now have powerful planning authorities, whose aim is to reconcile the desire of people to live in and near towns, while maintaining a pleasant environment. The following planning problems are common to many large urban areas.

1 The decline of the old city centre for housing, shopping, entertainment and cultural use.

2 The increased commuter traffic which is spread over a wide area can only be partly absorbed by public transport, and elaborate urban motorway systems have had to be built.

3 The rapid growth of housing and industry in small satellite towns and villages where communications, shopping and service facilities are inadequate.

Shape

The shape of a settlement is principally determined by the conditions responsible for its development. The expansion of a mining settlement is likely to follow the most favourable geological structure of the mineral resource, a port will develop its docks towards deeper water to accommodate the larger vessels, and a town which gains its importance from the roads that focus upon it is likely to expand along these routeways. Unless the site upon which the settlement is built is uniformly suitable for development, physical landforms are likely to be important factors in controlling shape. The indented island site of Stockholm, the morainic ridge above the damp North German Plain at Bremen and the narrow coastal plain at Genoa, all illustrate the control the physical landscape may exercise.

The most powerful recent influence on the shape of settlements is the motor vehicle, coupled with the construction of an increasing number of fast highways serving the urban areas. Together these developments have enabled people to live considerable distances from their place of work and to make daily journeys of up to one hour in each direction. In addition, a spacious location alongside the major roads has become important for factories using road transport for receiving raw materials and distributing their finished goods.

The combined result has been to encourage towns to build in narrow zones radiating outwards from their centres. Without planning control, nearby towns would soon become connected by built-up areas following the major roads, and the first stage in the evolution of a conurbation would have occurred. Along the Rhine valley, development of this kind has almost connected the towns of Duisberg, Düsseldorf, Cologne and Bonn.

The shape and distribution of settlements can be grouped into four categories: dispersed, nucleated, linear and planned.

1 *Dispersed.* Buildings are either isolated or loosely grouped within open areas.

2 *Nucleated.* A definite centre exists, often marked by an open market square surrounded by large buildings such as offices, shops and hotels. The urban area has grown concentrically around this core, sometimes industrial and residential development separately zoned, but in older towns existing side by side.

3 *Linear.* Settlements which have developed in a linear shape often have a small focal centre, but their main characteristic is that they straggle along a zone that is physically and/or economically attractive. Many nucleated towns have extensions of linear settlement along major roads.

4 *Planned.* New towns and large extensions to towns are usually planned to include commercial, industrial and residential zones incorporating open spaces and leisure areas. In most cases a compromise has to be made between the planner's ideal layout and the demand for building land. In developing areas, to accommodate overspill from large cities, attempts are usually made to make each new development an independent satellite community to reduce the daily movement of people into the centre of the city.

Good job opportunities have made towns and cities popular places in which to work, but few people live in the central areas. Here shops and businesses are located where the main road routes meet. With many business concerns competing for sites in the central area, land is usually too costly for houses and flats to be built. To satisfy the demand for a central location many tall buildings have been constructed in the centres of all the main West European cities and towns. Noise and atmospheric pollution are other factors which make the central areas less attractive than the suburbs for housing development. The central business district and the suburban residential area are features that have been encouraged by most European planning authorities, although it has created additional urban transport needs.

Function

The function or purpose of a settlement is to provide places to live and work and the services the community needs. These features can be observed in large and small settlements alike. In small settlements the residential, industrial and business zones are often less clear cut than in large towns, but even the rural village has a central area with a distinct function based upon shops and small businesses. The functional zones characteristic of towns are shown in Fig. 15.5.

While the area and population of a settlement are the factors which largely control the development of the functional zones, some settlements have grown around a specialist activity for which there are particular local advantages. Mining towns, fishing ports and tourist resorts are examples of settlements with a specialist business and industrial role welded to the basic functional town structure.

Questions

1. Choose *three* areas in Western Europe which have contrasted population densities and give an explanation of the differences.

2. (*a*) Draw simple sketch maps to show the shape of built-up land for each of the following patterns of settlement: dispersed, linear, nucleated, planned.
(*b*) Name *one* European town as an example for each of the types of settlement listed in (*a*) and describe and explain the factors which have influenced their development.

3. (*a*) Choose *three* of the following types of settlement site, and for each give *one* example of a European town that has been established on such a site: a river crossing point, an easily defended site, a location near a mineral resource, a sheltered port.
(*b*) For the towns named in (*a*) describe how their development has been influenced by the original site.

4. (*a*) With reference to the West European countries listed in the table on page 166 choose (i) a country with a low population total and a high population density, and (ii) a

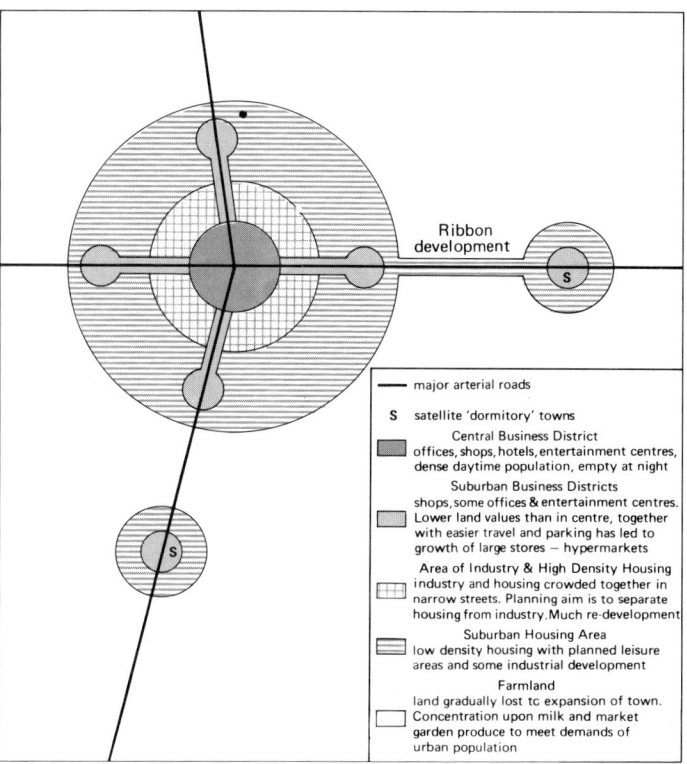

Figure 15.5 A model of the functions of an idealized town

— major arterial roads

S satellite 'dormitory' towns

Central Business District
offices, shops, hotels, entertainment centres, dense daytime population, empty at night

Suburban Business Districts
shops, some offices & entertainment centres. Lower land values than in centre, together with easier travel and parking has led to growth of large stores — hypermarkets

Area of Industry & High Density Housing
industry and housing crowded together in narrow streets. Planning aim is to separate housing from industry. Much re-development

Suburban Housing Area
low density housing with planned leisure areas and some industrial development

Farmland
land gradually lost to expansion of town. Concentration upon milk and market garden produce to meet demands of urban population

country with a high population total but a low population density.
(*b*) For each country chosen write a reasoned account of the factors which have produced the population pattern described above.

5. With reference to Fig. 15.4 and the text, give reasons to explain:
(*a*) the linear shape of the towns of Wuppertal and Hagen;
(*b*) the development of the conurbation in a predominantly east/west direction;
(*c*) the break in development between the main part of the conurbation and the towns of Dusseldorf, Wuppertal and Hagen;
(*d*) the discontinuous nature of the settlement along the banks of the river Rhine.

6. With reference to Fig. 15.5, answer the following questions.
(*a*) List the factors which might cause the zones in a particular town to be less regular than the idealized diagram shows.
(*b*) What urban transport would be needed?
(*c*) How could this be provided?
(*d*) Present a clear plan of the roles of public and private transport.

171

16 Selected settlement studies

Antwerp—A General Cargo Port

In 1973 the port of Antwerp handled 99.3 million tonnes of cargo, a figure exceeded only by Rotterdam among West European ports. The traffic is not wholly of Belgian origin, for within 300 km of the port live nearly 100 million people in one of the most densely industrialized regions of the world.

The port area is concentrated almost entirely on the deeper and more extensive right bank of the river Scheldt, while its seaward development is limited by the Dutch border. Dutch control over the estuary mouth restricted Antwerp's growth until the second half of the nineteenth century. They feared the emergence of a rival to the port of Amsterdam, and it was not until 1863 that the Dutch finally ceased to levy tolls on vessels entering the Scheldt.

The river estuary is sheltered and provides a dredged channel of 13·2 m, capable of accommodating vessels of over 70,000 tonnes. It is intended to improve the approaches for vessels of up to 125,000 tonnes. The clays of the low coastal plain have been excavated to form a series of connected tidal dock basins entered from the river by six lock systems. The small docks built near to the city date from Napoleonic times and are chiefly used by coasters and barges entering the Albert Canal. The major dock is the Canal Dock, which stretches for 8 km northwards to the Dutch border, and is lined by warehouses and industrial plants. It is entered by the Zandvliet lock with a capacity for 100,000-tonne vessels, and is the terminus of the Scheldt-Rhine Canal, completed in 1975.

The principal growth of the port of Antwerp has been achieved in the past 100 years, and it has been the result of the following factors.

1 *A network of road, rail and waterway communications have been developed to serve the port.* The inland navigation afforded by the river Scheldt is small when compared with the rival European rivers, Seine, Rhine and Elbe; and the construction of the Brussels–Charleroi Canal (1832, reconstructed 1960) and the Albert Canal (1940) to the Sambre-Meuse coalfield region have been essential to Antwerp's success in handling Belgium's heavy industrial traffic. Contact with the Rhineland has depended upon roads and railways. Although there have been several schemes for the construction of a waterway, they have understandably met with objections from the Dutch, through whose country the most easily-engineered route must pass. The railway to Liege, Aachen and Cologne, completed in 1844, provided the first major link, and this has recently been added to by the motorways to Duisburg and Cologne. The railway built in the 1860's from Brussels to Namur and Luxembourg was later extended to Nancy to tap the growing industrial region of Lorraine. In 1971, transit traffic, largely to West Germany (43%) and France (33%) comprised 23% of Antwerp's cargo movements. The port is the terminus of twelve important rail lines, including the recently built direct link to Ghent, and is planned to be at the crossroads of E10 (Paris–Amsterdam), E3 (Lille–Hamburg) and E39 (Antwerp–Cologne) motorways.

2 *The importance of foreign trade to the Belgian economy.* Antwerp, centrally situated to take advantage of European trade and facing North America and the large entrepôt port of London, was developed as Belgium's major port. The city is the home of the mercantile marine and a centre for ship repair, mercantile banking, commerce and insurance. Belgium's colonial involvement in the Congo (Zaire) has

Figure 16.1 Antwerp: vessels entering the Zandvliet locks

brought a range of port and industrial activities to Antwerp, notably processing diamonds, non-ferrous metals and tropical foodstuffs that would otherwise be little developed.

3 *The establishment of a wide range of industries.* The major industries are supported by imported raw materials, and include oil refining, flour milling, sugar refining, tobacco and food processing. The petro-chemical industry, although important, has not developed on the same scale as in Rotterdam, the limitations of the Scheldt navigation preventing the entry of the large tankers. In 1971, one-third of Antwerp's crude oil imports were received by pipeline from Rotterdam. The petro-chemical industry produces synthetic fibres, rubber, artificial fertilizers and a range of other chemical products. Several pipelines

have been laid in the industrial area for the transport of ethylene, other chemical raw materials and finished products. In addition to port industries, metallurgical and engineering industries rank among the most important, and include the car, tractor and motor vehicle component plants of the American companies—Ford, General Motors and Chrysler.

4 *A willingness to pioneer and develop new cargo-handling techniques.* Competition with the other North Sea ports has acted as a stimulus, and Antwerp has been at the forefront in the development of container services, roll-on/roll-off ferries and LASH* barges. Most of the container traffic is with North America

* Lighter Aboard Ship. The cargo ship carries standard-sized lighters (barges) which are discharged when the vessel docks.

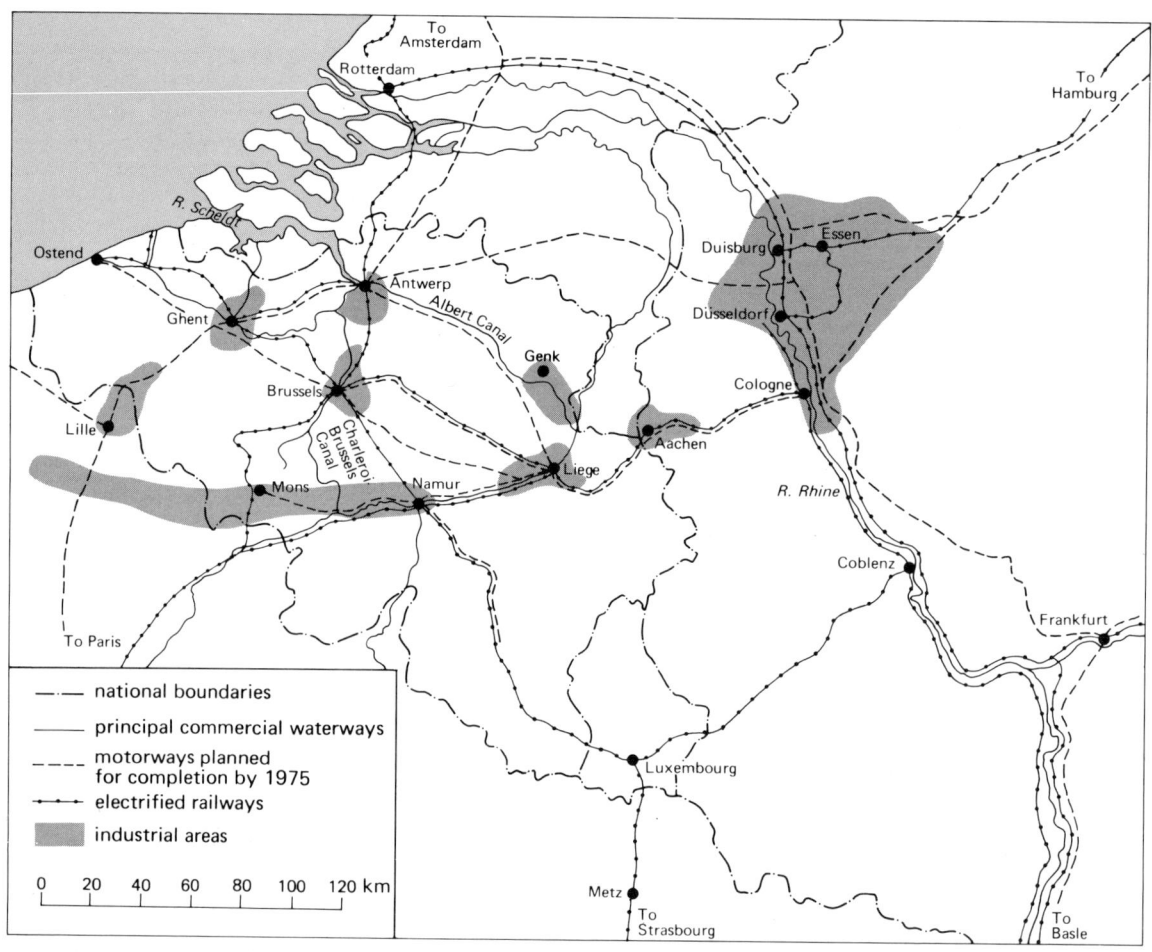

Figure 16.2 The hinterland of the port of Antwerp

(63%), and the containers are distributed across Europe by road and rail. The recent growth in Antwerp's container traffic is shown by the figures below:-

	1968	1971
Number of containers	57,447	133,443
Weight (in tonnes)	604,682	1,954,508
Total general cargo	22,093,000	23,996,338

The future trend of the port's development appears likely to show a further growth in general cargo traffic, particularly containers, with a slowing down in the growth-rate of bulk cargo, as the oil traffic is increasingly supplied by pipeline. Industrial growth has largely been a product of Antwerp's port and communication facilities but, in addition, the flat estuary sites and the availability of the major amenities, water, gas and electricity, have been influential.

Rennes (Brittany)—A Market Town and Regional Capital

Rennes is centrally sited in the largest area of lowland in Brittany, where the river Vilaine is joined by the Ille before continuing south to the Bay of Biscay. The Vilaine basin has a rolling landscape with hills rising to 100 m above the valleys. Surrounding the region is a distinct scarp edge which separates the harder igneous rocks of the moorlands from the various sedimentary rocks which form the floor of the basin. Although 60 m above sea level, the basin is sheltered from extreme weather conditions; while Brest receives 1090 mm of rain, Rennes has only 664 mm. The town is situated in a rich agricultural area at an important river-crossing point which acts as a focus for communication lines serving Brittany.

Rennes' pre-eminence among the several small towns of the lowlands was first established by the Romans, for whom it acted as the regional capital. In spite of a disasterous week-long fire in 1720, the town retained its importance, which was further strengthened by its development in the nineteenth century as a road and rail focus for routes crossing the Brittany peninsula. Although used primarily by pleasure craft today, the Ille–Rance Canal linking with the navigable river Vilaine provided an additional route across the peninsula. Projected motorway and rail electrification schemes planned to reduce the economic isolation of Brittany are to pass through Rennes en route to Paris.

The Vilaine basin is a region of mixed farming, with dairying, stock rearing, cereal production and market gardening all being important. The variety in the agriculture reflects the varied geology and soil structure of the lowlands. Many areas have remained wooded to form the characteristic 'bocage' landscape of small fields and scattered woodland. As the market centre for the region, Rennes has the markets and service facilities required by the farming communities for livestock, seed, fertilizer and machinery.

Most market towns with established communication facilities develop a number of other functions, and Rennes is no exception. With a population of 200,000 and transport services to draw its workforce from a wide area around, a variety of industries have

Figure 16.3 Antwerp: the Churchill dock container terminal

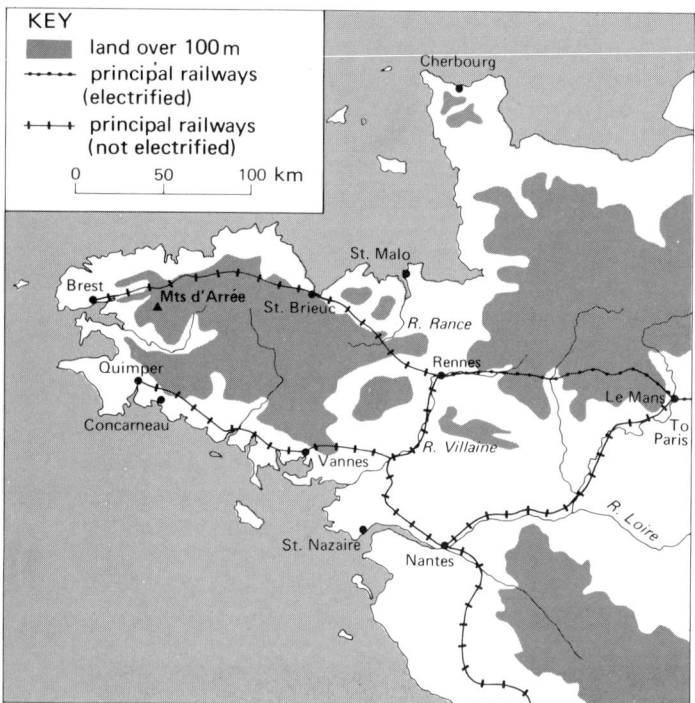

KEY

land over 100 m

····· principal railways
       (electrified)

+—+—+ principal railways
       (not electrified)

0   50   100 km

Cherbourg

St. Malo

Brest

Mts d'Arrée

St. Brieuc

R. Rance

Rennes

Le Mans

To Paris

Quimper

Concarneau

Vannes

R. Villaine

St. Nazaire

Nantes

R. Loire

Figure 16.4 The position of Rennes

become established. The most important of these are engineering—the Citroen factory, established in 1951, produces cars and components for other factories—building materials, electrical goods, chemicals and clothing. A shortage of raw materials and electrical energy held back industrial development in Brittany, but the improvement of communications and the construction of power stations, notably the Rance tidal barrage, have opened up new possibilities. Rennes, the most favourably sited of the Breton towns, has been planned as an industrial growth centre to stabilize the population loss the region has been experiencing.

The growth of industry at Rennes has resulted in the physical expansion of the town and much new building. It has not been allowed to damage the historic centre of the town or to reduce Rennes' administrative, educational and cultural functions. It is the capital of the Ille et Vilaine Departement, the centre for university education in Brittany, and houses the large regional RTF radio station. Clearly, the planned development of all Rennes' functions is necessary for the emergence of Brittany from its former isolation.

Paris, A Capital City

Paris illustrates how a city chosen as capital, and having many local advantages of site and position, can grow to dominate a country. It is believed that the original settlement was established approximately 2000 years ago by a Celtic tribe, the Parisii, on a small group of islands in a marshy stretch of the river Seine. The site provided for defence, water transport and a river crossing, factors which were to become the basis for the later growth of the town. Under the Romans the river was bridged at several points and an important military and administrative centre was built up. However, the first major development occurred in medieval times following the emergence of the House of Capet as Kings of France in 987 AD, with Paris as their chosen capital.

The city expanded from its site on the Ile de la Cité and grew across the river flood plain onto the low limestone escarpments that outcrop in the Ile de France region. The growth was in concentric bands, each stage of development marked by a perimeter rampart for defence. Many of these walls were demolished in the nineteenth century to provide the routes for the boulevards which encircle the city today. As the power and influence of France increased, the administrative and commercial functions of the capital city were extended. During the nineteenth century and since, the city has achieved its greatest period of growth, the population rising from 547,000 in 1801 (2% of the national total) to 8,197,000 in the 1968 census (17% of the national total). The cause of this rapid growth was the industrialization that occurred, particularly in the northern suburbs—an area benefitting from the docks at Gennevilliers—and the railways connecting with the Channel coast, the Nord coalfield and Lorraine. From its long history has evolved a unique role in French life—Paris is the administrative, commercial, industrial, cultural and communications centre of the country.

France has a highly centralized system of government; most decisions, even local ones, are made in Paris. Government and company offices, together with the university and associated libraries and institutes, are located in the central city area, chiefly on the south bank of the river. North of the river is a concentration

176

Figure 16.5 (*above*) The RTF building in Rennes

Figure 16.6 (*right*) Paris. View from Notre Dame on the Ile de la Cité showing several river crossings

of financial, banking and insurance establishments, together with an area of luxury shops. Daily transport into this congested central area is provided by the Metro and a system of suburban express railways and buses.

In any densely populated urban area, a large movement of goods takes place. The central position of the city within the saucer shaped depression of the Paris Basin syncline makes it the natural focus of routes using the valleys which breach the encircling chalk and limestone escarpments. In Paris, bulk transport is centered upon the river ports at Gennevilliers and Bonneuil, which handle over 20 million tonnes of cargo each year, the traffic being largely imports of building materials (sand, gravel and cement), fuel and petro-chemicals.

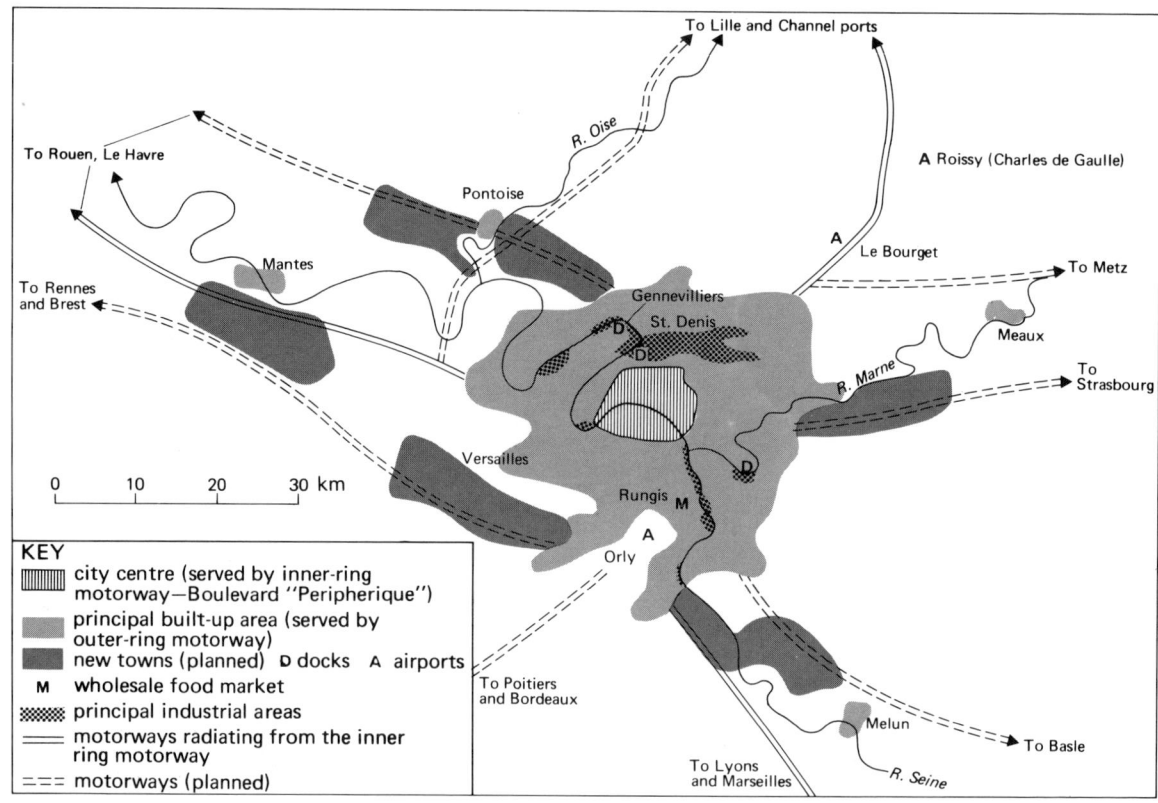

Figure 16.7 The site of Paris

The industrial districts of St Denis, Billancourt and Ivry are all conveniently located to use the 2000-tonne barges that the river can accommodate. Improved rail and motorway systems have been designed to serve the busiest industrial districts, the airports and the wholesale food markets. The recent transfer of the meat market to the surburb of Villette in the northeast, and the vegetable and fruit market to Rungis in the south, away from the congested central areas, illustrates the importance being given to the re-siting of major specialist activities in new accessible premises.

Like London, the industries of Paris are extremely varied. The port industries of chemicals, timber and food processing are supported by the bulk import of raw materials, by river and rail. The largest single employer of labour in the region is the engineering industry, which includes the Renault and Citroen motor vehicle plants at Billancourt and Grenelle respectively, and which have led to the development of many firms supplying components. Metal goods, machine tools, electrical machinery and appliances, foods, paper, printing, rubber, footwear, 'haute couture' clothing, cosmetics and jewellery are examples of the variety of industries located in the capital.

The historic and cultural associations of Paris make the city one of the world's great tourist attractions. Many thousands of visitors come each year to see such features as Notre Dame, the Eiffel Tower, the Louvre, the Arc de Triomphe and to enjoy a city that has both style and vitality. The new Charles de Gaulle airport at Roissy, the growing motorway system radiating from the 34.5 km inner ring motorway ('Peripherique'), additional hotels and car parks have made it possible to accommodate the tourist without making intolerable congestion in the central areas.

Milan—An Industrial City and Regional Capital

Milan is sited on the west bank of the river Lambro as it drains south from the Alps to

Figure 16.8 Paris: the industrial district of Billancourt. With reference to the photograph:
(**a**) draw a simple sketch map of the area including (i) the course of the river, (ii) the island, (iii) two bridges. Mark the extent of, and label, *three* different types of land use.
(**b**) What factors have favoured the development of industry at Billancourt?

join the river Po. The first settlement, Mediolanum, was founded by the Romans, and grew to be a city of great importance with a population of 100,000 in the first century AD. The invasions from the north by the Huns and Visigoths in the fifth century brought a decline in the life of the city, which was not halted until the Middle Ages. The revival (Renaissance) of Italian trade and influence stemmed from the ports of Venice and Genoa, but also stimulated commerce and industry on the plain. Here Milan's position, in a rich agricultural area and controlling routes northwards through the Alps, favoured its growth. Industries established at this time included textiles, particularly wool, silk and linen, and metal working; while control over the river and spring waters by the construction of canals† brought greater agricultural prosperity too.

†Milan is situated on the Fontanali line. See Fig 1.14

Since regaining its position of importance in northern Italy, Milan's development has suffered no serious setback and it is now the industrial and commercial capital of the country. As a major industrial city with a population of 1.7 million, its growth has been achieved without having the local coal resources that favoured such north European counterparts as Essen and Lille. The following geographical factors help to explain the industrial growth of Milan.

1 A position commanding the Simplon and St Gotthard passes through the Alps to France and Germany. Today Milan is the focal point of rail and motorway routes serving northern Italy.

2 Raw materials in the form of small deposits of iron ore from the Alpine foothills and locally produced flax, silk and raw wool, stimulated early industrial development in the region.

179

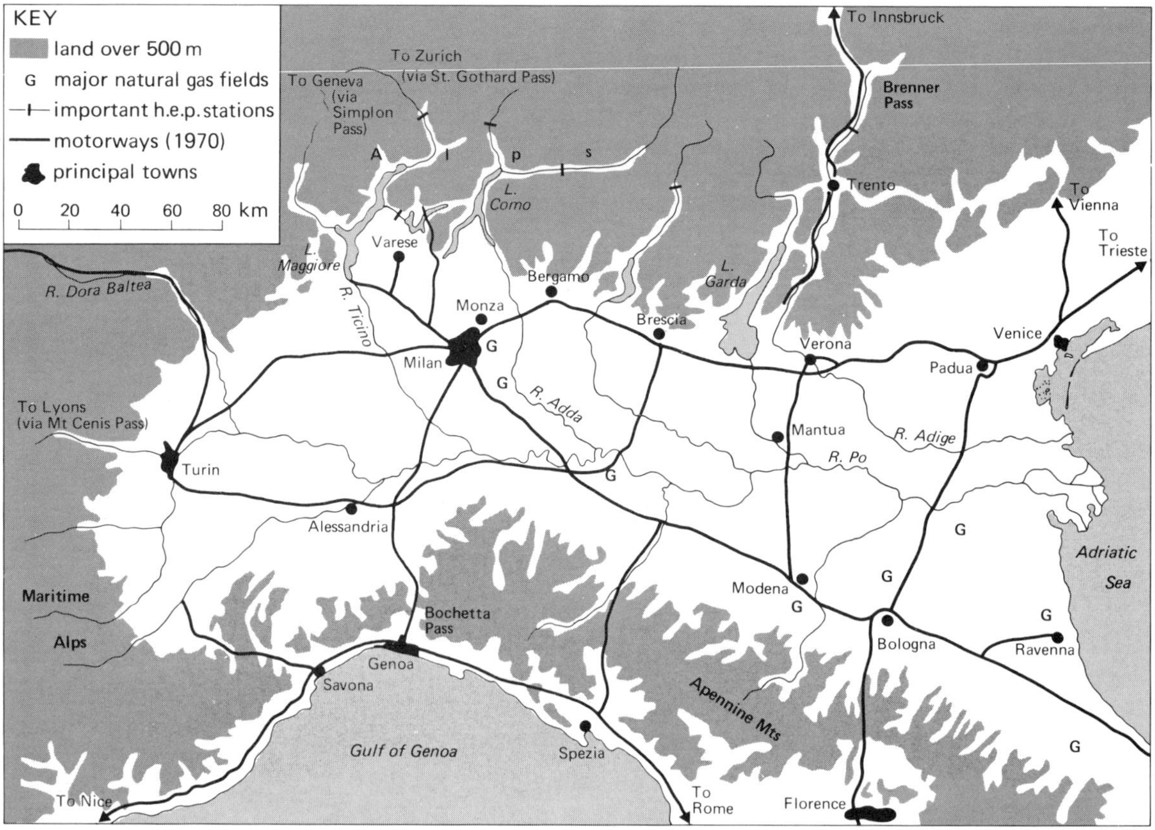

KEY

- land over 500 m
- G major natural gas fields
- ⊢⊣ important h.e.p. stations
- motorways (1970)
- principal towns

0 20 40 60 80 km

To Innsbruck

To Geneva
(via Simplon Pass)

To Zurich
(via St. Gothard Pass)

Brenner Pass

A l p s

L. Como

Trento

To Vienna

To Trieste

L. Maggiore

Varese

Bergamo

L. Garda

R. Dora Baltea

R. Ticino

Monza

Milan G

G

Brescia

Verona

Venice

Padua

To Lyons
(via Mt Cenis Pass)

R. Adda

Mantua

R. Adige

R. Po

Turin

G

Alessandria

Modena G

G

Adriatic Sea

Maritime

Alps

Bochetta Pass

G

Bologna

G

Ravenna

Genoa

Savona

Apennine Mts

Gulf of Genoa

Spezia

To Nice

To Rome

Florence

G

Figure 16.9 (*above*) The position of Milan   **Figure 16.10** (*below*) The Piazza Duomo, Milan

180

Figure 16.11 The Innocenti assembly line, situated on the outskirts of Milan

3 The early establishment of textile and metal working industries. Textile plants producing wool, cotton, silk and synthetic goods are located both in Milan and in the towns and villages to the north, Como and Varese being the most important.

4 The availability of hydro-electric power carried by high voltage transmission lines from plants in the Adda, Oglio and Adige valleys.

5 Natural gas, which is carried across the plain in a network of pipelines linking minor fields like the ones south of Milan, with the large producing areas at Ravenna. The gas is principally used for industrial and domestic heating and as a raw material for the chemical industry.

6 Access to the ports of Genoa and Venice for the import of bulk raw materials and the export of finished goods. Communications between Milan and Genoa are served by the electrified railway and motorway which cross the narrow Ligurian Apennines by the Bochetta Pass.

7 A labour force drawn in the nineteenth century from the rural villages of Lombardy, and in more recent years from the underdeveloped areas of southern Italy. In recent years, the prospect of high wages in the industries of Milan and other northern cities has drawn workers from the south at a rate of over 1000 each week. Many settle permanently in the north.

The industries of Milan are very varied and include a great number of small firms. Among the most important industries are steel, chemicals, engineering, machine tools, aircraft, electrical goods, textiles and food processing. Outside the city, but within its sphere of influence, are the towns of Varese, important for electrical engineering and domestic appliances, Monza with its large steelworks, and Como, a centre for textile fabrics and knitted goods. In addition to its industrial function, Milan is the administrative and commercial capital of the Lombardy region, and the communications focus for the whole of the plain. Linate airport provides a wide range of international services, and handled over 3 million passengers in 1974. However, aircraft using Linate airport are frequently diverted to other airports as atmospheric pollution from the factories of Milan, particularly bad in the damp conditions of winter, causes operations to be curtailed. Milan has the unwanted reputation of being the city with the third most-polluted atmosphere in the world, after Tokyo and Los Angeles. In some respects its industrial success has been at the expense of the urban living-conditions, and increasingly the wealthier members of the population are choosing to live outside the city and make lengthy daily journeys to work.

Bergen—A Fishing Port

The settlement was first established in 1070 around a natural fjord harbour, and has gradually spread northwards and southwards along the narrow platform that fringes the coast. Flat or gently sloping land is very limited and the town has straggled around the base of the steep Ulriken hills which rise to over 300 m in the east. In spite of this restricted site, Bergen has developed into one of the largest settlements in Norway, with a population of 120,000.

In addition to having a deep-water site, the port is sheltered from westerly storms by the 'skerry guard', a series of low, rocky islands

Figure 16.12 Bergen harbour: the indented coastline and offshore line of islands provide protection from storms

which lie parallel with the coast. Although offering protection, the islands make for a difficult approach into the port for large vessels. Like other Scandinavian ports, the mild influence of the North Atlantic Drift and the south-west prevailing airstreams keep the port ice free. Bergen, situated near latitude 60°N, is on the same latitude as the north coast of Labrador in North America, where the harbours are closed for six months each year, while Montreal, at latitude 45°N, is closed for four months.

Bergen's position within easy reach of the rich cod and herring fisheries of the North Atlantic was the dominating factor in the early growth of the port. Situated near to the densely populated countries of Western Europe and facing the Americas, Bergen developed important trade in fish and timber, while remaining relatively isolated from the rest of Scandinavia by the mountainous interior. It was an important member-port of the medieval Hanseatic League, a group of Scandinavian and north European ports which successfully controlled maritime trade from northern Europe. The Hanseatic League lost significance in the eighteenth and nineteenth centuries with the growth of ports serving the newly-industrialized regions of Europe. However, as an established port in a region with few natural resources, Bergen's role has been extended to include the following functions.

1 *Fishing port.* The principal catch of the Bergen fleet has been the winter herring and mackerel, but with the depletion of the herring shoals a wider range of fish is being landed from larger vessels fishing distant waters. The Norwegian Directorate of Fisheries and the Institute of Marine Research are located in Bergen, indicating the importance of the fishing industry there. Processing plants include the manufacture of fertilizer, fish meal, oil and the freezing and packaging of fish.

2 *Ferry port.* Services from abroad are most frequent during the summer season when vessels from Newcastle, Rotterdam and New York bring tourists to visit the fjords of western Norway. The daily service along the coast from Oslo to the North Cape connects

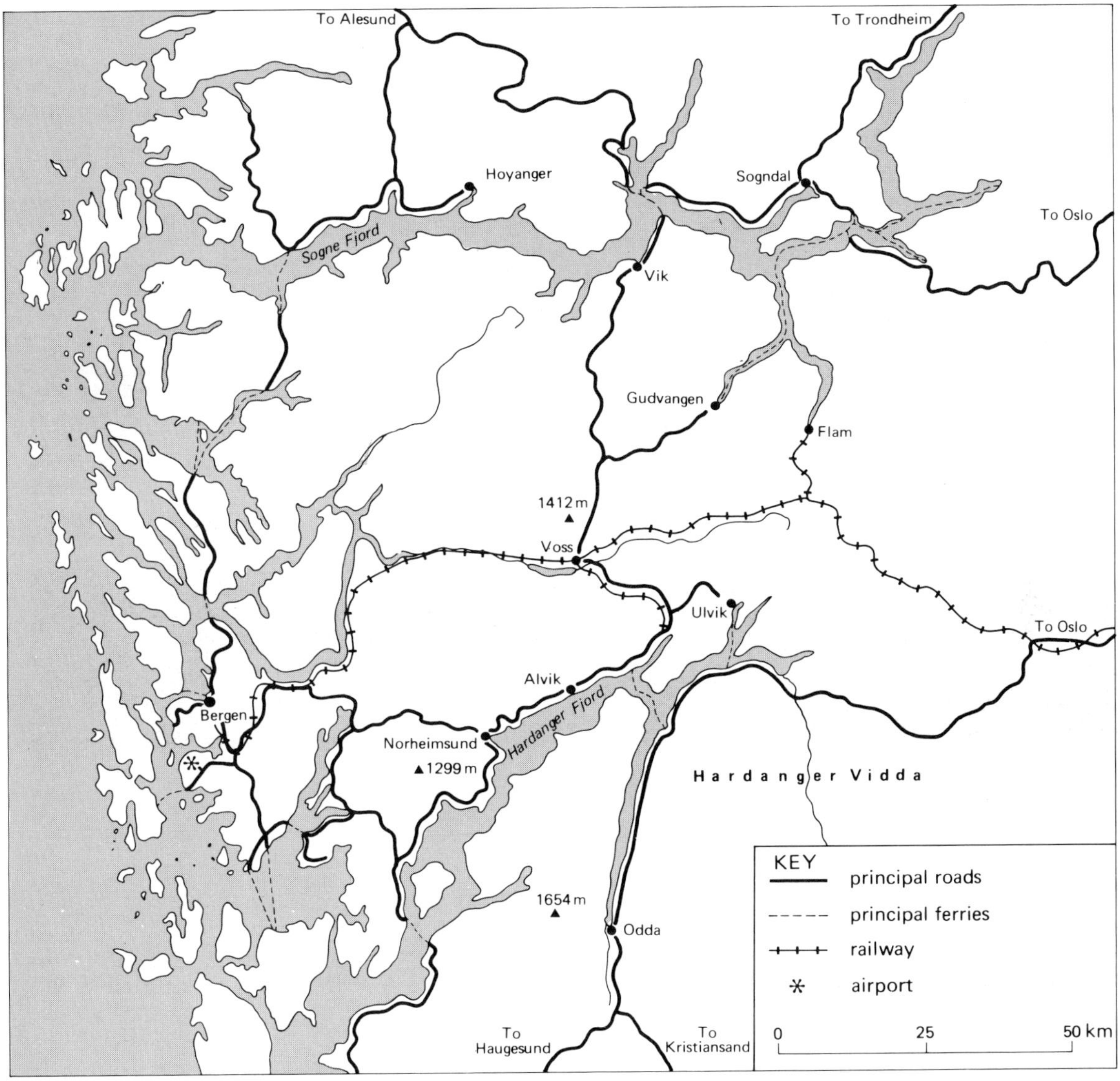

Figure 16.13 The position of Bergen

Bergen with other Norwegian ports. International air services operate from the major European airports and connect with the domestic services to Oslo, Stavanger, Kristransund and Trondheim.

3 *Communications centre.* Land communications are difficult and mountain roads leading inland from Bergen are often closed in winter by snow drifts. The limited volume of road traffic and the severe effects of freeze/thaw weathering on tarmac surfaces mean that roads outside Bergen are narrow, with dirt surfaces which are periodically scraped to remove ruts and pot-holes. The

important road to Oslo has been reconstructed in recent years and now provides a fast, reliable routeway. The electrified railway, completed in 1909, to Oslo offers a more reliable service and links Bergen with the winter-sports resorts of Voss and Geilo on the Hardanger plateau. These towns are situated at over 1000 m and rely upon the rail services. The inland communications extending from Bergen connect the scattered farming, industrial and tourist communities of the Veslandet province, but they are often most effectively supplied by the commercial steamer services operating along the fjords.

Figure 16.14 Bergen. Hansa warehouses lining the water-front

4 *Tourist centre.* Bergen is the principal entry point for tourists visiting the Hardanger and Sogne fjord areas, and throughout the summer many visitors in transit stay in the town. Bergen is on an attractive site and has many buildings of historical significance.

5 *Industrial centre.* Although primarily a town providing services for the fishing fleets, its thinly-populated hinterland and tourists, some manufacturing industry has been developed in recent years. The reasons for this development are (a) the Norwegian government wish to have an urban growth centre in the fjord country to reduce the drift of population to Oslo, and have encouraged industrialists to develop there; (b) an abundant supply of electric power from the many h.e.p. stations; (c) a thriving commercial port to provide a link with raw materials and markets; (d) relatively cheap labour in an area where the opportunities for regular all-year-round jobs

are limited, Industries which have become established are timber processing, cotton and woollen textiles, engineering and shipbuilding. In common with the other ports of south-west Norway, Bergen has benefitted from the discovery of oil in the Norwegian sector of the North Sea. Service and supply industries have grown up and a new oil refinery has been built at Mongstad, north of the town.

6 *Administrative centre.* Bergen has always been the most important town in the south-west of the country. It is a regional centre for local administration and houses the offices of many of the industrial companies which have built factories in the area.

The Costa del Sol in Southern Spain, a Tourist Region

The area stretches from Malaga to Gibraltar, the coast plain backed by mountains rising to

Figure 16.15 The Costa del Sol; hotels, apartment blocks and chalets compete with 'huertas' for the flat land of the coast plain

2000 m. Sandy beaches alternate with occasional rocky headlands, a pattern which becomes more prominent east of Malaga as the mountains approach the sea. The level alluvial coast plain offers fertile farmland which is intensively cultivated in small farms, or 'huertas', of up to 5 ha in size. The land is irrigated from wells and springs issuing from the limestone hills behind the plain. Superimposed upon the farming and fishing communities has been the construction of numerous hotels, chalets and apartment blocks. Much of the farmland has been built upon, but what remains helps to provide fruit, vegetables and salad crops for the tourist population. Tourist development has chiefly been centred upon the established villages of Estepona, Marbella and Torremolinos, which are located along the coast road west of Malaga. Development has been rapid since 1960 and a narrow but almost continuous ribbon of building extends for 50 km along the coast.

Most visitors to the area come from northern Europe; in 1973, 70% of the 11·5 million tourists who visited Spain came from the United Kingdom, West Germany, France, the Benelux countries and Scandinavia. Entry to the Costa del Sol is principally by air to Malaga airport, which received over 2·4 million passengers in 1972, compared with 27,000 in 1962. Before the closure of the border with Gibraltar in 1965 many visitors entered Spain by this route.

In common with most of Spain the summer is the popular season for visitors to the region. The imbalance also explains the effort of the Spanish Tourist Board to attract visitors by offering reduced terms for holidays taken during the October–May period when the hotels and tourist facilities are under-used.

Number of foreign-tourist arrivals in Spain in 1973 (in millions)

J	F	M	A	M	J	J	A	S	O	N	D	Total
0·4	0·5	0·6	0·9	1·0	1·2	1·7	1·8	1·	1·0	0·5	0·5	11·5

185

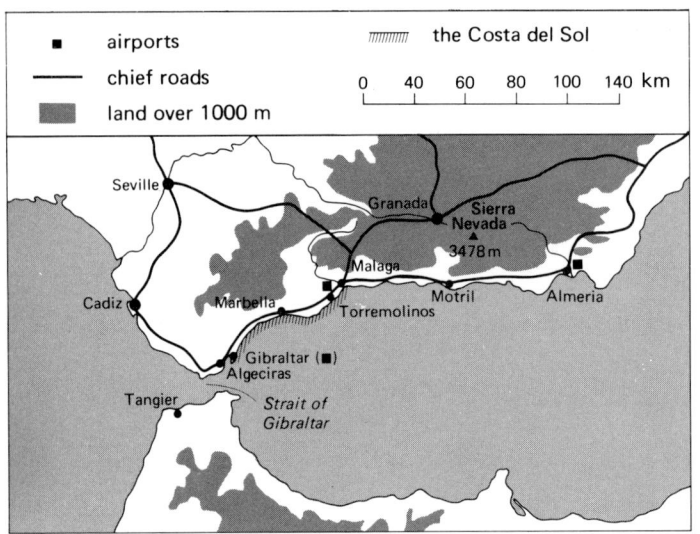

Figure 16.16 The Costa del Sol

The following factors explain the attraction of the Costa del Sol.

1 Hot, dry summers with 9–10 hours sunshine each day, and mild, fairly dry winters. The average January temperature is 11°C and average July temperature 25°C; rainfall 635 mm (25″).

2 Extensive beaches which alternate with rocky headlands along the coast.

3 The relatively low cost of accommodation and transport by air charter has enabled tour operators to offer cheap standardized package holidays.

4 The variety of inland and coastal scenery, which includes the mountains of the Sierra Nevada, and the vast limestone caves at Nerja.

5 The historic towns of Malaga, Granada and Seville are accessible for day visits from the resort area and offer excellent shopping facilities, as well as the opportunity to visit a bullfight and to see beautiful buildings dating from the Moorish occupation.

6 The modern, self-contained hotels provide most of the facilities the tourist requires.

7 The opportunity of taking a short flight to Tangier from Malaga airport.

The growth of tourism has been very rapid and problems have inevitably occurred. One of the most difficult is the provision of a reliable water supply, needed by the influx of the many thousands of people during the dry summer months. The construction of reservoirs and water-supply systems has been extensive in the mountains inland. Secondly, the loss of coastal farmland and the crowding together of buildings on the most favourable sites has damaged the scenic appearance of the area. However, the area is now developed, and while holidays can be offered which are relatively cheap to the north European, many thousands will continue to visit the Costa del Sol.

The Reclamation and Settlement of the Zuyder Zee

The Zuyder Zee (or Southern Sea) was enclosed in 1932 by building a barrier dam across the 32 km of open sea between north Holland and Friesland. The plan for the enclosed area has been to reclaim five polders, each surrounded by a high dyke, and to leave a freshwater lake—Ijsselmeer. Sluices in the barrier dam are opened at low tide to drain the excess water accumulated from the rivers, canals and pumping stations emptying into Ijsselmeer.

Before reclamation, the Zuyder Zee was a shallow bay bordered by fishing and farming communities, who lived with the continual fear that the protecting dykes would be inadequate to resist floodwaters. The barrier dam has given complete protection and the economy of the region has been revitalized. Although fishing has declined in importance with the closure of the Zuyder Zee and the more difficult exit for vessels through the locks in the dam, farming has improved and extended and the population increased. The settlement of the polders has been carefully planned by the Dutch government, each scheme drawing from the experience gained in laying out the farms and villages on earlier polders.

The area of the Zuyder Zee chosen for empoldering was that part underlain by boulder clay, while Ijsselmeer occupies the area floored by infertile sands. Once the barrier dam was completed, successive dykes were constructed around each area and pumping stations were built to raise water from 4 m below sea level into Ijsselmeer. A bare muddy surface was left, across which large earth-moving machines cut a network of canals and ditches, directing water to the pumping stations and providing the first transport routes

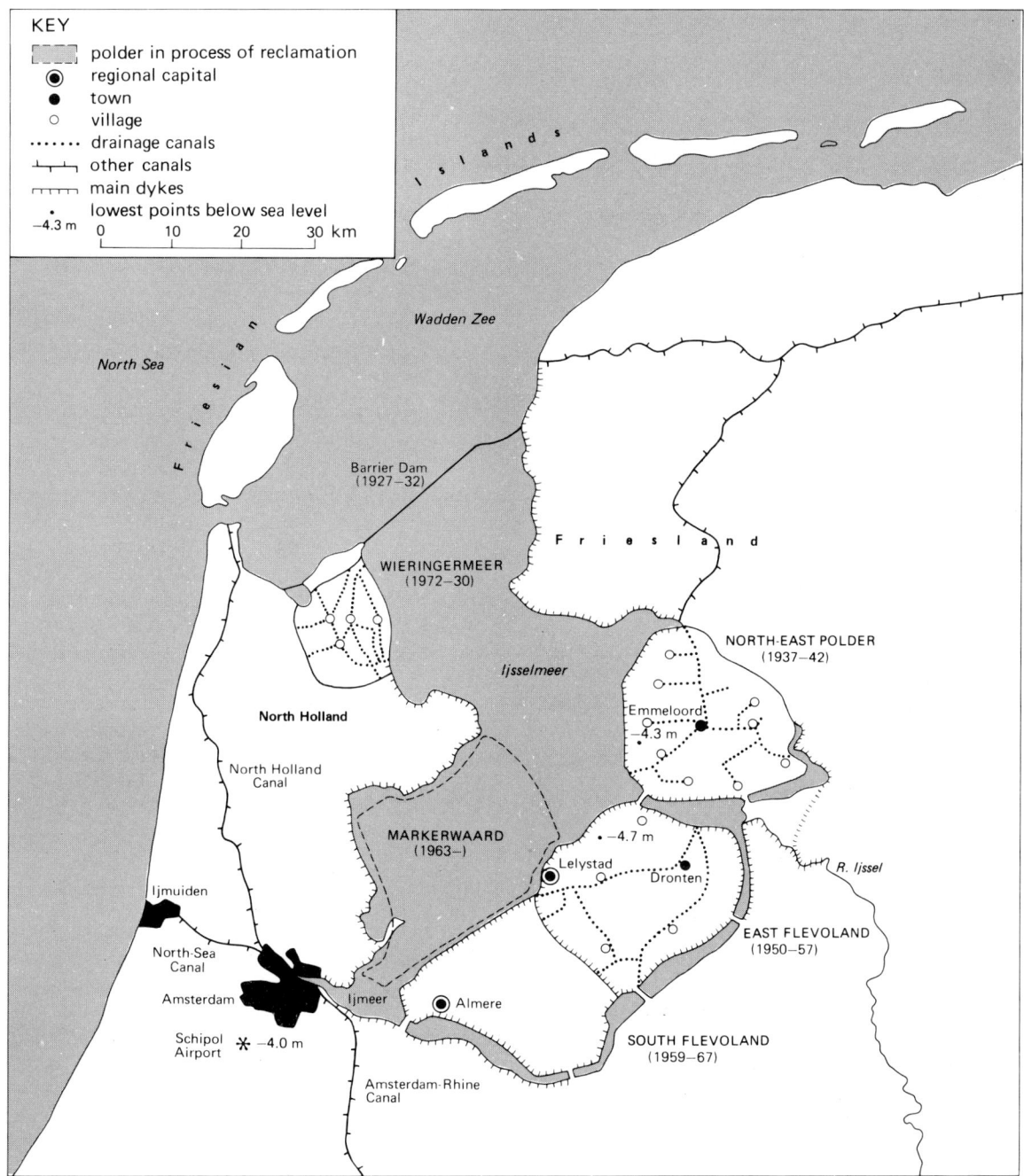

KEY

polder in process of reclamation
⊙ regional capital
● town
○ village
········ drainage canals
⊢┬┬┤ other canals
┬┬┬┬ main dykes
• lowest points below sea level
−4.3 m

0   10   20   30 km

I s l a n d s

North Sea

F r i e s i a n

Wadden Zee

Barrier Dam
(1927–32)

F r i e s l a n d

WIERINGERMEER
(1972–30)

Ijsselmeer

North Holland

North Holland
Canal

NORTH-EAST POLDER
(1937–42)

Emmeloord
−4.3 m

MARKERWAARD
(1963–)

• −4.7 m

Lelystad

Dronten

R. Ijssel

EAST FLEVOLAND
(1950–57)

Ijmuiden

North-Sea
Canal

Amsterdam

Ijmeer

Almere

SOUTH FLEVOLAND
(1959–67)

Schipol
Airport   ✳ −4.0 m

Amsterdam-Rhine
Canal

Figure 16.17 The reclamation of the Zuyder Zee. Markerwaard: 60,000 ha; East Flevoland: 54,000 ha; North East Polder: 48,000 ha; South Flevoland: 44,000 ha; Wieringermeer: 20,000 ha

across the polder. To prevent the land being colonized by undesirable marsh plants, reed seed was sprayed over the land surface from light aircraft and helicopters. The reed thrives in the wet, salty soils, which its roots open up and ventilate to encourage evaporation and

187

Figure 16.18 The Wieringermeer polder: dykes protect the low polderland, from which the Lely pumping station removes surplus water. The village of Medenblik existed as an island settlement before the reclamation began in 1930, and can be seen on the left of the photograph

drying out. The tall reeds can easily be removed and their decay helps to establish a humus element in the soil. Saline soils were only a problem in the reclamation of the first and second polders, as the enclosed water became progressively fresher. Ijsselmeer is also important in combating the flow of salt water into the polders from the Rhine distributaries and the North Sea Canal. Where salt water seeps into arable or pasture land from high level drainage canals and rivers, falls in crop and milk yields occur.

All the initial work on the Zuyder Zee polders has been undertaken by the government; the cost of reclamation and settlement being beyond the resources of private organizations. Government teams laid out and harvested the first crops, but gradually houses

and roads were built and the farm plots marked out, each polder entering full production approximately ten years after enclosure. The farms are leased to tenant farmers and the flat, open land is principally used for crops of potatoes, sugar beet and wheat, with some market gardening.

The settlement pattern decided on at Wieringermeer was for 512 farms of 20 ha and three villages. In the light of this experience the pattern was modified in the larger North-east Polder, which has 1800 farms of 12, 24, 36 and 48 ha units and 250 market gardens served by ten villages and one centrally situated town, Emmeloord. This has proved to be a settlement magnet to the detriment of the villages, and in the East Flevoland polder the pattern has been modified again. The varied farm size has been retained, but the urban pattern is based upon four villages and two towns, Lelystad and Dronten, the former acting as the regional capital for the Zuyder Zee polders with a range of industrial and commercial activities. South Flevoland has not yet been settled, but the south-west corner is designated to become an urban area for Amsterdam overspill.

Crop yields on the polders have risen steadily as the soils have improved in quality through cultivation and fertilization, while complete control over water management allows for irrigation at critical stages in a plant's growth. In addition to benefitting agriculture and water management, Zuyder Zee reclamation has:

1 increased the land area of the Netherlands by 10%;

2 improved flood protection by reducing the length of the sea dykes from 320 to 32 km;

3 provided a major road link between the eastern and western Netherlands along the barrier dam;

4 enabled the development of such leisure pursuits as sailing and water ski-ing for the crowded urban population around Amsterdam.

Although originally conceived primarily as a scheme for increasing the agricultural land of the Netherlands, different objectives have emerged in the final stages of the Zuyder Zee reclamation. Today, the main consideration in the East Flevoland and South Flevoland polders is to house overspill population from the Amsterdam area. Little progress has been made towards draining the Markerwaard polder and its reclamation may be postponed indefinitely—the area acting as a freshwater reservoir for the Amsterdam conurbation. Even if reclamation does go ahead, the area of the Markerwaard polder is certain to be much reduced.

Planned Economic Development in Southern Italy

In Italy, the difference between the way of life in the north and in the south is very marked. People in the northern cities have always looked towards the industrial areas of Western Europe, while those in the south identify more with the agricultural life of the Mediterranean lands. As northern Italy has become increasingly industrialized, the gap between living standards in north and south has widened. Many southerners have migrated to the industrial centres of the north, while in the south the established commercial and industrial cities of Rome and Naples have attracted people from the poor, hill regions. The lack of balance in the Italian economy can be judged from the fact that 50% of the working population in the south is involved in agriculture, compared to 19.3% for the whole country.

The reasons for the lack of development in the south are as follows.

1 A predominantly steep, mountainous terrain with the Apennines rising to over 2000 m in Abruzzi and Calabria.

2 The low coastal plains which lie between the mountain spurs have coarse, stoney soils and are frequently affected by spring floods. Settlements are built on hillsides to avoid the lowland floods and malaria, which has been rife in the mosquito infested marshes of the rivers and coast.

3 The dry summer climate makes large-scale cultivation difficult without costly irrigation schemes.

4 The absence of extensive mineral deposits. The only resources which have been worked are the coalfield in the south-west corner of Sardinia, the sulphur of Caltanissetta in southern Sicily, and the scattered natural gasfields in Sicily and the peninsula.

Since 1950 the Italian government has had a policy for the economic improvement of the south, but its progress has been hampered by limited financial resources, and the movement to the north has continued—six million people had left their southern homes in the period 1950–70. However, the amount of money allocated for the development of the south has been steadily increased, the amount for the period 1972–77 being £4,800 million. The progress so far falls into three distinct periods.

1950–60. The plan was to establish a sound structure of motorways and major roads, water provision and control systems and an electric power network.

1960–70. The attraction and development of major industries.

1970–77. The aim is to attract smaller industries and services and develop tourism. These activities are expected to have a greater

Figure 16.19 The North-east Polder; the land lies about 3 m below sea level. The regular pattern of settlements, with the village of Luttelgeest in the foreground, can be clearly seen. With reference to the photograph:

(a) what are the main features of the physical landscape?
(b) Describe the distribution of houses and farms.
(c) How is the farmland used?
(d) Estimate the approximate population of Luttelgeest.
(e) Explain how the drainage system of a polder operates

impact on the region than the large, but often isolated, project.

Although industrial development has quadrupled and agricultural output doubled in the past twenty years, the aim is also to raise general living standards. The elimination of malaria and the lowering of the level of illiteracy is being achieved; new hospitals and schools are being built; and higher personal incomes are reflected in increased expenditure on food, drink, clothing and leisure activities.

The development of the south is being accomplished by improved administration, and the establishment of schemes for agriculture, industry and tourism.

Administration

The development area of southern Italy is known as the Mezzogiorno, and the administration of the government funds allocated was centred upon Rome. Gradually the administration has been decentralized and in 1972 fifteen new regions were established to develop agriculture, industry and tourism in the south. In addition to the finances allotted by the Italian government, grants have also been received from the EEC Farm Fund which have amounted to 25–65% of the capital cost of approved measures.

Agriculture

Farming in southern Italy is dominated by hill

Figure 16.20 The recently completed motorway and improved rail track near Reggio, Calabria

Figure 16.21 Mechanized fruit picking in southern Italy

farms with small fields of wheat, vines, olives and fruit supplemented by a few sheep, cattle or goats. The farms are small; in 1970 two-thirds were under 10 ha in size, while EEC policy is for a minimum size of 12 ha. The following schemes are supported by financial aid from the Farm Fund.

1 The modernization of holdings by the increased use of machinery,‡ irrigation and drainage.

2 Assistance to enable older farmers to give up farming, and their land sold to adjoining farms or used for forestry. Afforestation has been carried out in the mountain districts of the south on abandoned hill-farming land. A typical development is the Cosenza district of Calabria where extensive areas have been planted with oak, chestnut and beech trees.

3 The establishment of technical training schemes. The overall plan is to reduce the number of people dependent on farming, and

‡ In southern Sicily there is an average of one tractor/100 hectares, compared with one tractor/15 hectares in Denmark.

to raise the standard of living of those remaining. For this to be successful and not cause further migration to the north, alternative employment in industry and tourism is needed in the south.

Industry

The provision of power is being achieved by the construction of hydroelectric power dams, many of which are an integral part of a water-management system. In the mountains of Calabria, where the annual rainfall often exceeds 1000 mm, power plants have been built on the rivers Neto and Mucone to serve the metal smelting and chemical industry at Crotone and the towns of Cosenza and Catanazaro. Lacking a large source of power, the Mezzogiorno area has become increasingly dependent on electricity generated by the oil-fired thermal power stations at Naples, Bari, Brindisi, Palermo and Catania. These centres of power production, together with Taranto, Latina and Pescara, have been developed as the major industrial areas of the south.

Naples: oil refining, metal smelting, iron and steel works, shipbuilding, motor vehicles (Alfa-Romeo, Fiat).

Taranto: oil refining, iron and steel works, shipbuilding (naval vessels).

Brindisi: oil refining, petro-chemicals, engineering.

Bari: oil refining, motor vehicles (Fiat), engineering.

Pescara: chemicals, engineering.

Latina: nuclear power generation, chemicals, engineering, metal smelting.

Catania/Syracuse: oil refining, chemicals, pharmaceutical goods.

Palermo: oil refining, chemicals, iron and steel works, engineering, metal smelting.

The present aim is to supplement these large industrial developments with light industry and services, which it is hoped will raise the income level of a wider section of the southern community.

Tourism

Italy has the largest tourist industry in Europe, receiving over 30 million foreign visitors each year. The Naples–Salerno area is the only long-established tourist district in the south, but since 1950 other coastal areas have been developed, often with the same sprawl of hotels and apartments as found on the Mediterranean coasts of Spain and France. By decentralizing the administration of the Mezzogiorno it is hoped that the expansion of tourism and industry can be achieved without drastically damaging the coastal scenery of the south. Tourist development is mainly for foreigners and is seen as an important means of attracting income into the south. In addition to the coastal scenery, tourists are attracted to the many historic buildings and spas of the mountain regions. An untapped market for the tourist industry is the Italian population, only 60% of whom take a regular annual holiday. One cause of this is that July–August is the traditional period for Italian holidays, when the country has many foreign visitors and prices are high. Greater flexibility in arranging industrial and school holidays could result in the all-year-round use of the country's extensive tourist facilities.

The economic improvement of the south through the development of agriculture, industry and tourism has already been considerable, and it is hoped that gradually the bar-

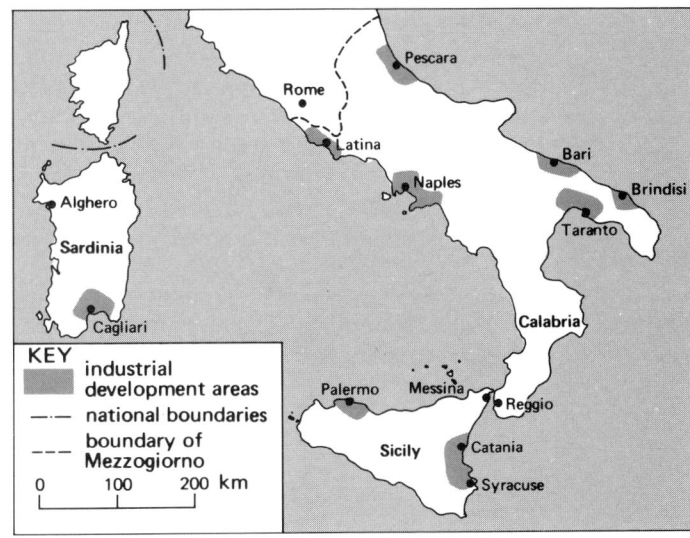

Figure 16.22 The industrial development areas of southern Italy

riers that exist between people from the north and south will be broken down. The wide cultural differences are illustrated by the way southern migrants to Turin have crowded together in old property near the cathedral to establish their own distinct community, while at Gela in southern Sicily technical staff recruited from the north to operate a petro-chemical plant are housed in a separate estate outside the town. It is in blending these distinct peoples, who were unified into one nation in 1870, that the Italian government faces its greatest challenge.

Figure 16.23 The Bay of Naples, showing the shipyards in the foreground and the silhouette of Mount Vesuvius

193

Questions

1. Between 1801 and 1968 the proportion of the total French population living in Paris increased from 2% to 17%. What factors explain the attraction and growth of Paris during this period?

2. Rotterdam and Antwerp broadly serve the same hinterland of the Low Countries, northern France and the Rhineland. Suggest reasons to explain why Rotterdam relies more upon inland waterway transport and Antwerp more upon roads and railways.

3. What are the chief benefits that have resulted so far from: (*a*) the reclamation of the Zuyder Zee, and (*b*) the redevelopment of southern Italy? Arrange your answer under the following headings: agriculture, industry, communications.

4. (*a*) Refer to the Table on page 185 and construct a bar graph to show seasonal variation in the number of tourists visiting Spain. (*b*) Describe and give reasons to explain the seasonal variation in the number of tourists received.

Conversion tables

Temperature

°C	°F	°C	°F	°C	°F
−30	−22	6	43	16	61
−20	−4	7	45	17	63
−10	14	8	46	18	64
−5	23	9	48	19	66
0	32	10	50	20	68
1	34	11	52	21	70
2	36	12	54	22	72
3	37	13	55	23	73
4	39	14	57	24	75
5	41	15	59	25	77

Length and Distance

Millimetres	Inches	Metres	Feet	Kilometres	Miles
10	0·393	5	16·41	1	0·62
25	0·974	25	82·05	5	3·11
50	1·958	50	164·10	10	6·21
100	3·916	100	328·20	50	31·10
250	9·790	500	1,641·00	100	62·10
500	19·580	1000	3,282·00	500	311·00
1000 (1m)	39·160	5000	16,410·00	1000	621·00

Area

Hectares	Acres	Sq. kms	Sq. miles
0·4	1·00	1·00 (100 ha)	0·38
1·0	2·47	2·59	1·00
10·0	24·70	10·00	3·80
50·0	123·50	50·00	19·00
100·0 (1 sq. km)	247·00	100·00	38·00
200·0	494·00	200·00	76·00
500·0	1235·00	500·00	190·00

Weight

Kilograms	Pounds
0·45	1·00
1·00	2·20
10·00	22·00
50·00	110·00
100·00	220·00
1000·00 (1 tonne)	2220·00
1016·00	2240·00 (1 ton)

List of abbreviations used in the text

mm	milimetres
cm	centimetres
m	metres
km	kilometres
ha	hectares
k/h	kilometres per hour
°C	degrees Centigrade (Celsius)
°F	degrees Fahrenheit
$m\,m^3$	million cubic metres
T cal	Terra calories
kW	kilowatt

Index